GODS
OF THE NORTH

BRIAN BRANSTON

THAMES AND HUDSON

TO ROBERT WALLER

© Copyright 1955 and 1980 by Brian Branston
First paperback edition published with revisions in
the USA in 1980 by Thames and Hudson Inc,
New York

Library of Congress Catalog
card number 79-66130

Printed in Great Britain by Biddles Ltd, Guildford,
Surrey

Bound in Great Britain

CONTENTS

Contents

Contents

Note

All the drawings in this book were executed by the author

Thanks are due to the following for supplying photographic material: National Museum, Copenhagen (1 and 5); Edwin Smith (2); Royal Library, Copenhagen (3); British Museum, London (4 and 7); Biblioteca Medicea-Laurenziana (6); Associated Press Ltd (8).

Guide to the Pronunciation of some Old Norse Consonants and Vowels

Þ, þ   like *th* in *thin*

Ð, ð   like *th* in *the*

J, j   like *y* in *yes*

AE, æ   like German *ä*

Ö, ö ⎫
Ø, ø ⎬ like *-er* spoken with rounded lips

The acute accent over a vowel indicates length.

INTRODUCTION

THE NORTHERN MYTHS

MYTHOLOGY is every man's business, whether it be of the private kind called psychology or the collective kind which manifests itself in stories of the gods.

Mythology has come to mean for many a collection of rather childish tales about the gods and goddesses of ancient Greece and Rome, well suited to the nursery and the infant class but not really worth remembering after leaving school.

However, since psychologists such as Jung have drawn our attention to the matter we have come to realize that both myth and nursery rhyme have a significant meaning for every man and woman. We begin to suspect that a myth may well have not only a social value but also a practical value, giving us a deeper insight into our own make-up if we can only read its meaning.

A myth is like a dream; it is a direct expression of the unconscious mind, and the events of a myth, its characters and symbols are to the human race as the events, characters and symbols of his dream are to the individual. Like a dream the myth may ignore the conventional logic of space and time relationships, of events following one another in a causal sequence. Nevertheless, a dream has a meaning which can be made plain; and so has a myth.

It is not easy to interpret the myths of our own race, for our near ancestors – those of a thousand-odd years ago – were persuaded to forget them or to relegate their broken remnants to the nursery. Once upon a time the Gods of the North were the gods of our forefathers. The fossilized remains of these deities survive in place-names where the Angles, Saxons and Jutes settled, as Wansdyke, Wednesbury, Wensley, Tuesley and Thundersley; in the names of the days of the week, as Sunday, Monday, Tuesday, Wednesday, Thursday and Friday; in carven scenes, such as that of Thunor fishing for the World Serpent on the Gosforth cross in Cumberland or the hamstrung Wayland, the gods' smith, on the Franks Casket in the British Museum; in folklore and fairy tale, with their stories of pucks, witches on broomsticks and the Wild Rider with his belling hounds. Such remains are, on their own, largely useless as an aid to reconstructing the mythology of our forefathers; if we want to do that we can call in archaeology and philology but mainly we must rely on a literature which grew, first orally and then in manuscript, in Iceland.

THE NORTHMEN

The basic written authority for early English history is the *Old English*, or *Anglo-Saxon*, *Chronicle*, a sort of national diary. This diary begins with a summary of history in Britain from before the invasion by Julius Cæsar down to the year AD 1, when it records:

> Octavianus reigned 56 years and in the 42nd year of his reign Christ was born.

Scanty annals follow up to the year AD 449, when the coming of the Angles, Saxons and Jutes to Britain is recorded. From then on the entries become (in general) more detailed and longer. Today there exist seven known manuscripts of the *Old English Chronicle*. All are derived as far as the year AD 891 from a set of annals written (in the English language of the time) in the reign of Alfred the Great (*d.* 26 October 899). Soon after 891 the *Chronicles* begin to differ from one another, presumably because they were sent out to different churches for their continuation. Still, up to the year 915 the *Chronicles* have much material in common. After the Norman Conquest they begin to peter out.

The entry in the *Old English Chronicle* (Laud Ms) for the year AD 787 runs:

> This year Beorhtric took to wife Eadburg daughter of King Offa. It was during Beorhtric's days that three

ships of the *Northmen* first came here from Hörthaland. The reeve galloped to meet them, intending to drive them to the king's town (Dorchester, Dorset) for he did not know who or what they were. They killed him.

These were the first ships of the *Danes* ever to seek England.

It is instructive to note that the *Chronicle* does not use the name Vikings: it says they were "Northmen", "Danes" and that they came from "Hörthaland", which is in fact a district on the west coast of Norway. The name Hörthaland is equivalent to "Lancashire", "Yorkshire" or any other of the English counties with a coastline. No doubt the English Dorset folk of the time recognized that their assailants came in general from Scandinavia or Denmark, but for them to remember, and for their clerks in holy orders to put on record, the actual name of the district whence the strangers came argues two things: first, that the speech of both peoples was near enough for them to understand each other and second, that some of the Dorset men asked the mariners where they came from and were told in reply "Hörthaland".

Can we picture the scene when (round about A D 787) the three keels ran easily on to the flat expanse of Weymouth sands? A fair amount of inquisitive chat must have gone on between the crews and the local yokels while word was sent up to Dorchester ten miles away to warn the officials of the arrival of armed strangers. King Beorhtric of Wessex's representative in Dorchester was his reeve Beaduheard. The reeve, "with a few men",[1] trotted out of Dorchester town for the last time: he passed (probably without a thought) the monuments of former peoples, the grass-grown Roman amphitheatre on his left, the long hog-back of the prehistoric earthwork, Maiden Castle, on his right. It is said that he thought that "the newcomers were merchants rather than enemies. He addressed them in a commanding tone and ordered them to be brought to the king's vill. But he was killed there and then, and those that were with him."[1]

If these pugnacious sailormen actually came from Hörthaland on the west coast of Norway then the *Chronicle* is right to refer to them as "Northmen" but wrong to call them "Danes". Is there any meaning behind this confusion? Perhaps we can get further light from another entry, the annal for the year AD 793 (Laud Ms), which calls the attackers of Lindisfarne "heathen".[2]

This new designation "heathen" emphasizes two points: at the time of the raid on Lindisfarne and for many years to come the invaders *were* heathen, while the invaded had for two centuries been Christian. The terms "Northmen", "Danes", "heathen" are employed by the *Chronicle* writers imprecisely without their taking much account of whether the invaders were Norwegians, Danes or Swedes. Another frequent *Chronicle* label for this thorn in the flesh was the Old English word *here* meaning "army" or "host", particularly an enemy host. A word found in Old English glossaries dating from the eighth century is *wícingsceaða*; the first part of this word is related to Old Norse *víkingr*; but the term "viking", which has been in fashion for only a little over a century and a half, came into vogue with the Victorians.[3] "Viking" really refers to a way of life lived by some of the members of all four of the countries Denmark, Sweden, Norway and Iceland between the years AD 700 and 1100.

The historical Norse saga writers use the term "Northmen" (O.N. *Norðmenn*) to include the natives of Denmark, Sweden, Norway and Iceland; this is equivalent to the *Old English Chronicle's Norðmenn* and to the monks' medieval Latin *Northomanni*. In this book "Northman" or "Northmen" will be used as a blanket term, except where it is necessary to indicate a Northman of the raiding, trading, colonizing years AD 700–1100, and except where it is necessary to indicate Icelander, Norwegian, Swede or Dane.

BACKGROUND

LINKS: LANGUAGE

English people are vaguely aware of their mixed descent. They may even remember Tennyson's "Saxon, Norman and Dane are we", which reminded our grandfathers that our "Saxon" ancestors in England had received a double transfusion of Northman blood. We ourselves may be dimly aware that the forbears of these same "Saxon" ancestors were first cousins in Europe to the forbears of the Northmen. In other words, the Northmen who invaded and settled England after 787 as vikings and after 1066 as Normans were already our second cousins. There were other cousins too who remained behind in Europe.

The peoples who can be included in the Continental family are the tribes which went to make up, among others, the races whom we call today Germans, Dutch, Danes, Swedes, Norwegians, Icelanders, English and any of their extraction. The earliest accepted collective name for these related peoples was the Latin word *Germani*, "Germans". But if we use the word "Germans" now, we cannot avoid ambiguity since it is often difficult to know whether the whole or the part is intended. A more suitable term for our Continental ancestors would be one derived from their homeland namely "North West Europeans". The least doubtful link between the various tribes is not one of skulls, hair, colour or blood group: it is a link of language. The supposed common language of these peoples has been called Primitive Germanic. To avoid the ambiguity already mentioned, a better phrase for the language would be Primitive North West European (sometimes called Gothonic).

The speakers of Primitive N.W.European were linked again by language to a dozen or so other groups of peoples talking tongues which in the dim and distant past derived from one single parent language. The more important of these groups include Celtic, Italic, Greek, Slavonic, Baltic, Indic (Sanskrit and Prakrits) and, what was only recognized some seventy years ago, Hittite.

The mother tongue or group of close-knit dialects from which all these languages sprang is nowhere extant in rock-carved inscription or written document for the good reason that writing had not been invented before the original speakers split up and wandered far apart. Distance and time are the great changers of tongues. This is especially so when communication between the original speakers becomes sporadic or stops altogether. Nevertheless, the mother tongue from which N.W.European, Celtic, Italic, Greek, Slavonic, Baltic, Indic and Hittite ultimately derive can be reconstructed, because although languages change apparently out of all recognition, the changes are of a regular order and in the case of phonetic changes follow certain "laws".

It is convenient to call the parent tongue Indo-European (it used to be called Aryan) and in discussing words in the following pages, I shall where necessary indicate the source

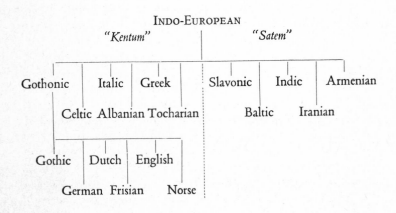

FIG. I THE GOKSTAD SHIP

A restoration of the vessel discovered in a "ship burial" mound at Gokstad on Oslo fjord in 1880. Length 78 ft., greatest beam 16 ft., depth 4 ft. (Oslo)

of the word by an abbreviation, such as I.E. = Indo-European; or O.E. = Old English = Anglo-Saxon; or O.N. = Old Norse. When a word is a hypothetical one, that is to say nowhere recorded but in the form which according to phonetic laws we should expect to find it, then this will be indicated by an asterisk in front of it, e.g. I.E. *djevs.*

2

LINKS: OLD HOME OF THE NORTH WEST EUROPEAN NATIONS

Indo-European is a linguistic term and not a racial one. No archaeologist digging in the ground has ever run his spade, or ever will, against the skull of an Indo-European. But there can be no doubt that many of the languages of present-day Europe and India have developed from an original tongue sufficiently homogeneous to be called Indo-

European and to be regarded as one language. The date at which this language was spoken can only be guessed at; and as good a guess as any is that we have to go back to 4000 B C to find Indo-European still a linguistic unity. The problem as to whether the speakers of this Indo-European originated in Europe or Asia has not been satisfactorily solved; nor for our present purpose is the problem acute. The vocabulary of original Indo-European indicates that the speakers had reached a general level of culture of the Later Stone Age: there are words of common origin suggesting that their earliest weapons and tools were made of stone (e.g. Lithuanian *akmuo* "stone" = Greek $\overset{\prime}{\alpha}\kappa\mu\omega\nu$ "anvil" = O.N. *hamarr* "hammer"). They may have used bows and arrows; they certainly knew the ox, cow, horse, dog, sheep and pig as well as the goose and duck; they did not know the ass, camel, lion, tiger and elephant; they were cattle rearers and knew the use of milk as well as how to plough, sow, reap, and grind grain. It is interesting, and will be important later, for us to know now something of their family relationships: Delbrück showed in 1889 that the words for father, mother, brother, sister, son, daughter and grandchild are all original Indo-European. "Widow" is original and so is "daughter-in-law" but not "son-in-law". The deduction was that among the Indo-Europeans when a son married he took his wife into his father's house and continued to live there, while married daughters went to live with their husband's parents. We know little more of their tribal government than that they had chiefs. Of their religion we may discover something as we go on.

I have suggested that original Indo-European was being spoken round about 4000 B C. About a thousand years later in 3000 B C writing was invented in the Near East, probably in Mesopotamia. The oldest recorded Indo-European language is Hittite. It is found written in styles known as cuneiform and hieroglyphic. Cuneiform was first produced by pressing the wedge-shaped end of a cut reed into soft clay and got its name from Latin *cuneus* = wedge or nail. This style of writing never lost its wedge and line appearance. Hieroglyphic began as a system of pictures or

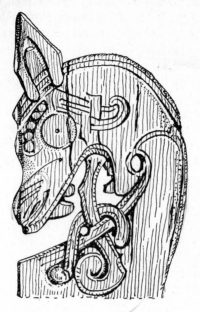

FIG. 2   DRAGON'S HEAD
Wood carving from the furniture of the Gokstad ship. (Oslo)

pictographs, but from it there was eventually developed in Egypt a cursive system of writing called hieratic, and, later still, hieratic was simplified and stylized into demotic. Hittite hieroglyphic is still not completely deciphered, but we know enough from Hittite and Egyptian texts to realize that around 1500 BC the Hittites were one of the "world" powers rivalling and sometimes out-shining the Egyptians and other nations of Mesopotamia. They had already developed a high culture and a literature at a time when our own North Western European ancestors were living in a state of non-literate barbarism. The illiteracy of our forbears was to persist for another 2000 years, for the oldest graphic remains of the North West Europeans are inscriptions in runic dating from about AD 200 and, in writing, an incomplete translation of the Gospels into Gothic by bishop Ulfilas about AD 500. Nearer home, the oldest extant manuscripts of the Anglo-Saxons date from the seventh century and of the Northmen even later, from the twelfth century AD.

If written records tell us (as they do) that Indo-European offshoots were flourishing in Crete in the Middle Bronze Age (the Mycenians) and in central Turkey, with a capital city Hattusas near what is now the village of Bogăzköy (the Hittites) in the second millennium BC, it is safe to assume with Childe[4] that, wherever they came from originally, the dispersion of the Indo-European speakers had begun by 2500 BC.

The European part of the original peoples we can regard without controversy as stemming from Europe: we need go no further back in time than when Europe *was* their old home, for the native traditions of the North West European peoples claim for themselves an old home in North West Europe. Such traditions are first quoted by the Roman historian Tacitus in his *Germania* of AD 98 and by Jordanes in the sixth century. In a famous passage, Tacitus records the claim of the North West European peoples to be descended from their god Tvisto, who sprang from the earth on the spot:

> In their ancient ballads, their only form of recorded history, they celebrate Tvisto, a god sprung from the earth, and they assign to him a son called Mannus, their progenitor through his three sons.[5]

Jordanes calls Scandinavia *officina gentium*, "a factory of peoples" and *vagina nationum* "a womb of nations". In addition to the ancient beliefs of the Goths, Gepidae, Burgundians and the rest of the family of tribes in a "Scandza insula", "Scandinauia", "Scadin-auja" or "Scandanan", we have these beliefs first echoed in our own ancient epic *Beowulf* with its story of Scyld Scefing, who had come as a baby alone in a boat from the sea and when he died he was laid in his boat and returned to the sea:

Nalæs hi hine læssan
lacum teodan,
  þeodgestreonum,
  þon þa dydon
þe hine æt frumsceafte
forð onsendon
  ænne ofer yðe
  umborwesende.

With no less gifts
they girded his body,
  with splendid dues,
  than they had done
who at the first
had sent him forth
  alone o'er the waves
  as a little waif.
    (*Beowulf* 43–46)

This tradition must have been brought over from Europe to England with the original Anglian settlers and kept alive orally. When William of Malmesbury refers to the tale, in his *Gesta Regum Anglorum*, II, 116, he is no doubt cribbing from Jordanes. William writes:

> They say Sceaf as a boy was wafted in a boat without oars to a certain island of Germany called Scandza (the same of which Jordanes speaks).

It is the nature of colonizers to carry the well-loved place-names of their homeland to the new country. Forms of the name "Scandza" crop up in new settlements made by the North West European tribes who wandered from their old home: just as *New* Amsterdam and *New* York cropped up in the New World, so when they left home the Goths founded Gothi*scandza*, the Langobards *Scatenauga* and the Burgundians changed their name to *Scandauii* in their new abode.

Traditions of an original northern home of the North West European nations, which at present answers to

Scania (southern Sweden), but which at first included Danish islands and possibly the Danish mainland as well, are given confirmation by place and river names. The archaic Scandinavian tribal names belong to the Bronze Age and have clearly come into being on the spot: Firðir from "fiords", Skeynir from Skaun "the fair districts", Fervir from Fjære "the ebb strand".

Further confirmation of a northern starting point for the wanderings of the North West European peoples and of a continuous southern trend is given by history after about 200 BC. From then right up to the eleventh-century expeditions of the Viking Age the movement of peoples has been a definite fanning out from north to south. When, as an apparent exception to the rule, there is a migration from south to north (for example, that of the Erules from the Middle Danube to Scandinavia, AD 505, or the Saxons from Italy to the districts of the Middle Elbe, AD 572), such a movement on closer inspection always shows itself to be a return home.

When Jordanes called the Jutland Peninsula, southern Norway and Sweden "a womb of nations" he was speaking truer than he realized. It was a womb that eventually was to people a large portion of the world. For, as I have suggested, not only did the early migrations of Angles, Saxons and Jutes, Visigoths, Ostrogoths, Vandals, Franks, Gepidae, Erules, Burgundians, Langobards and later the vikings populate or impregnate southern Europe, western Russia, North Africa, Britain, Iceland and Greenland, but their much more modern descendants colonized huge tracts of the world from North and South America to Africa, Australia and New Zealand. Nobody so far has satisfactorily explained why this tiny womb of a Jutland Peninsula, its islands and the neighbouring tips of southern Scandinavia should have been so fecund. Perhaps a familiarity with the ancient Gods of the North may suggest a few reasons.

3

MIGRATIONS OF THE NORTH WEST EUROPEANS

Having indicated the early links of language (and, by implication, of thought), habitat and pursuits of eleven peoples deriving from the Indo-European complex, it is now time to turn the spotlight on the North West European branch and in particular the one race among them, the Northmen, with whose gods we are especially concerned.

The North West Europeans were established in their "old home" in Denmark and southern Scandinavia before 1800 BC. By that time they were entering into the Bronze Age which is reckoned in those parts to last down to 600 BC. Shortly after 1000 BC, certain North West European tribes began pushing west and south-west from their "old home" into the territories of the Celtic peoples until, by about 200 BC, they had reached the Rhine and Main, and in the first century AD had occupied most of what is now southern Germany. This was the *Western* branch; these were the tribes from whom were to spring the modern Frisians, Dutch, Germans and Anglo-Saxons.

Another group of North West European tribes, the *Eastern* branch, began migrating from the southern Scandinavian peninsula somewhere about 500 BC. They crossed the Baltic and made their way into the region between and around the rivers Oder and Vistula, gradually trekking southwards in the next two hundred years until they had reached the foothills of the Carpathian mountains. These tribes included the Lombards from Scania, Burgundians from Bornholm, Rugians from Rogaland and Goths from Östergötland and Västergötland in Sweden. There were in addition Vandals, Gepids and Erules. A steady and continuous advance was maintained right across Europe up to the shores of the Black Sea. The first tribes to reach its shores were the Sciri and Basternae between 200 and 150 BC.

The importance of this south-eastern penetration for those of the North West European peoples left behind in

Scandinavia and Denmark is twofold: first, in the very contact of the Sciri and Basternae with other peoples such as Dacians and Greeks from whom new cultural and religious ideas were assimilated; and second, in that these new ideas were able to travel back to the "old home" in Scandinavia and the Prussian amber coast by way of the migration and trade routes. We have, therefore, no need to be surprised to find religious conceptions and even gods and goddesses of Asia Minor and Egypt bringing an exotic beam of the Middle Eastern sun to the cold northern latitudes.

The thrust to the south-east continued until about 113 BC, when the Cimbri left Jutland and attacked the Celtic inhabitants of Bohemia without much success. The stream then turned south-west from the Danubian countries and, from 109 to 101 BC, the Cimbri and Teutons harried Gaul and northern Italy. From this time down to 58 BC there appears to have been a general bulging westward from the Baltic to the Black Sea, a bulge which was shored up by Julius Cæsar and his legions when, in that year, they drove Ariovistus, king of the Suebi, across the Rhine. After 58 BC, the North West European nations became permanent neighbours of the Romans, and very soon the frontiers of Rome reached from the Rhine mouth to that of the Danube.

The next great move of the *Eastern* branch of the North West Europeans that is of importance to us is that of the Goths who had reached the districts of the lower Danube by AD 238, who conquered Dacia about AD 250, who made expeditions to Thracia, Asia Minor and Greece from AD 267 and who founded a kingdom in south Russia after AD 300. It is important to note once again the name of the Erules from south Scandinavia who rowed and sailed over the Black Sea, in company with the Goths; for after AD 500 the Erules turned about-face – having been forcibly persuaded to do so by the Langobards – and made their way back to Scandinavian parts, no doubt carrying with them much of what they had learned on their travels.

A furious wave of droop-whiskered, slant-eyed, butter-

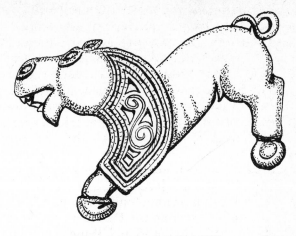

FIG. 3   ANIMAL PLAQUE

Part of a silver hoard left by the Goths near Kanef on the river Dnieper below
Kiev. Fifth century A.D. (British Museum)

faced horsemen next appeared in the shape of the Huns,
galloping at speed from the east. In A D 363 they hurled
themselves from the shores of the Caspian westwards and
forced the North West European tribes into their great
invasions of the Roman Empire. About the year A D 375,
the Huns forced the passage of the Don and overthrew the
empire of the Goths in south Russia. Ostrogoths, Visigoths
and Lombards made for Italy; Visigoths, Vandals, Burgundians and Franks invaded Spain, the Vandals even
continuing to North Africa. When, in the midst of this
pother and turmoil, the order went out from Rome at the
turn of the fourth century for the withdrawal of the legions
from Britain, the Angles and Saxons seized the opportunity
of changing their hit-and-run raids on the "Saxon shore" of
Britain into a permanent occupation.

In the first half of the fifth century, the restless Huns,
influenced by the subjected North West European peoples
and by contact with the Roman Empire, formed an organized state which was unified by Attila in about 445. Attila

pushed westward and crossed the Rhine in the spring of
451. The Roman Commander in north eastern Gaul,
Aetius, with an army of Romans, Burgundians and Visigoths, stopped the Huns outside Orleans, forced them back
and, on 14 June, defeated them near Troyes in Champagne.
The Huns brought off an orderly retreat, but in 453 Attila
died suddenly and the North West European peoples,
subdued but not assimilated, rose up and threw the Huns
back towards the lower Danube and the Black Sea Steppes;
so that in less than a century the thunder of the Hunnish
storm had rolled away into the distant east. But it is
unnecessary to trace the fortunes of the rest of Europe: the
centre of interest moves to Scandinavia itself, to the north
and west even as far as the coast of North America.

4

THE VIKINGS: SETTLING IN ENGLAND

The North West European races who overran the rest of
Europe as well as parts of North Africa in the fourth and
fifth centuries settled their peoples in those countries we
now call Italy, France, Spain and so on. Except for Anglo-
Saxon England, however, they failed to turn the regions
they conquered into a North West European empire or an
extension of the North West European world; on the
contrary, it was they who were assimilated by the Latin
populations they had conquered. The language and culture
of Italy, France and Spain have remained "romance"
down to the present day.

As for the branches of the North West European tribes
who sat back in the "old home" in Denmark and Scandinavia, it was not to be until just before A D 800 that they
became a terrible and disturbing factor in Western Europe.
In their harsh northland they lived the lives of relatively
uncultured pagan farmers-cum-fishermen: they were Iron
Age peasants occupying long low houses, "halls", perhaps
30 metres in length with aisles and "lock-beds" down the

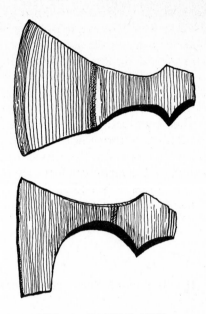

FIG. 4 BATTLE AXES

Above: half þynna; *below:* skeggøx or "bearded axe". The skeggøx was recommended for sea-fights, presumably because the beard was useful for grappling.
(After Rygh)

sides and a long-fire of wooden logs and turf down the middle. Each farmer had to be self-supporting, each man a stock-breeder and farmer as well as (if possible) a fisherman, which is as much as to say a boat-builder and seaman. Every housewife had to know how to spin and weave, to make cheese, butter and other dairy products. All clothes, furniture, utensils, ironwork, gear and fishing tackle had to be home-made. It has been suggested that the invention of the iron axe really touched off the viking expansion, for with it forests were cleared for new farms and planks were hewed for ships.

In character, these Northmen were brave, fiercely independent, hard, often cruel, grimly humorous, industrious, enterprising, active, selfish, faithful to death. Their dispositions were shaped by the barren soils, rocks, moors and mountains and the sea fiords, curled fingers reaching far into their homeland and beckoning them away. Their deeply indented coastline was vast, endless. The ocean washed up to their very doors, and the mountains at their back nudged them into it. All this was particularly the case in Norway. Forced to be fishermen, the Northmen spent half their working lives at sea. It was natural for them to expand over "the whale's way" and to fight if they were opposed. They sailed out of the dawn and they bullied their way west, leaving their starved stony farms, to look for living space. The poor crops of oats and rye, which were late to ripen and ticklish to harvest, and a primitive animal husbandry, eked out with sea fishing, provided a fare so meagre that the expanding population was driven "west-over-sea". Just opposite the bulge of the Norwegian peninsula lie the Shetland Islands, beyond them, to the north, the Faroes, to the south the Orkneys and Hebrides: they were like stepping-stones leading to better lands. The first navigations, gathering strength in the eighth century, were made by colonizing farmers. Later, kings and jarls, together with their retainers, realized the value of the stepping-stones as bases for plundering expeditions, and the rich churches and abbeys of Ireland yielded, from AD 803 onwards, a living far less laborious, far more exciting, than farming and fishing. The northern stream of vikings was met, in the middle of the ninth century, by a southern stream proceeding from Denmark down the Channel round Cornwall and into the Irish Sea. For a time the Danes (called by the Irish "the Dark Strangers") got on top, but the Norwegians ("the White Strangers") were reinforced by a fleet under Olaf the White, who made himself a king and ruled for twenty years in Dublin (833–871). England suffered because she lay between the claws of the attack.

The history of the viking raids on England may be divided into five phases between 787 and 1066. The first four fall into cycles of roughly thirty years each. In the first thirty years, from about 787, there were pinpricks (com-

FUThORCGWHNI
J I
A H
PXSTBENgDLMŒAY Ea

FIG. 5 SCRAMASAX

A *scramasax* or short one-edged sword (ninth century) found in the Thames at Battersea. The ornamental inlay of silver, copper and bronze incorporates a runic alphabet or *futhorc*. (British Museum)

pared with the wrath to come), minor raids on establishments at or near the coast. The objectives were rich monasteries or abbeys with portable plunder in the form of silver plate and gold. There was no question of staying. Once the ships' crews' bellies and gunny-bags were full they lugged their booty aboard and pulled away before any counter attack could be organized, threshing the waves with their thin-bladed oars in time to some wild heathen ditty in praise of Odin. "Cattle die," they sang, "kindred die, we ourselves die: but I know one thing that never dies – the fair fame of him who has earned it. . . . Never put your trust in a flying spear, a falling wave, a one night's ice, a coiled serpent, a broken sword or a woman's bed-talk." G. K. Chesterton caught the spirit of these times in his *Ballad of the White Horse*:

The Northmen came about our land
  A Christless chivalry:
Who knew not of the arch or pen,
Great, beautiful half-witted men
  From the sunrise and the sea.

> Misshapen ships stood on the deep
> Full of strange gold and fire,
> And hairy men, as huge as sin,
> With hornèd heads, came wading in
> Through the long, low sea-mire.

Though the prayer, "O Lord save us from the fury of the Northmen!", began to rise along the stricken shores of England and France, in these first years the vikings were a nuisance rather than a permanent oppression.

In the second thirty years, the vikings brought their bags and made some attempt to unpack them. Egbert, king of Wessex (*d.* 839), and his son Athelwulf (*d.* 858) were equally determined to see the unwanted squatters off. The *Old English Chronicle* contains entries like this:

> ANNO 851 This year Ceorl the aldorman fought the Heathen at Wembury in Devonshire and beat them after a bloody fight.
>
> The Heathen took up winter quarters on Thanet.
>
> This same year 350 ships entered the Thames estuary and took Canterbury by storm. They routed Beorhtwulf king of Mercia at the head of his army; then they crossed the Thames southward into Surrey to fight at Oakley against the Wessex levies led by king Athelwulf and his son Athelbald. Here the slaughter of the Heathen was more terrible than we have ever heard before and the English won a great victory.
>
> Again this year king Athelstan [of Kent] and aldorman Ealhere took part in a sea battle at Sandwich killing many of the invaders, capturing nine ships and putting the rest to flight.

If we count an average of forty men to a ship we can calculate that the expedition which captured Canterbury and was cut to pieces at Oakley numbered 14,000 men. A formidable host, just about double the estimated size of William the Conqueror's army which took England in 1066.

In the third period of about thirty years, the vikings really did move in lock, stock and barrel to East Anglia and Northumbria. The year AD 865 is as important in English history as 1066, for then the "Great Army" (as it came to be called) invaded and occupied the little kingdom of East Anglia. The Great Army's leaders appear to have been sons of Ragnar Shaggybritches, a viking of the epic kind, supposedly put to death by king Ælla of Northumbria who had him cast into a pit of venomous snakes. If it was so, the two sons, Ivar (with an equally romantic nickname, the "Boneless", perhaps because he was double-jointed) and Halfdan, later joined by a third brother, Ubbi, took an equally epic and savage revenge, first by laying the foundations of a "Danish" kingdom in England and then by making a martyr of the East Anglian king, Edmund, whom they tied to a stake and shot full of arrows.

The generals of the Great Army based their campaigns on the seizing of positions with natural defences, which they turned into strongholds from which they ravaged the surrounding countryside. Frequently, their earth-banked and palisaded forts were sited by navigable rivers. Their longships, whose dragon figure-heads had for years terrified look-outs and peoples of coastal areas where the boats could easily run ashore, as at Weymouth, were equally well suited for river penetration, and the Great Army worked its way inexorably into the body of eastern England up its river arteries. These vikings were bold and imaginative improvisors sometimes corralling the nags they had rustled into their narrow ships to move them from one area of plunder to another. Nor did they stop, if the need arose, at portaging their ships. They were always prepared to stand fast in defence, skilfully constructing earthworks (as at Benfleet in Essex) to protect themselves and their families. In addition, they knew well how to attack and break into fortified towns by brute force, stratagem or simple wiliness.

For a year after their invasion (for it was no less) Halfdan and Ivar the Boneless with their Great Army remained in East Anglia, stealing and rounding up the horses they needed for the expansion of their enterprise.

KAMB: KOTHAN: KIARI : THORFAST R

FIG. 6   BONE COMB

Back of a bone comb of viking type found at Lincoln. It bears the runic
inscription: "Thorfast made a good comb." (British Museum)

They also made raids which were immensely profitable in
two ways, first for their raw booty and second for the
protection money the raided were willing to pay to escape
further depredations. For the vikings were big-bodied men
with immoderate appetites for food as well as bloodshed,
not to mention women, but they were also businessmen
frequently willing to be bought off. "Danegeld" is a word
for protection money, which became common early on in
the English language. In any case, these payments never
work and it took the English many years to discover (as
Kipling sang):

> You will find it better policy to say:
>
> "We never pay *any*-one Dane-geld,
>   No matter how trifling the cost;
> For the end of that game is oppression and shame,
>   And the nation that plays it is lost!"

For ten years the Great Army retained the initiative in the
struggle for conquest and in fact, together with its reinforce-
ments, became so firmly ensconced in the land north of a
line drawn from the Thames estuary to the Mersey mouth
that this area became known as the "Danelaw".

Later in this third period of thirty years the vikings tried by force and stratagem to overrun the whole of southern England into the bargain. But the little kingdom of Wessex proved unconquerable, and her king, Alfred the Great (*d.* 899), defeated the "Danes" and had their leader Guthrum baptized. For the English, one of the most heartening entries in the *Chronicle* for this third phase of viking attack is that for the year 878:

ANNO 878 This year, in midwinter just after Twelfth Night the invaders came slyly to Chippenham [Wiltshire] and charged down on the West Saxons in a determined attack so that many were forced to flee overseas and the rest they conquered and enslaved except for King Alfred. He, with a small troop, escaped by the skin of his teeth to the woods and the desolate moors.

This same winter, the brother of Ivar and Halfdan [Ubbi] landed on the Devonshire coast in Wessex with 23 ships and was killed there together with 840 of his men.

That Easter, King Alfred and his handful of retainers threw up an earthwork at Athelney and, helped by the men of the neighbouring parts of Somerset, made forays from it on to the Danes. The seventh week after Easter he rode to Brixton-Deverill (Wiltshire) on the east of Selwood forest, to which spot there came overjoyed to meet him all the men of Somerset, Wiltshire and Hampshire who had not fled overseas. He left the town after one night and went to Iley; and the night after that to Ethandune, where he attacked the whole Danish army and put them to flight, pursuing them as far as their dug positions which he surrounded for a fortnight. The invaders then gave him hostages and swore great oaths promising to leave his kingdom as well as that their own king should be baptized: all of which they kept to.

Three weeks later, Guthrum and thirty of the most notable of the Danish army came to Alfred at Aller opposite Athelney and were received in baptism by the king. The ceremony of loosing the christening fillet was carried out at Wedmore. Guthrum stayed for twelve nights with the king who honoured him and his comrades with gifts.

In the fourth phase of viking attack on England (ending about AD 926) the Northmen still continued to settle in the Danelaw; but Alfred's successors established nominal rule over the Danelaw, which nevertheless retained its viking "law" – its customs and usages. King Alfred's famous daughter Athelfled, "the Lady of Wessex", and his son, Edward the Elder, between them annexed to Wessex every "Danish" colony south of the Humber. Edward the Elder's son, Athelstan, won a resounding victory in 939 over a combined army of "Danes" and Scots at Brunanburh. The *Chronicle* celebrated the victory in epic alliterative verse but the site of the famous battle is uncertain to this day. Perhaps it was Burnswork Hill in Annandale, six miles north of the Solway Firth. Its importance is in no doubt: "the question as to which Power in Great Britain should rule the destinies of the Island was put and settled once and forever" (Sir James Ramsey). The victor, Athelstan, was succeeded by Edmund and then Eadred, who in 954 drove out the last foreign kings of York and broke the viking power for the time being.

After a quarter of a century of peace there came to the English throne in 978 a boy of ten. This was Ethelred (whose name meant "noble counsel" and whose nickname was a pun on it, "Redeless" meaning "no counsel at all" or in the modern idiom "not a clue"): his main claims to fame are his five whacking payments of protection money to the "Danes" and the fact that when he was driven from his kingdom in 1013 he was followed by the first Danish king of England namely Swain of Denmark. This last phase of viking assault on England, then (from about 980–1066), saw a Danish dynasty on the throne: yet the reigns of Swain, Canute, Harald Harefoot and Hardicanute did not have the far-reaching effects of the previous peopling and farming of the Danelaw by Northmen. English kings returned in the persons of Edward the Confessor (1042–66) and Harold, who stopped the last true viking invasion of England at Stamford Bridge eight miles from York. On that hard fought field opposing Harold were Northmen led by the finest filibuster of his day, Harald Hardradi "the Headstrong", king of Norway, one-time Commander of the Emperor of Constantinople's Varangian guard, who had been the Empress Zoe's lover (they said in the north) and who was the hero of a thousand swashbuckling adventures. Although sixty years old, King Harald Hardradi was no weakling: he swung a double-headed axe (often in one fist) as though it were a rush. Snorri Sturluson says he was a handsome dignified man with yellow hair, yellow beard and long moustaches. One of his eyebrows was somewhat higher than the other which gave him a quizzical look. He had large hands and feet but was a well-proportioned man, for he was seven and a half feet tall. Fighting alongside Harald Hardradi at Stamford Bridge that September in 1066 was Harold of England's outlawed brother Tostig. On being offered peace to himself, Tostig asked what Harald of Norway was to get for his trouble in coming all the way to England. The reply, according to *Heimskringla*, shouted by King Harold of England himself, between the drawn up lines, was, "Hasn't the same man said something about wanting to peg a claim to English soil? Very well then: he shall have a seven foot plot – or as much more as he is taller than other men!"

Harald Hardradi got his plot of English ground and Tostig got one as well, but Harold of England was unable to follow up his success a few days later at Senlac. As the leaves turned brown, William the Norman, a Frenchified Northman with true Frenchmen as well as Normans in his train, began the last successful invasion of England to date.

Before leaving the viking attacks which led to settlement of parts of England it will be useful to consider the fortunes of religion in the country.

The Ancient Britons had been converted to Christianity. The Angles, Saxons and Jutes, who persecuted and gradually overran them after AD 450, were heathens. That is to

say, like the Northmen who were to give them the same
kind of medicine they had served out to the Britons, they
professed a different religion from Christianity. Their
heathendom seems to have existed on two levels and the
division was broadly one of class, each level of belief
according well with the life style of its adherents. There was
the aristocratic level with a family of gods and goddesses
from whom kings and eorls claimed descent, and whose
chief representatives were Woden and his wife Frigg. This
level had a recognizable cosmography in which the world
of men was Midgard, "the Middle Enclosure", with heaven
above and hell beneath. This was the heathendom of kings,
noblemen, professional warriors and poets in particular;
underneath there was the more robust, practical, stronger
heathendom of the peasant farmer, of village life, of the soil
with its rites reaching back into who knows what dim
distances of man's antiquity, rites to appease the gods of
the sun, rain and vegetation, rites such as the charming of
the plough (now the Christian *blessing* of the plough) on
Plough Monday, the charming of the sea and river to give
forth fish, of orchards to swell with fruit and fields to ripen
with grain, May Day and harvest festivals and offering
cakes to the sun and blessing and decorating wells to
persuade their Powers never to let them run dry. The
fertility aspect of this northern heathendom had been noted
down as far back as Roman times when Tacitus described
the rites accorded to Mother Earth, Nerthus, in the land
we now call Denmark. Mother Earth was worshipped in
England well after Norman times if her starkly naked
images on eleventh- and twelfth-century Christian churches
are any guide. Such images still survive on some twenty
known Romanesque churches in England, Wales and
Scotland. Good examples are at Whittlesford, Cambridge-
shire; Kilpeck, Herefordshire; Llandrindod Wells, Powys;
and Taynuilt, Muckairn, Scotland. Nor is documentary
evidence lacking for the worship of Mother Earth as for
example a twelfth-century medical treatise (Ms Harl.
1585, fol. 12a):

I MAN OF THE NORTH

Mummified head of a naked man found preserved in Tollund bog, Jutland, in May 1950 and thought to be some 2000 years old. 'Tollund Man' had been hanged, perhaps as a sacrifice to Odin.

2 MAES HOWE

In the great chamber of this Bronze Age tomb in Orkney there are twenty-four inscriptions cut by passing Vikings. Four of these say that *Jórsalafarar*, 'Jerusalem farers', i.e., Crusaders, broke into the Howe and removed the treasure. One such exploit is usually identified with the expedition of Jarl Rögnvaldr and Einðriði the Younger, which wintered in Orkney in 1150-1.

Holy goddess of Earth, parent of Nature, who dost generate all things, and regenerate the planet which thou alone showest to the folk upon earth. . . . Thou givest us food in safety by a perpetual covenant; and when our soul fleeth away, it is in thy bosom that we find our haven of rest. Thou too art called by the loving-kindness of the gods, the Great Mother, who hast conquered the god of Mighty Name. (G. G. Coulton, *Life in the Middle Ages*, Cambridge 1930, Vol 1, p. 41)

The heathendom represented at this level lives on to the present while Woden has long since gone and Thor and Tiw and Frigg: they have been overtaken by a Ragnarök, a Doom of the Divine Powers quite different from that described by the northern poets. They have simply been replaced and forgotten. How else can we account for the relative scarcity in England of place-names containing the names of the old North West European gods, or the comparative ease and speed of the conversion of the Angles, Saxons and Jutes to Christianity? Out of the thousands of Saxon place-names only half-a-dozen (it has been calculated) include Woden's name and only nine Thunor's.[6] Examples of each are Wednesbury in Stafford-shire and Thundersley in Essex. Other gods have left even fewer traces: we have Frigg's name in Friday and Tiw's name in Tuesday and possibly Tuesley in Surrey. As R. H. Hodgkin wrote:

> The world of Woden was ready to become a world created by an Almighty Father; dominated by his wonder-working saints, and tended by his bishops and clergy. The heavenly powers might change, but the underworld of monsters and evil spirits could remain to be marshalled by Satan into a host of demons [*Unholden*], the enemies of Christian men.[7]

There is no need here to follow in detail the conversion of the English; it is enough to indicate the significant dates. Augustine landed in Thanet in AD 597 with a mission to convert the English. At this time they were practically surrounded by Christian peoples in the Celts of Cornwall, Wales, Ireland and Scotland and the Franks across the Channel. When King Ethelbert of Kent heard of Augustine's arrival he had him fetched to Canterbury. Signs of the times were that Ethelbert had for nine years been married to a daughter of Charibert of Paris, namely Bertha, who remained a practising Christian and who had brought with her to Ethelbert's court bishop Liudhard of the Franks. Ethelbert gave the mission supplies, a dwelling in Canterbury and permission to preach. He himself was baptized, his lead being followed by his nobles and people, so that Augustine could claim that 10,000 men of Kent had been baptized by the end of the first year of his mission. Christianity spread to the other kingdoms of the country, to Northumbria, to Mercia, to Wessex, and, in spite of backslidings and returns to paganism in odd corners, the country could be claimed to be Christian by the year of the Synod of Whitby, AD 663. The descendants of the warlike heathen nobles who had wrested the land from the Christian Britons now supplied the Church with militant princes. As time went on, such a one was Wulfstan, Archbishop of York (1002–23), who pointed the irony of the wheel come full circle in a sermon delivered "to the English at a time when the greatest persecutions were put upon them by the [heathen] Danes". In these fiery words he fulminated from his minster pulpit in York:

Alas! for the misery and worldly shame the English must now endure through God's anger: often a couple of Northmen (or shall we say three?) will drive a whole gaggle of Christian folk huddled together out through the very heart of our nation from one sea coast to the other. O! what a shameful thing it is to us, if we could sincerely feel any shame or could be brought to an understanding of what is right! Instead, all these insults which we daily endure, we pay for with fawning on those who injure us: we continually give them protection money and daily they make us smart for it! They harry and they burn, they pillage, plunder and carry off to shipboard! And tell me! What else is it plain to see in

these events over all this nation but the wrath of God?
. . . There lived during the time of the Britons a sage
called Gildas, who wrote concerning their wrongdoings,
how with their wicked sins they drew down the wrath of
God upon their heads. In the twinkling of an eye, He
allowed the army of the Angles to overrun their land and
to kill the flower of their race. This came to pass
(according to Gildas) through the transgressing of laws
both holy and man-made; through plundering of the
kingdom and through covetousness of other people's
property; through the bad laws of princes and through
twisted judgments; through the sloth and unwisdom of
bishops; and through the wicked cowardice of God's
messengers who were far too frequently silent when they
ought to have trumpeted forth the truth, who mumbled
in their teeth when they should have shouted from the
house-tops; and it came to pass too, through the foul
wantonness of ordinary people, through their gluttony
and manifold sins, that they brought their land to utter
ruin and they themselves perished. . . .

Archbishop Wulfstan was preaching in York, the very
centre of the old Danelaw, somewhere about the time of the
expulsion of Ethelred the Redeless (1013) when the Danelaw had been lost and won back again but before the
Danish dynasty sat on England's throne. It seems that the
Northmen who had settled in England were converted
early to Christianity: there are even slighter traces of their
heathendom in place-names than there are of the heathenism of the Saxons. It is doubtful whether any English place-
name contains the name of the viking god most popular
among ordinary folk, *Þórr*: the Thurlstones and Thur-
golands are the *tuns* and *lands* of settlers named after the
god. It may be that O.N. *Óðinn* is to be found in Onesacre
and Onesmoor (Yorkshire), and O.N. *Vanir* in Wayland,
formerly Waneland (Norfolk). But there is evidence to
show that (as with the Anglo-Saxons) the under level of
heathen belief lived longer and is to be looked for in place-
names (quite common) which include elements like *elf*,
thurse (O.N. *þurs*, giant) and *troll*.

5

THE VIKINGS: SETTLEMENT OF ICELAND

The vikings flooded through the world of their time like a terrifying tidal wave engulfing parts of England, the coasts of Wales, Scotland, Ireland, Frisia and France. Northmen colonized the Faroes, Iceland and Greenland and no bones about it; gained a foothold on the Wendish and Prussian coasts and formed the nucleus of the Greek Emperor's bodyguard at Constantinople, even trickling into Spain and Italy and as far as the New World. But like the tide that spreads over a porous land and, except for isolated pools, disappears, so disappeared the Northmen, or seemed to do so as they merged into the peoples they had briefly dominated. Only the pools remained – the Faroes, Iceland and for a long time, nearly 400 years, Greenland.

Of these latter three places, Iceland is most important, for Iceland became the cradle of the written records of the traditions concerning the Gods of the North. These traditions are mainly contained in two literary works knows as the *Eddas*. The *Verse Edda* is a collection of ancient poems by unknown authors, and the *Prose Edda* a story book of Norse myth combined with a poet's handbook written by a famous Icelander, Snorri Sturluson (*d.* 1241).

It seems that the Northmen first discovered Iceland by chance: a Norwegian called Naddod was driven by contrary winds on to the coast; then Gardar a Swede drifted there from the Pentland Firth. Flóki, another Norwegian, attempted to settle in Iceland but, deceived by the mild summer climate, neglected to make hay to over-winter his cattle. He was forced to leave. Before he did so, he climbed a mountain and saw a fiord filled with pack ice: he called the country, rather spitefully, Iceland. These visits took place round about AD 860, five years before the gangster-like sons of Ragnar Shaggybritches and their "Great Army" descended on East Anglia and began the foundation of the Danelaw in England. Some ten or twenty years later a significant and famous battle took place in Norway at Hafrsfiord[8] when Harald Fairhair (son of King Halfdan

the Black) after fifteen years of fighting broke the resistance
of the west Norwegians and made himself king of all
Norway. It appears that the threatened loss of independence
drove many of Harald's defeated enemies to emigrate and
most of them went to Iceland, the first settler (following in
the footsteps of Naddod, Gardar and Flóki) being Ingolfr.
This Moses of the Icelandic people:

> settled in the south, in Reykjavik. He first touched land
> at a spot now called Ingolfr's Head east of Minthakseyr;
> and he laid claim for ever to Ingolfr's Fell west of Ölfossa.
> At that time Iceland was well wooded between the fells
> and the sea shore. (*Libellus Islandorum*, by Ari Thor-
> gilsson, writing between 1122 and 1133)

Further on in the same work, Ari Thorgilsson writes:

> There were living in Iceland at that time those Christian
> folk whom the Northmen called *papishers*.[9] But they
> afterwards went away, not liking to remain here with
> heathens though they left behind them Irish books,
> bells, and croziers: and this was sufficient evidence of
> their being Irish monks. After that there was a great
> flitting of people from Norway out here until King
> Harald [Fairhair] put a stop to it for fear of depopu-
> lating the homeland.

Ingolfr settled at "Reeky Bay" now Reykjavik, the
capital, about the year 874; Ari Thorgilsson says it took
another fifty years to colonize the island completely. A
traveller of a later day has left a description of the
topography of Iceland:

> Imagine to yourself an island, which from one end to
> the other presents to your view only barren mountains,
> whose summits are covered with eternal snow, and
> between them fields divided by vitrified cliffs, whose
> high and sharp points seem to vie with each other to
> deprive you of the sight of a little grass which scantily
> springs up among them. . . . Rivers and fresh water
> lakes abound; the latter of very considerable extent and
> well supplied with fish; the former . . . much obstructed

by rocks and shallow. [And, he might have added, piercingly cold and milky white from the melt-water of the glaciers, but embellished with some of the most wondrous waterfalls and cataracts in the world.][10]

The traveller who wrote of Iceland was William Jackson Hooker, who, thirty years later, in 1841 became the first director of Kew Gardens. He describes the barren moors, morasses, volcanoes, sulphur springs and boiling fountains; he mentions what the main items of the native diet were, and there is little reason to suppose these items had changed a great deal since Ingolfr's days – fish and butter. The fish was eaten mostly dried and uncooked (it frequently is today), and the butter was made without salt and with all the whey and superfluous moisture pressed out (so that if necessary it could keep indefinitely – ideal provender for long sea voyages). Milk was converted into *syra*, or sour whey, preserved in casks until it fermented. This mixed with water was called *blanda*. Then there was *striugar*, whey boiled to the consistency of curd; *skyr*, which was *striugar* with the moisture squeezed out. The flesh of sheep and bullocks could be eaten only by the well-to-do.

It is important to remember that not all the first colonists of Iceland came from Norway, Denmark and Sweden. Many emigrated from the colonies of Northmen in the British Isles, especially from the settlements in the Hebrides and Ireland. Even if these Northmen themselves had no Celtic blood in their veins, many of their descendants had, their fathers having married or entered into concubinage with Celtic women; and a childhood spent at a Celtic knee meant for the child an absorption of Celtic lore and culture. Evidence of links between Iceland and the Celtic countries can be seen in the names of Celtic origin borne by famous Icelanders of the tenth century, Njáll, Kormákr, Kjartan; and by such stories as that of Helgi the Lean, who settled in Iceland and whose mother was Rafarta (Irish *Rafertach*) daughter of an Irish king, Kjarvalr, said to be Cearbhall, king of Ossory who died in 887. Many of the Icelandic thralls obviously came from Ireland or the Hebrides: they had such Celtic names as Dufan and Melkólfr, while the Westman Islands off Iceland's south coast still retain the name of the rebellious thralls who once set up a brief republic there. A fair sprinkling of Icelandic place-names are of Irish origin, and how are they to be explained except as the abodes of Celts or Northmen with Celtic links? Examples of such place-names are Papey, Pappabýli, Patreksfjörðr, Minþakseyrr (near Ingolfr's first landing place), Brjánslœkr and Dufgusdalr. Everyday contacts resulted in Irish words being adopted into Old Icelandic, as for instance *slavak* (from Ir. *sleabhac*) chickweed; *súst*, a flail (Ir. *súiste*); *tarfr*, a bull (Ir. *tarbh*). This evidence of Celtic links is important when one comes to consider whether or not the Old Icelandic eddaic verse holds notions deriving from Christianity through the Christian Irish.

Still, the bulk of immigrants to Iceland came from Norway bringing with them, besides their pots and pans, a fierce spirit of independence, a love of adventure and a superb seamanship to back it up. They brought, too, long memories and to assist those memories a strong mould of genealogical lines and another strong mould of alliterative verse, both of which gave and kept shape to their oral tales and unwritten ballads. Ten centuries later a visitor to Iceland was struck forcibly by the tough fibre of this oral tradition:

> Scarcely a man in Iceland bears the same surname as his father. Only a few householders have a family name and they are all recent arrivals. A man whose name is Eric Sigurdsson may have his son baptized Olaf, and this child will all his life bear the name of Olaf Ericsson. If, in turn, Olaf gives the Christian name of Haukur to his son, that fellow will have as his full name Haukur Olafsson. . . .
>
> This would be a shiftless arrangement were it not for the genealogical interest which each man takes in his forefolk. They can all tell you their ancestors' names for the last thousand years, and are thus conscious of

living, not in the current generation but a river of
personal life. "I am the thirty-fourth generation since
the immigration", one will tell you. The immigration is
the year 874, when the first of them landed on their
empty island.[11]

The strength of tradition (and the Icelander's respect
for it) is contained in that sentence, *They can tell you their
ancestors' names for the last thousand years*; and there is not the
slightest doubt but what that tradition was just as strong
and just as respected among those first immigrants themselves.

At first, none of the traditions was warped or transmuted
(according to the way you look at it) by Christianity, for
the settlement of Iceland as an outpost of heathendom
continued for over a century. Then, at a famous meeting of
the Council of the country, the *Althing*, in A D 1000 it was
decided officially to accept Christianity.

The Althing was set up about 930, after the Icelandic
góðar, who were both secular chiefs and pagan priests, had
appointed one of their number, Ulfljót, to draw up a code
of laws, which he did after spending three years as an
observer in Norway. A president over the Althing, called
the Lawspeaker (*lögsögumaðr*), was appointed for a term of
years, and one of his duties was to recite the laws (or part of
them) at the yearly meeting. This meeting always took
place on the Thingvellir (or Thing Plain, east of Reykjavik)
in the summer time. Few details of the ancient laws remain,
but enough to show they were given some force by heathen
oath and ritual.

The Althing played an important part in the conversion
of the country. To all intents and purposes Iceland
remained pagan from its first colonization by the Northmen
in 874 down to the year 1000. Some of the earlier settlers
were indeed Christianized emigrants from Ireland or the
Hebrides, such as Helgi the Lean (already mentioned) and
Aud the Deepminded, widow of Olaf the White, viking
king of Dublin (page 15). Helgi made the best of both
worlds: he believed in Christ and called his estate in
Iceland *Kristnes* (Christ's Headland), its name to this day;

but in any tight corner or when he was at sea he never
neglected to invoke the help of Thor. Aud, on the other
hand, was a devout Christian who set up crosses near her
home at the spot which thenceforward to the present has
been called *Krosshólar* (Cross Mounds). Aud's nephew,
Ketill, was nicknamed "the Fool" by his heathen neighbours because of his religious observances as a Christian;
but Helgi the Lean's descendants returned to paganism.
So, though at first some settlers were Christian and some
others were influenced by Christianity, it would seem that
after a generation the pagan gods reclaimed their own, and
throughout the ninth century heathenism was general in
Iceland.

How far the Icelanders of these early years could be
called practising pagans is something of a puzzle. Probably
(and I write without irony) with as much truth as one
could call the population (the *native* population, that is) of
Great Britain practising Christians today. The pagan
religion (in contrast to Christianity) had no dogma and
appears to have made few moral or ethical demands on its
subscribers. The poem *Völuspá* does indeed speak of oath-
breakers, murderers and possibly adulterers as persons
who must tread the Helway after death. But in general, the
pagan ritual of Iceland seems to have called mainly for
propitiation of the gods by prayer and sacrifice. The centre
of the organized religion was the temple, a simple rec-
tangular building. Remains at Hofstadir, near Mývatn in
the north of Iceland, show a building oriented north–south
with two rooms, a main one and a smaller one at the north
end where (it seems likely) were set up wooden figures
representing the god or gods. Round the walls of the main
room there were benches for the worshippers. In *Eyrbyggja
Saga* there is a description of furniture used in a temple
dedicated to Thor and built by Thórólfr, a settler in the
Broadfirth region who had come from Norway. In the
middle of the small room, standing on the floor, was a
pedestal (like an altar) on which lay a great arm ring
"without join". This ring weighed twenty ounces and all
oaths had to be sworn on it. At public gatherings the

temple priest had to wear the ring on his arm. Animals were sacrificed and their blood caught in a bowl which also stood on the pedestal; in the bowl was a sacrificial twig like the aspergillus used in the Roman Catholic Church to sprinkle holy water over the congregation: but the twig spattered blood. This blood was called *hlaut*; and according to *Eyrbyggjar Saga* the effigies of the gods stood around the altar-like pedestal. A remarkable survival from the heathen age in England, a similar stone pedestal, still stands in the lovely old Romanesque church of Saintfield, near Broadway in Gloucestershire. Perhaps more remarkable, there is in the same remote church an image of the pagan mother goddess of fertility set in a splay of one of the south windows. We need not therefore be surprised that as late as AD 1013, after 400 years of nominal Christianity in England, Wulfstan, Archbishop of York, was bearing witness to heathen customs which he must have observed in the Danelaw or heard of being practised in the northern countries; he says, in the course of the sermon already quoted on page 24.

> Among the heathen Danes no man dare withhold one jot or tittle laid down for the honouring of their idols: but we everywhere far too frequently fail to render God His lawful dues. Nor among the heathen dare men desecrate inside or out the offerings or sacrifices laid before their graven images: but we have stripped clean God's Church of every due, out and in. Everywhere (or nearly so) the servants of God are deprived of the respect and reverence which is their right: yet men say among the heathen nobody dare as much as offer to hurt their priests. . . .

Of course, we have to remember that Wulfstan was very likely exaggerating his contrasts for effect; and he shows no evidence of understanding the peculiar position of the heathen priest as a temporal as well as a spiritual leader.

The gods who were actively worshipped in Iceland appear to have been few in number. The favourite (if personal and place-names are anything to go by) was Thor. Thor was a favourite in Norway and the preponderance of his devotees in Iceland is another indication that the majority of settlers came there from Norway. Frey was the favourite in Sweden; in Iceland he was commemorated in place-names, had temples dedicated to him and was patron of a famous saga *góði* called Hrafnkell (nicknamed *Freysgáði*) and of a family called *Freysgyðlingar*. Njörðr is remembered in such place-names as *Njarðvík*; and there is slight evidence of a cult of Týr and Balder. As in Anglo-Saxon England, there was an underground religion and there were "heathen" heathens like the Icelandic family notorious for worshipping a stallion's penis, obviously a form of fertility rite. The phallus (whether of horses or men) had always attracted veneration as is attested by the phallic wooden effigies dug up from Danish bogs, and the famous idol of Frey at the temple of Uppsala dignified with what Adam of Bremen called "a gigantic erect penis".[13] There were witches about too. One kind of witchcraft mainly practised by women was called *seiðr*; it was a type of sorcery which even found its way into Asgard as is told in a dramatic episode in *Völuspá*. In this case the witch was punished by being spitted on an arch of spears over the long-fire in Valhalla and burnt to death. People believed that spirits could return from the dead, the Icelandic ghost being more akin to the West Indian zombie, a corpse-like walker after death rather than a transparent wraith. Such a ghost required a macabre ritual before it could be laid: reburial at a cross-roads (a Christian influence?) with a stake through the heart. Those whose passage from this world to the next went smoothly appear to have had a long journey before them. Some were provided with special shoes, others with a boat-shaped grave or an actual boat. The destination of the traveller could be either hel or Asgard; though many saga personalities are pictured living a sort of sedentary existence in their grave mounds. From belief in spirits in grave mounds to spiritualism was no doubt an easy step. There is an account in the *Saga of Thorfinn Karlsefni*[14] of how in the Greenland colony round about the year 1000 a "prophetess", little different from a modern spiritualist medium, got in touch with those "on the other side". It may be objected that *Thorfinn's Saga* first found itself in manuscript form some 300 years after the event and reflects later ideas; however, in rebuttal, we do know from Irish sources that a similar "séance" took place in Ireland as early as 841, when Aud, the wife of a Norwegian viking Thorgest, sat up on the high altar at Clonmacnoise and scandalized the clergy by going into a mediumistic trance.

No matter how the missionaries tried they would never stamp out the smouldering underground beliefs. Perhaps the first attempts to convert Icelanders to Christianity were made shortly after AD 980. An account of such attempts is given in *Kristni saga* (*Saga of Christianity*) and in *Þorvalds þáttr Víðförla* (*Story of Thorwald the Wanderer*). Both date from the thirteenth century and, while unreliable as connected historical accounts, they probably have a basis of truth. If one person could be called responsible for the conversion of Iceland, that one must be Olaf Tryggvason, a very famous Norwegian viking who made himself king of Norway in 995. During the five years of his reign, Olaf Tryggvason is said to have made Christians of six nations (according to *Agríp*), namely the peoples of Norway, Iceland, Greenland, Faroe, Shetland and Orkney. It is told how Olaf, while harrying from a base in the Scilly Isles, played a similar sort of trick on a Christian hermit as Charles the Dauphin and Gilles de Rais are said to have played on Joan of Arc. The disguise of Olaf's impersonator was spotted at once and the hermit (to give good measure) foretold happenings which took place in the next few days and convinced Olaf of the genuineness of the new religion. He is said to have been baptized. At all events, Olaf Tryggvason appears in English records accompanied by Swain Forkbeard in an attack on London (8 September 994). King Ethelred the Redeless bought his peace by the pound (16,000 pounds of silver) and stood sponsor for Olaf to be confirmed into the Christian religion. When Olaf Tryggvason returned to Norway the next year, 995, and made himself king, he took with him a bishop (sometimes called Jón, sometimes Sigurd) and a number of other priests. There can be little doubt that Olaf preached Christianity in Norway with fire and sword wherever he met opposition: he himself went out like a light, dowsed in the waters of the Baltic when his longship the *Long Serpent* was ambushed by one Eirík. Fifteen years after Olaf's death, the interior of Norway was completely pagan while the people of the coastal districts, although baptized, knew little of Christian teaching. It was left to St Olaf, king of Norway, who worked on much the same lines as Olaf Tryggvason, to complete the conversion before he was killed at the battle of Stiklastadir in AD 1030.

As to Iceland, one of the six countries claimed as proselytized by Olaf Tryggvason, conversion dates from the year 1000. That year, at the June meeting of the Althing, the pagan party and the Christian party declared each other outlaws, each electing its own Lawspeaker. But moderation prevented bloodshed and finally the parties agreed to abide by the decision of the pagan Lawspeaker, a man of recognized integrity called Thorgeir. Thorgeir retired into his booth and pulled a cloak over his head; he spoke to nobody for a day and a night. He then came out and ascending the Lawrock announced his decision: all Icelanders were to be Christian in name and to be baptized, but at the same time, those who desired it were to be allowed to observe their pagan rites in private. It was to be some years before these observances were forbidden.

It is instructive to compare the tolerance meted out to paganism in Iceland with the intolerance it received in Norway. Although paganism as a religion lived on longer in Norway, when it did come to be dealt with it was fanatically and fiercely burnt and cut out: that treatment effectively suppressed pre-Christian religious traditions in Norway. But in Iceland those traditions lived on, at first orally, then to this day in written edda and saga.

6

THE EDDAS

The main literary sources of information about the Gods of the North are two: the *Verse Edda* and the *Prose Edda*. A third important source is the first nine chapters of the *Danish History* by Saxo Grammaticus. To these may be added the sagas and the skaldic poems. The *Verse Edda* must be regarded as the primary source for two reasons: it is the oldest of this kind of source and the majority of its poems had taken shape before the pagan period ended. The most informative poems of the *Verse Edda* can be dated to the ninth century, while both the *Prose Edda* and the *Danish History* were composed about the year 1200, i.e. 200 years after the introduction of Christianity to Iceland.

The *Prose Edda* was written by Snorri Sturluson, a famous Icelander who lived from 1179 to 1241. The superscription of the manuscript copy in the *Uppsálabók* set down about half a century after Snorri's death runs, "This book is called *Edda* which Snorri Sturluson composed." The meaning of *Edda* has caused considerable argument. The word occurs in the old poem *Rígspula* where it seems to mean "great-grand-mother". Jacob Grimm's suggestion was that, as used in *Uppsálabók*, "edda" meant "tales of a grandmother". Nothing could be less appropriate to the subject matter. It seems obvious now that Eirikr Magnússon's explanation[12] must be the right one: that *Edda* is the possessive case of the place-name Oddi. It was at Oddi in the south-west of Iceland that Snorri lived from his third to his nineteenth year, under the tutelage of the grandson of Sæmund the Learned, who had founded a school at Oddi. *Edda* is thus taken to mean the "Book of Oddi".

But Icelandic tradition persisted in ascribing an *Edda* to Sæmund the Learned himself and this ascription became all the more puzzling when Arngrimur Jónsson proved early in the seventeenth century that Snorri was indeed the author of the *Edda* which bore his name at the head. Clearly, if Sæmund had written one, then there must be another *Edda*. There seemed little doubt that this *Edda* had been found, when in 1643 Brynjólfr Sveinsson, Bishop of Skálholt in Iceland, discovered a manuscript dating from 1300 and containing twenty-nine poems (more or less intact), some of which had actually been quoted by Snorri. Brynjólfr called the manuscript *Sæmund's Edda*, but while it is improbable that Sæmund composed any of the poems, it is almost certain that the book was at one time part of his library at Oddi. This treasure found its way to the Royal Library at Copenhagen where it was known as *Codex Regius* (R2635). It has formed the basis of all published editions of the *Verse Edda*, though a few poems of similar character, found elsewhere, have been included until most editions now contain thirty-four poems. Any open-minded student of the *Verse Edda* is bound to come to a number of conclusions: while the style and subject matter of these poems have enough in common to set them apart from all the rest of extant Old Norse poetry, they are not the work of a single poet. In fact, many of the pieces are a patchwork of incomplete poems in different verse forms by different hands; some of the verses were composed in Iceland, others hail from Scandinavia and still others possibly from Greenland – some may even come from the Norse settlements in the British Isles. The poems fall into two types: those dealing with the world of the gods (the mythological poems) and those dealing with the world of men (the heroic lays); both types are allusive in the extreme and rarely tell a connected tale from beginning to end. There is still a good deal of disagreement about the interpretation of much of the *Verse Edda*.

Snorri's *Prose Edda* is really a handbook for poets, or skalds. There are four parts to it: first, a short Prologue which is an amalgam of Bible story, pagan myth, the "Matter of Troy" and popular history, in which Snorri rationalizes the old gods into a kind of supermen, who became the ancestors of Scandinavian kings; next, a connected account of myths of the Northmen based on oral tradition, on the poems of the *Verse Edda*, and other poems of a similar kind no longer extant, and on poems by ancient skalds. Th s part of Snorri's *Edda* is called *Gylfaginning*, or "The Tricking of Gylfi", Gylfi being a legendary Swedish king who journeys to Asgard and who by dint of numerous questions put to High, Even-as-high and the Third (Odin regarded as a trinity) elicits the mythological information. The third part of the Prose Edda is *Skáldskaparmál*, "The

Poetry of Skalds", which in addition to more myths contains a treatise on the conventional vocabulary, phraseology and figures of speech fit to be employed in skaldic verse by budding poets. The fourth and last part, the *Háttatál*, or "Enumeration of Metres", gives examples by Snorri himself of 102 separate metric types or sub-types of stanza.

Snorri Sturluson's familiarity with what we now call the *Verse Edda* is shown by his frequent quotation from poems in the collection, such as *Völuspá, Hávamál, Grímnismál, Vafþrúðnismál, Alvíssmál* and the complete version of *Grottasöngr*. He knew *Lokasenna*; possibly by heart and not from referring to a manuscript, for he quotes a stanza made up of lines from three others. The measure of wonderful material lost to us is brought home by Snorri's quotations from seventeen other poems similar to those in the eddaic collection but now no longer extant; and he mentions one title, *Heimdalargaldr* (*Lay of Heimdallr*), which tells of another missing piece.

There are aspects of both *Eddas* which it will be more convenient to discuss in the mythological chapters of this book; but there are two general matters which will be better discussed now than later, namely the verse forms of the *Versa Edda* and Snorri's treatment of his sources.

The verse forms are important, first, because they are set in a mould which is not easily broken, so that the original composition is given a great chance of continued existence; and, second, the student can see when the mould *has* been broken and knows at once to suspect loss, addition or tampering, and he may be guided to correct emendation. The verse form may be sometimes a rough guide to age, as for instance in the poem *Þrymskviða*, which in the manuscript begins:

> *Reiðr vas þá Vingþórr*
> *es vaknaði.*

We suspect that when the poem was composed the word *reiðr* (our word *wroth*) was pronounced *vreiðr* with a *v* which alliterated with the *v* in *Vingþórr* and *vaknaði*. If we know

3 VÖLUSPA

A page from the *Verse Edda* manuscript known as *Codex Regius* (R 2365), in the Royal Library at Copenhagen. This particular leaf is from *Völuspá* and recounts the Doom of the Gods, beginning with the god Heimdallr's sounding the call to arms.

4 HELMET FROM SUTTON HOO

An ornamental helmet of the kind Odin is supposed to have worn, with the exception that Odin's helmet was of gold and this one is of iron overlaid with silver and gilt-bronze. The helmet was discovered in 1939 at the excavation of the Sutton Hoo ship burial and is similar to others found in Swedish boat graves at Vendel and Valsgärde. They were probably worn on ceremonial occasions.

when speakers got into the habit of dropping such a *v* then we know the poem was in all likelihood composed before that date.

Before discussing the metrical forms of the *Verse Edda* I want to call attention to the fact that verse as a means of expression is of extreme antiquity among the descendants of the Indo-Europeans. Correspondences between the metres of ancient verse forms such as the Hindu Vedas, the Iranian Gathas and the Greek lyrics suggest some form of common metrical tradition inherited from an earlier epoch. The tradition was one of metres depending on a regular structure with a set number of syllables to a line. A specialized development among the speakers of the North West European group of languages is thought to be due to the preference those speakers had for placing the main accent on the first syllable of any word. This specialized development is *alliteration* – the repetition in two or more words of the same initial sound, especially where the alliterating sound bears the stress.

Alliteration is one of the four main attributes of the old North West European versification, the other three being stress, arrangement into lines and the grouping of lines into stanzas. Both Old Norse and Old English verse share these attributes, though Old Norse tends more to arrange the lines into groups of four. Nowadays, English speakers are apt to look down upon alliteration (once the mainstay of ancient versification) as a bit of fun left over from the nursery, a tongue-twister, or as a poor joke on a par with a pun – "Peter Piper picked a peck of pickled peppers"; for the Norman Conquest put the old metre out of tune by hastening the inflexional breakdown of Anglo-Saxon – words lost their old endings – and by introducing French vocabulary and end-rhyming verse forms. Nonetheless, English poets never allowed alliteration as an integral part of poetical form (and not a mere ornament) to die, as a couple of examples chosen at random with five centuries separating them will demonstrate:

> *R*obin, *t*ak *t*ent unto my *t*ale,
> And wirk all as I *r*eid,

> And thou sall *h*aif my *h*eart all *h*aill
> Eik and my maiden-*h*eid.
> (*Robin and Makyne*,
> Robert Henryson, fifteenth century)

> Daffodil *b*ulbs instead of *b*alls
> *S*tared from the *s*ockets of the eyes!
> He knew that thought clings round dead *l*imbs
> Tightening its *l*usts and *l*uxuries.
> (*Whispers of Immortality*,
> T. S. Eliot, twentieth century)

In the *Verse Edda* the bulk of the lines are divided into two half-lines by a definite pause or "caesura". Each half-line has two heavily stressed syllables:

> crág peaks crásh as   the kóbolds scúttle . . .

There is no need for all four stressed syllables to alliterate, though in strictly regular verse the *third* syllable should always do so. Snorri Sturluson called this third stressed syllable the "head" stave or letter and said it dominated in recitation. Either or both of the first and second stresses could carry alliteration, the fourth one rarely. All vowels alliterate with each other and for this purpose *h* and *j* are counted as vowels.

The three verse forms exemplified in the *Verse Edda* are called Old Story Measure, Speech Measure and Song Measure:

(1) Old Story Measure (*Fornyrðislag*) has stanzas of four lines, each with four main stresses and the caesural pause. In strictly regular metre not more than three unstressed syllables are permitted in each half-line. An example is stanza 51 of *Völuspá*:

> From the *s*óuth drives *S*úrtr   with the *s*cóurge of fórests,
> the *b*áttle-god's sún   *b*lázes from his swórd,
> *c*rág peaks *c*rásh as   the *k*óbolds scúttle;
> déad tramp the *H*élway   and *H*éaven crácks.

Old Story Measure is sometimes called epic metre, and the eddaic poems whose subject matter is concerned with the affairs of the North West Europeans on the Continent – the memories of the heroic age of the Goths and Burgundians and Attila the Hun – are all composed in either Old Story Measure or Speech Measure:

(2) Speech Measure (*Málaháttr*) is similar to Old Story Measure except in one respect: more unaccented syllables are permitted in each half-line. In the regular form there may be three or four of these unaccented syllables in a half-line which gives a more rapid colloquial rhythm, e.g. stanza 39 of *Atlamál*:

Högni put his *s*póke in,   he *s*pát at thought of yíelding,
he *f*éared not a jót   what *f*áte had in stóre.
"Trý to make us *w*índy!   You'll *w*áste your bréath and
time,
I *t*éll you all your *t*álk   won't *t*álk you out of déath."

(3) Song Measure, sometimes called Chant Measure (*Ljóðaháttr*), differs from the other two metres in that the second and fourth lines of each stanza have no break or caesura. These unbroken lines normally have three stressed syllables, two of which regularly alliterate. In the half-lines there should be no more than two or three unaccented syllables (as in Old Story Measure). An example is stanza 41 of *Grímnismál*:

Out of Ýmir's flésh   was the éarth fáshioned,
from his gúshing góre the séas,
hill tóps from his bónes   trées from his háir,
héav'nly *s*ky from his *s*kúll.

In my translations I have tried to fit the sense into the appropriate verse form without unduly contorting the English. I have adhered to lines and alliterating pattern except that sometimes I have allowed the fourth accented syllable to alliterate; also on occasion I have let in more unaccented syllables than the strictly regular form permits. Both these irregularities are frequently met with in the original Icelandic verses.

It will be useful to say what some of the eddaic lays of the gods are about, since they are to be one of the windows

through which we can look back on to northern myth.
Völuspá, or *The Spaewife's Prophecy*, is perhaps the most
magnificent poem of them all. In it Odin, chief of the gods,
has spirited from her grave a *völva* (translated spaewife,
sybil or seeress), who tells him of the past during which the
world was created, of the first man and woman, of the
World Ash Yggdrasill and of the war between two rival
factions of gods, the Æsir and Vanir; she then tells of the
future, prophesying the doom of the gods and the destruction by fire and flood of heaven and earth. This is not quite
all: a new and beautiful universe is to arise with new men
and women and both new and old gods. *Völuspá* stands at
the beginning of *Codex Regius*, but another version (found in
Hauksbók, compiled about AD 1300) gives many stanzas in a
quite different order. There are what seem to be interpol-
ations in both versions, such as the extended list of dwarfs'
names (stanzas 11–15 inclusive), and, throughout, missing
lines and corrupt passages which defy translation. One
important point should be made: *Völuspá* is allusive and
episodic to an extent that would be extremely baffling had
no other mythical sources survived; it is certain that the
poem was intended for an audience which was well able to
fill in the gaps. No doubt such an audience existed when
Völuspá was composed, but when was that? Not later than
1064, for an echo of *Völuspá* is found in a poem by Arnórr
Jarlaskáld in honour of the Orkney Jarl Thorfinnr who
died in 1064. Arnórr sings:

> *Björt verðr sól at svartri   søkkr fold í mar døkkvan*

which clearly recalls Snorri's quotation from *Völuspá*,

> *sól tér sortna   søkkr fold í mar.*

The internal evidence suggests that the poem was
composed in Iceland, and Iceland was not colonized until
after 874: so we are left with a period, 874–1064, in which
Völuspá could have been composed, and the present con-
census favours a date about AD 950.

Another poem, *Vafþrúðnismál* (*The Words of Vafþrúðnir*), is
an encyclopedia of mythological information framed as a

question-and-answer contest between the giant Vafþrúðnir and Odin (in disguise). Each wagers his head on the result of the contest and Odin wins when he asks, "What did Odin whisper into the ear of his son [Balder] before he was burnt on the pyre?" *Vafþrúðnismál* is contained in *Codex Regius* and from stanza 20 on is also included in the *Arnamagnaean Codex*. The date of its composition is believed to have been near that of *Völuspá*, i.e. about 950.

A similarly encyclopedic poem is *Grímnismál* (*The Words of Grímnir*, i.e. the "Masked One"). Odin appears as usual in disguise at the court of an earthly king, Geirröðr, who has been warned against a stranger. He has Odin seized and pinioned between two fires. The father of the gods is slowly scorched but is given relief in the form of a horn of ale by Geirröðr's son (some say brother) and recounts to him the mythological stories. In the end, Odin throws off his disguise and Geirröðr in terror falls upon his own sword. *Grímnismál* is introduced and concluded by a prose narrative in both manuscripts (*Codex Regius* and *Arnamagnaean Codex*) in which it occurs. The prose was written (no doubt by the compiler of the eddaic corpus) in the twelfth or thirteenth century; the poem itself was composed about 950. The prose narrative suggests two important conclusions: first, the point I have already made, that the eddaic poems in their episodic and allusive treatment of myth presuppose an audience which already knew the background story; and second, that after 150 to 250 years of Christianity (i.e. when the eddaic poems were brought together in manuscript) the audience for the *Verse Edda* had forgotten or was forgetting the background of the myths.

Altogether there are some fifteen lays of the gods in the eddaic collection. Since Snorri made extensive use of them when he came to write his *Prose Edda* it is important to form a true opinion of his treatment of the extant poems as sources, especially as by analogy we can decide how he treated sources no longer available to us except through his writings.

Scholars' opinions of the mythological value of the *Prose*

Edda have been almost amusingly diverse. Writing simul-
taneously in the last quarter of the nineteenth century,
Rydberg and Vigfusson held views as opposite as the poles.
Viktor Rydberg in *Teutonic Mythology* (published in English
in 1889) used Snorri's work when it suited his book but
otherwise did not hesitate to slight *Gylfaginning* as being
"produced in the thirteenth century by a man who had a
vague conception of the mythology of our ancestors" (page
380). Vigfusson on the other hand claimed that *Gylfaginning*
"rested upon a purer, fuller, and earlier text" of *Völuspá*
"than any other version preserved"; and that Snorri,
"though basing his work most largely on the two Sybil
Songs [i.e. *Völuspá* and the *Shorter Völuspá*] *plus* Wafthrudni's
and Grimni's Lays", has "not scrupled to omit or re-
arrange where it suited his purpose, though he has *not*
falsified or defaced his authority".[15] Snorri did make
mistakes, but I find myself in a greater measure of agreement with Vigfusson than with Rydberg.

Here are some of my own arguments to support the belief
in Snorri's probity in dealing with mythological material.
Respect for tradition was and still is a national characteristic of the Icelanders: we have seen it noticed by the
traveller in 1953 who said, "They can tell you their
ancestors' names for the last thousand years"; we can see it
in such early writers as Ari Thorgilsson, who habitually
quotes a string of authorities for statements he makes.
Snorri's authorities are the ancient verses, and in
Gylfaginning alone he supports his account by quotation
from the old poems on at least fifty-two separate occasions.
In a number of places Snorri makes it plain in what light he
regards the old poetry: he says in his Preface to *Ynglinga
saga*, "We rest the foundations of our story principally upon
the songs which were sung in the presence of the chiefs
themselves or their sons, and take all to be true that is
found in such poems about their feats and battles."[16] It
could be objected that this refers only to historical and not
mythological material; but in *Skáldskaparmál I* Snorri
adjures young poets "not so to forget or discredit these
traditions as to remove from poesy those ancient metaphors

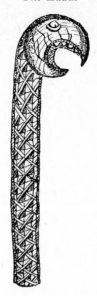

FIG. 7 OAK STERN-POST
Found with ship's timbers in the river Scheldt near Termonde, Belgium.
Ninth century A.D. (British Museum)

with which it has pleased Chief Skalds to be content; nor on the other hand, ought Christian men to believe in heathen gods, nor in the truth of these tales otherwise than precisely as one may find in the beginning of this book."[17] What exactly is Snorri saying here? The "beginning of this book" to which he refers is the *Prologue* to the *Prose Edda* in which he gives a euhemeristic account of Odin and the other deities. As I have already said, this is a rationalized account of the gods as men who came from Asia, and is bolstered up with such popular and false etymologies as AEsir = men from Asia; it is such an account as that which he gives in greater detail when he purports to write a truly historical work, namely the *Ynglinga´ saga*. But nothing could be more striking than the difference in his treatment of Odin, Thor and the rest in the *Prologue*, on the one hand, and in *Gylfaginning*, on the other. In the *Prologue*, Thor is a grandson of Priam of Troy and Odin his descendant in the twentieth generation; in *Gylfaginning* Odin is a god, a son of Bor, a son of Búri who was licked out of the primeval ice by the mythical cow Audhumla.

What Snorri is saying, then, is that the heathen lore is to be treated on two levels; first, without alteration by the poet, and, second, with legitimate manipulation by the historian who must make the most reasonable account he can from the materials at hand: for whereas the audience for myth would be willing to suspend disbelief, the audience for history must be reasoned into belief.

If we accept these arguments, then Snorri in *Gylfaginning* and *Skáldskaparmál* becomes a more important source than the *Verse Edda* in spite of the fact that he wrote some 250 years after the poems had taken shape and some 200 years after the conversion of Iceland. For Snorri reproduces most of the mythological material contained in the *Verse Edda* and, in addition, a good deal no longer extant in verse: for example, what we know of Niflheim and Muspellheim (names nowhere mentioned in the *Verse Edda*), most of what we know about Hvergelmir (mentioned only once in the *Verse Edda*), the attributes of the god Heimdallr (except for *Þrymskviða's* information that he is "the whitest of the gods"), the fact that Geri and Freki are wolves and Huginn and Muninn ravens, that Balder was kept in Hel because Loki disguised as Þökk would not weep for him – and so on.

In the account of the Gods of the North which follows, I treat the two *Eddas* as of almost equal importance, but check one against the other and both against Saxo, the skalds, philology and archaeology.

CHAPTER I

In the Beginning

ALLFATHER

In answer to the question "Who is the One who was there from the beginning of time? Who is the oldest of the gods?"† Snorri Sturluson replies, "He is called Allfather (so the story goes) and in the Ancient Asgard he had twelve names: first Allfather, second Lord (or Lord of Hosts), third Lord of the Spear, fourth Smiter, then All-knowing, Fulfiller of Wishes, Farspoken, Shaker, Burner, Destroyer, Protector and twelfth Gelding."

Snorri gives this further information: "He lives through all time and he rules his kingdom with absolute power over all things great and small. . . . He created heaven and earth and sky and everything within them . . . but most wonderful was when he created man and gave him spirit which shall be eternal and never fail though the body drop to dust or burn to ashes. Aye, all men shall live who live with right and decency and be with him in that place called Gimlé or Vingólf; but the wicked shall descend to Hel and from there to Niflhel which is indeed in the depths, nine worlds down."

Snorri adduces one other fact in answer to the enquiry "How did he pass his time before heaven and earth were made?" "All those aeons of time he was with the Frost Giants."

In this myth of Allfather we meet at once with confusion. Allfather is said to be "the oldest of the gods", to have been "there from the beginning of time", to have "created heaven and earth and sky and all within them", to have "created man", to be the ruler "of his kingdom with absolute power"; and yet he shares some of these attributes with the god called Odin. For,

† *Gylf.* III.

as we shall see in detail later, Odin (with his two brothers) is said to have created heaven, earth and man, and like Allfather is called at one time or another by the twelve names used for Allfather. In fact, in both *Eddas* "Allfather" is taken to be synonymous with "Odin". But Odin did *not* live from the beginning of time; he was born of the union of Bor and a giantess Bestla; nor did Odin "rule his kingdom with absolute power"—he was at the mercy of fate: both Snorri and the ancient verses are agreed on these points. There can be no doubt but that Allfather and Odin (no matter how they have got mixed later) were originally two different personages.

Then who *is* Allfather? Since Snorri was nominally a Christian, writing in Iceland two hundred years after Christianity had been officially accepted there, it was to be expected that commentators would claim to find Christian traits embodied in his *Edda* and in particular in the conception of Allfather. Put the name "Jehovah" in place of "Allfather" in the passages I have quoted, substitute "heaven" for "Gimlé" or "Vingólf" and "hell" for "Niflhel", and a good Christian would find nothing to strain his conscience or beliefs. Even the very phraseology smacks of the Bible—except of course, the remark about the Frost Giants and one or two of Allfather's special names such as "Gelding". The Christian doctrines dealing with the creation of man, the spirit of man, punishment in hell and reward in the New Jerusalem seem to be sharply reflected in Snorri's description of Allfather.

And yet we must exonerate Snorri from the charge of Christianizing heathen myth: for in this instance we can trace his sources to the pagan poems which were in existence 250 years before Iceland officially adopted Christianity: to *Völuspá* 63 for instance:

Sal sér hon standa	A hall she sees stand
sólu fegra,	fairer than the sun,
golli þakðan,	thatched with gold
á Gimléi;	in Gimlé;

þar munu dyggvar	there shall they dwell
dróttir byggva	the doers of right
ok of aldrdaga	and ever and ever
yndis njóta.	enjoy delight;

and to *Völuspá* 36 and 37:

Sal sá hon standa	A hall she saw stand
sólu fjarri	far from the sun
Náströndu á,	with doors facing north
norðr horfa dyrr;	on Nástrand;†
fellu eitrdropar	drops of poison
inn of ljóra,	dripped through the smoke-hole,
sá's undinn salr	the hall is wickered
orma hryggjum.	with the backs of snakes.

Sá hon þar vaða	She saw there wade
þunga strauma	through weltering waters
menn meinsvara	men forsworn
ok morðvarga	and murderers too;

and to *Vafþrúðnismál* 43:

níu komk heima	to nine worlds I came
fyr Niflhel neðan	to Niflhel beneath
hinig deyja ór helju halir	where dead men drop from hel.

Of course, it has been argued that *Völuspá* and other of the pagan poems are themselves affected by Christian doctrine; that although they were composed some fifty years before Iceland officially accepted Christianity, nevertheless, there had been Christians in Iceland before the ninth century, and Northmen in the Western Isles and Ireland were avowed Christians from before the time of the Icelandic settlement. My own view (and for the moment I put it forward simply as a view) is that some of the eddaic poems were affected by *recent* Christian teaching and (what has not been properly recognized) that for some centuries on the Continent the thought out of which the poems

† Corpse strand.

flowered had been affected by Christian doctrines. In spite of
these Christianizing influences it is possible to adduce evidence
to show that Snorri's Allfather is basically a pagan conception
of a primitive deity.

There is among the twelve names applied by Snorri to the
Primal Deity one which sticks out like a sore thumb: it is the
twelfth name, *Jalkr*, the Gelding. Nowhere in either *Edda* or in
any folklore of the Scandinavian peoples does there appear to be
an explanation of *Jalkr*, of why the Allfather should be called a
Gelding. But there *is* an echo in one of the myths of another
Indo-European people, the Greeks:

> Ouranos, the god of the sky, came in the night to his
> wife, to the Earth, to the goddess Gaia . . . being inflamed
> with love, [he] covered the earth and lay all across it, the
> son [Kronos] thrust out his left hand from the place of
> ambush and seized his father. With his right hand he took
> the huge sickle, quickly cut off his father's manhood, and
> cast it behind his back.[18]

Ouranos was god of the sky. There is no doubt that Snorri,
at any rate, regarded Allfather as god of the sky. He says in the
Prologue to his *Edda*, speaking of mankind in ancient days:

> the thought stirred within them that there might be some
> governor of the stars of heaven: one who might order their
> courses after his will; and that he must be very strong and
> full of might. This also they held to be true: that if he
> swayed the chief things of creation, he must have been be-
> fore the stars of heaven; and they saw that if he ruled the
> courses of the heavenly bodies, he must also govern the shin-
> ing of the sun, and the dews of the air, and the fruits of the
> earth, whatsoever grows upon it; and in like manner the
> winds of the air and the storms of the sea. They knew not
> yet where his kingdom was; but this they believed: that
> he ruled all things on earth and in the sky, the great stars
> also of the heavens, and the winds of the sea.[19]

In his book *The Aryans* Professor V. Gordon Childe says on page 5 "It is certain that the great concept of the Divine Law or Cosmic Order is associated with the first Aryan [Indo-European] peoples who emerge upon the stage of history some 3,500 years ago. Even the original Aryans [Indo-Europeans] themselves worshipped at least one deity, a Sky Father." The name of this deity comes from an Indo-European form which according to Schütte[20] is debatable; either it is I.E. *Djevs* which gave rise to O.Ind. *Dyaus*, Gr. *Zeus*, Lat. *Ju(piter)*, Gothonic *Tiwaz*; or it may be I.E. *Deivos*, cf. Lat. *divus* "divine", *divum* "sky", Lithuanian *dẽvas* "God "and "sky" (Finnish loan word *taivas* "sky"). The idea behind the original word *Djevs* appears to have been "shining" and the later development "sky">"God" and not "God">"sky", or the opposite to the development outlined in the quotation just given from Snorri's *Prologue* to the *Edda*.

This interesting word is common Gothonic, appearing as Gothic *Tyz* (name of a rune), O.H.G. *Ziu*, O.Fris. and O.E. *Ti(w)*, O.N. *Týr*. It is the name forming the first element of Tuesday. In the pantheon of the North, Týr is regarded as the god of war; he is no longer the "sky father", although clues to his former identity still remain. The name Týr itself is sufficient to identify its bearer with *Djevs*; in addition, there is Snorri's reminder in *Skáldskaparmál* that the old poets frequently use the word "*týr*" as a synonym of "god"; and the main myth by which Týr is remembered shows him as the guardian of the sky against the wolf Fenrir and his sons who will shut off the "shining" of the heavens by gorging the sun and moon. Týr, then, the Northmen's god of war, was originally Allfather, the sky father, and Odin is a deity who at some period has usurped his position and many of his attributes.

It may be helpful to speculate on when Týr sank in the social scale. As I have said, the Old English form of his name is fossilized in Tuesday. Tuesday is an adaptation or translation of the Old French name for the day of the week named after Mars, the modern French *mardi*, Mars' day. Tiu or Týr is taken to be the equivalent of Mars the Roman god of war. But the seven-day week was adopted in Rome only as late as *c*. A.D. 300. The suggestion is, then, that by round about this date the original Allfather of Indo-European myth had completed his development into the Northern Týr, god of war. How much earlier the change took place I shall hope to enquire later on.

2

GINNUNGAGAP

In the beginning there was nothing but a Yawning Gulf, a mighty void called Ginnungagap. Snorri says so in *Gylfaginning* IV, and to emphasize the nothingness in contrast with the something of our everyday experience he quotes a stanza from *The Spaewife's Prophecy*:†

> In ancient days
> existed nothing,
>   neither sand nor sea
>   nor swelling billows;
> there was no earth
> there was no heaven
>   not a blade of grass
>   but a Yawning Gulf.

This chaotic region, this Ginnungagap, was nevertheless not empty. Snorri goes on to say that there were two contrasting regions in Ginnungagap: to the north lay Niflheim (the home of fog) which had existed "countless ages before the earth was created"; and to the south lay Muspellheim (the home of the destroyers of the world). These two regions contrasted even as ice and fire, for Niflheim was compact of freezing and fog while Muspellheim was full of flame and heat.

In the centre of Niflheim there surged and boiled up the mighty fount of all waters, a well called Hvergelmir, the

† *Völ.* 3.

Roaring Cauldron. Hvergelmir is not mentioned in *Völuspá*, nor indeed in any other poem of the *Verse Edda* except *Grímnismál*, where it is described as the source "whence all rivers run" followed by a catalogue of some forty river names. Snorri contents himself at first with a list of eleven rivers by name, Svöl, Gunnþrá, Fjörm, Fimbulþul, Slíðr, Hríð, Sylgr, Ylgr, Víð, Leiptr and Gjöll "which is the one nearest Hel Gate Bars"; but later on† he gives an account of twenty-five such rivers. Eleven, twenty-five or forty, it is evident that Hvergelmir the Roaring Cauldron was no trickling spring but a mighty geyser of tumescent, tumultuous waters.

Hvergelmir bears a distinct family resemblance to that ancient stream of Greek myth, Okeanos, to which Homer refers as "the origin of the gods"[21] and "the origin of everything".[22] In his *Gods of the Greeks* Kerényi says of Okeanos that "Ever since the time when everything originated from him he has continued to flow to the outermost edge of the earth, flowing back upon himself in a circle. The rivers, springs and fountains—indeed, the whole sea—issue continually from his broad, mighty stream."

But what connection there is between Hvergelmir, the rivers which issue from it and another important stream called Élivágar or Icywaves, we are left wondering. Of the importance of Élivágar there can be no doubt for, says Snorri,‡ it "had welled up from its source from time immemorial, and yeasting through it a poisonous scum which set like the slag which runs out of a furnace. This hardened into ice. When the ice stopped and flowed no further it hung suspended where the spume rising from the poison scum froze into rime. And this congealed fog grew and spread over everything in Ginnungagap." The result was that "the Yawning Gulf which lay to the north quarter was filled with heavy and crushing ice and frost from the drizzling rains and blasts; while in contrast, the southern sky of the Yawning Gulf glared with sparks and molten gases gushing out of Muspellheim." There is this further to add, that the

† *Gylf.* XXXIX.   ‡ *Gylf.* V.

"region to the south (now called Muspell) was nothing but fiery heat, where the skyline flared and flamed so as to bar the way to strangers and such as have no stake there."†

3

YMIR

It seems that the first living creature was a giant: his name was Ymir.

The third stanza of *Völuspá* as we have it in the *Verse Edda* begins not as the version from Snorri already quoted, but like this:

> Long aeons ago
> was Ymir created:
> no sand was, nor sea,
> no swelling billows . . .

and so on. The ancient poem *Vafþrúðnismál* adds a little more information when it says:‡

> the poison drops
> dripping from Icywaves
> waxed till a giant was.

The poems do not actually say that Ymir was created within the Yawning Gulf though they strongly suggest it in speaking of him in *Völuspá* 3 in close conjunction with Ginnungagap, and in *Vafþrúðnismál* 31 by indicating that he arose from Icywaves. Snorri fills out the picture:§ "Just as cold and all terrible things blow up out of Niflheim, so the entire neighbourhood of Muspell was of heat and flame. But the Yawning Gulf was as mild as the windless air, and where the freezing met the livid heat it melted and dripped away. From the fermenting drops fusing to life by virtue of the power which threw up the heat, there was shaped the likeness of a man. He is called Ymir: though the Frost Giants called him Aurgelmir [Mud Seether] for from

† *Gylf.* IV.   ‡ *Vaf.* 31.   § *Gylf.* V.

him their race claimed descent. . . . He was no god but a creature of evil, and so was all his get: we call them Frost Giants" says Snorri. "It's said that as he lay sleeping, Ymir began to sweat and under his left hand there grew a male and a female; then his one foot gat a son upon the other and from these sprang all the legion of Frost Giants." The ancient verses agree with Snorri's description of the origin of the Frost Giants, and the hermaphrodite quality of Ymir is strongly brought out in this question and answer from *Vafþrúðnismál*†

> Odin: How gat he bairns
> that giant grim
> who never a giantess knew?
>
> Vafþrúðnir: They say neath the hand
> of the giant of ice
> grew maid-child and man together;
> one foot on the other
> of the wise giant fetched
> a son who bore six heads.

The giant with six heads was called *Þrúðgelmir*, the Mighty Roarer, an apposite title for one with six throats and six tongues, and who himself was father to Bergelmir the Noah among the giants.

There is no doubt about the antiquity of the ground-work of this myth of Ymir, though time has wrought some changes: many strands of crumpled weft and cryptic woof have gone into the weaving of the tale before we get the version unfolded in the two *Eddas*. Earlier, Ymir seems to have been the ancestor of humanity, "the maid-child and man" who grew under his hand. By "earlier" I mean in and before the first century A.D. Our Eddaic sources show us a creature coming from the frozen earth, a creature with hermaphroditic qualities, who from his own body gives birth to *man* and woman. A creature, similar in each of these three respects is described by Tacitus (A.D. 98) in chapter 2 of his monograph on our continental ancestors the

† *Vaf.* 32, 33.

Germania: *Celebrant carminibus antiquis, quod unum apud illos mem-
oriae et annalium genus est, Tvistonem, deum terra editum, et filium
Mannum, originem gentis conditoresque.* "In their ancient ballads,
their only forms of recorded history, they celebrate Tvisto, a god
sprung from the earth, and they assign to him a son called
Mannus, the founder of their race." We have here, as with
Ymir, the creature coming from the earth who gives birth to
"Mannus", i.e. *man*, and whose name Tvisto emphasizes his
hermaphroditic quality: for in the circumstances the Tvi- of
Tvisto can only be cognate with the Indo-European prefix
meaning "double" which is found in O.N. *tví-*, O.E. *twi-*,
Sanskrit *dvi-*, and Mod. Eng. *twin*. There seems little doubt that
Mannus = man is to be discovered among the Indo-Iranian
branch of the Indo-Europeans. There is an Indian primeval
ancestor Mānus with a son Mānavas and a daughter Mānavī
and descendants called Mānušas; and there is an Iranian
primeval ancestor Mešia married to Mešianě.

It will be instructive to look closer at the Iranian version of
the story which is preserved in *Bundehesh* 15. A primeval being
in human form, Gaya Maretan (Gayomert) was created from
sweat but was slain by the evil Angra Mainyu. There sprang
from Gaya Maretan a plant (*rheum ribes*)† with a single stalk. A
man and a woman developed within the plant and in such unison
with each other that it was impossible to see which was which,
and they were holding their hands over their ears. Then Ahuramazda said to them, "Be human beings and bring forth the race
of mankind!" After this they separated and took on the form of
human beings, when Ahuramazda enjoined them to think good
thoughts, speak good words and do good deeds. It was not long,
however, before they thought an evil thought and became sinners.

The parallels between the Nordic and Iranian versions of this
creation-of-man myth indicate that they originate from the one
source: we shall soon see similar myths of the Northmen which
also derive from that source.

† genus "rheum" = rhubarb, a plant of Asiatic origin which is propagated by
splitting the root, cf. mandrake.

That Ymir was at one time believed to be the progenitor of mankind (rather than of the giants) is suggested by his name. "Ymir" looks as if it might come from Old Swedish *ymu-man* "man from Umeå Lappmark" and is part of the body of evidence to show that the ancient Scandinavians derived their primeval ancestors from the Finns. We shall be fairly safe in assuming that Ymir-Aurgelmir = Tvisto was regarded in the North as the progenitor of mankind down to as late as the end of the first century A.D. But after that date a new god, Woden-Odin, was to oust the old Indo-European Sky Father (*Tiwaz-Týr-Tíw*), and, as the new Allfather, Woden-Odin had to take his place in the creation myths which were modified to accommodate him. So according both to Snorri and the *Verse Edda* Ymir is no longer the ancestor of mankind; he is no longer a god though he is still *terra editum*; instead he is a creature of evil and for that reason a suitable first parent for the race of giants.

Before Ymir gave birth to the Frost Giants provision was made for his own sustenance. Snorri gives without explanation a story which has its origin in the common stock of early Indo-European myths: he says "the very next thing after the rime dripped down, there solidified from it the cow called Auðumla [Nourisher] from whose teats spirted four rivers of milk: she fed Ymir." Without trying the ins-and-outs of the tale one might observe that the cow, the supplier of the primal food, milk, is an obvious fertility symbol.

4

THE SONS OF BOR

The cow Auðumla also needed to eat. "She licked the rocks of ice which she found salty. When she licked the rocks on the first day there appeared out of them by evening the hair of a man; the second day, a man's head; the third day, a man complete. He is called Búri, beautiful to look upon, great and mighty. He begat a son called Bor who took to wife Bestla, daughter of the giant Bölþorn [Evil Thorn]: they had three sons called Odin, Vili and Vé."†

In this account Snorri was evidently able to draw on other local sources no longer available to us, for there is no mention of the cow Auðumla nor of Búri in the *Verse Edda*. The father of Odin, Vili and Vé, i.e. Bor himself is introduced twice in the ancient verses (*Völuspá* 4 and *Völuspá hinn skamma* 2) and then merely as the father of Odin; while *Hávamál* (140) is the only eddaic poem to speak of Bölþorn and his daughter Bestla (without adding much to our information). The fact that neither Snorri nor the *Verse Edda* gives us much information about Búri, Bor, Bölþorn and Bestla might indicate that there was never very much information to give; this suggestion is supported by the knowledge that the names Búri and Bor mean practically the same thing, "born" or "created" ; and when we ignore for the moment Bestla and Bölþorn, we find we have the old creation myth mentioned by Tacitus. For, to give it in full, Tacitus' story‡ goes "In their ancient ballads, their only form of recorded history, they celebrate Tvisto, a god sprung from the earth, and they assign to him a son called Mannus, the founder of their race, and to Mannus three sons, their progenitors, after whom the people nearest Ocean are called Ingævones, those of the centre Herminones, the remainder Istævones." If we set the three versions of the myth side by side we can easily see the points of resemblance:

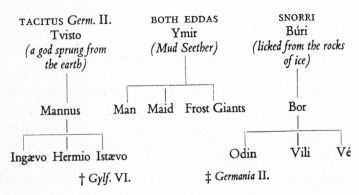

† *Gylf.* VI.   ‡ *Germania* II.

In putting these genealogies alongside each other I am not of course suggesting that Búri= Ymir-Tvisto or that Odin, Vili and Vé are Ingævo, Hermio and Istævo. What I am suggesting is that there is a strong connection between all three myths and an ancient Indo-European myth dealing with the creation of gods and men: nor are we finished, for we shall find yet other variants of the tale.

According to Snorri the story goes on that the sons of Bor (Odin, Vili and Vé) and the old giant Ymir fell at loggerheads.† "The sons of Bor knocked the giant on the head, and when he keeled over, so much blood poured from his wounds that every man-jack of the Frost Giants got drowned except one. He just managed to escape with his family. The giants call him Bergelmir. He scrambled on to a mill together with his wife and they were both saved: from them springs the race of Frost Giants, as this rhyme will tell‡

> Unnumbered winters
> ere world was made
>   then was Bergelmir born;
> I mind first of all
> the wise old monster
>   who was made to lie on a mill."

Odin, Vili and Vé then§ "took Ymir's carcass and flitted it to the middle of the Yawning Gulf and made the earth out of it. And from his blood they created the lakes and seas. In actual fact, the earth was made from his flesh and the mountain crags from his bones; rocks and screes they made from his toes, his double-teeth and bits of splintered bone."

A new race now came into being.|| "The dwarfs had first taken shape and life in the carcass of Ymir and were at that time like maggots; but at a word of the gods they became conscious with the intelligence of men and had human form. They lived in the earth and the rocks." Four of these dwarfs were marked out for important work.

† *Gylf.* VII.　　‡ *Vaf.* 35.　　§ *Gylf.* VIII.　　|| *Gylf.* XIV.

The sons of Bor† took Ymir's "skull and made it into the heavens, poising it high over the earth with a dwarf stationed to hold it aloft at the four corners. These dwarfs are called East, West, North and South (*Austri, Vestri, Norðri, Suðri*). They then took the glowing cinders and sparks which are thrown up and blown up out of Muspellheim and set them in the midst of the Yawning Gulf, both alow and aloft to give light over heaven and earth. They appointed their steadings to all the stars: some in heaven, some to pass backwards and forwards under the heavens; and they stablished their places and laid out their paths. According to the ancient traditions, from this labour came the tally of nights and days and the measuring of the years."

There is this further information: "the earth is round, and about it lies the deep blue sea. Along the outward shores of the ocean Odin, Vili and Vé gave a grant of land" which came to be called Jötunheim "to the race of giants to settle in. But towards the centre of the earth they built a fortress wall encircling the region against their giant enemies: and to make it they employed the brows of Ymir, and called their stronghold Midgard. They took his brains too and flung them to the winds and so created the clouds."

As authority for these statements, Snorri quotes from *Grímnismál* 41, 42:

> Out of Ymir's flesh
> was the earth fashioned
>   and from his gushing gore the seas;
> mountain tops from his bones
> trees from his hair,
>   heavenly sky from his skull.
>
> Then out of his brows
> the joyous gods built
>   Midgard for the sons of men;

† *Gylf.* VIII.

and from his brains
there burgeoned all
   the soul-encooping clouds.

Similar confirmation is given in *Vafþrúðnismál* 21; but *Völuspá* makes no mention of Ymir's corpse having been used in the creation: it says†

   Then Bor's sons lifted
   the level land,
      Midgard the mighty
      there they made;
   the sun from the south
   warmed the stones of earth
      and green was the ground
      with growing leeks.

There are a number of curious points in Snorri's account of the creation of the world from Ymir's body: on some of these it will be worth while to speculate. For instance, Snorri, in his account of the flood which overwhelmed the giants, evidently pictured Bergelmir and his wife (the only survivors) as escaping by clambering on to a mill. But there are strong doubts as to whether the earliest version of the myth contained any such suggestion. The word "mill" occurs as *lúðr* in connection with Bergelmir in both *Vafþrúðnismál* 35 and in Snorri. But this stanza from the *Verse Edda* which Snorri has quoted to support his story of Bergelmir's escape has no reference at all in the poem to the flood which drowned the giants: Vafþrúðnir simply says "My earliest memory is of the giant Bergelmir who was laid on the mill." Snorri could get no other meaning out of this than that Bergelmir and his wife "scrambled on to a mill", i.e. a spot higher than flood level, and so were saved. Modern commentators and editors[23] have twisted the original meaning still further and for "mill" read "boat" so that Bergelmir has become a northern Noah and his *lúðr* an Ark. The emendation

† *Völ.* 4.

"boat" is first found in the Resenian edition of Snorri's *Edda* (Copenhagen 1665) where Snorri's *fór upp á lúðr sinn* "scrambled up on to his mill" is changed to *fór á bát sinn* "went into his boat". We can be certain then that Vafþrúðnir is not connecting Bergelmir with the flood and that there is some other meaning (which we will leave for the moment) about the giant's being "laid on a mill".

Nevertheless, there is confirmatory evidence that the story of a flood drowning the giants was known to other of the Gothonic tribes. It was certainly told among the Anglo-Saxons for we find it preserved in *Beowulf* where (suitably Christianized) it is mentioned as the theme of decoration on the golden hilt of the gigantic sword found by Beowulf in the cave of Grendel and his mother. The hero Beowulf shows the hilt to Hroðgar king of the Danes:†

> Hroðgar spoke
> when he saw the hilt,
> the ancient treasure.
> Of old had been traced there
> a struggle of antiquity
> when a storming flood,
> a roaring sea,
> slew the giant race.
> They had lived with pride,
> that people estranged
> from eternal God
> Who gave as reward
> this final requital
> a mighty flood.

A second reference occurs at lines 113–114 where the poet speaks of "the giants who for a long time struggled against God." In *Beowulf* the giants' adversary has become the Hebrew deity Jehovah; just as in the *Prose Edda* the giants' adversary has become Odin (together with his brothers); but the myth is far

† *Beowulf*, 1687–1693.

older than Odin's assumption of first place among the gods of the northern pantheon, and the war of the giants was originally a war against Allfather, the Indo-European Sky Father (as seen in the parallel Greek version of the war between Zeus and the Titans). Despite the flood the giants were not annihilated: they appear in Anglo-Saxon folklore and play a most important part in late northern pagan myth. The story of Bergelmir's survival is an attempt to explain rationally how the giant race was carried on after the great flood and bears all the marks of a late addition and one probably influenced by the Old Testament tale of Noah.

There is one other great work for which the sons of Bor are said to be responsible—the Creation of Mankind. When, according to *Gylfaginning*, Gylfi king of Sweden had heard of the wonders of the creation of the world he remarked† "It seems to me the gods had done quite a bit when heaven and earth were created, when sun and moon were set in their courses, and day and night given their appointed span. But now may I ask where did the Men come from who peopled the world?"

This was the answer he received, "As the sons of Bor strolled along the deep sea strand they stumbled across two logs of driftwood and picked them up and whittled them into humankind. The first son gave them soul and life; the second, understanding and the power to feel; the third, form and the faculties of speech, hearing and sight. They gave them clothing and called them by their names, the man Ash and the woman Elm (*Askr, Embla*). These two brought to birth all mankind who were given a dwelling place in Midgard."

The story of the creation of mankind in *Völuspá* 16–17 is substantially the same as that just quoted except that there is no mention of whittling the logs or clothing the man and woman; and most important, the names of the sons of Bor are given not as Odin, Vili and Vé but as Odin, Hœnir and Lóðurr:

> Then came three
> out of the throng

† *Gylf.* IX.

of the mighty and gracious
gods at home;
they found on the land
empty of force,
Askr and Embla
empty of fate.

They had no spirit,
no five senses,
no heat, no motion
no healthy hue;
spirit gave Odin,
sense gave Hœnir,
heat gave Lóðurr
and healthy hue.

There is one further difference between the two accounts, namely, that *Völuspá* suggests the other gods are already in being, while Snorri has nothing to say of any except Odin, Vili and Vé. It is easy to impute the differences to rationalizing, as for instance, in the details he gives of the whittling of the logs and the clothing of them. But it happens that there is still extant a snatch of ancient verse which again vindicates Snorri of the charge. The title *Hávamál* means "the Sayings of the High One", i.e. Odin, and the "saying" in stanza 49 goes

My garments once
in a field I gave
to two men made of trees:†
with these clothes they knew
they had donned nobility—
the naked man is naught.

This stanza can refer only to the northern myth of the creation of man and taken together with the other versions presents parallels which show the original closeness of this and the Iranian tale already mentioned on page 56. If we put the two side

† *tveim trémönnum.*

by side, we can see that there must have been a common Indo-European myth which told of the creation of humankind from trees or plants. The extraordinary viability of these tales is borne out not only by such extant literary remains as I have just discussed but also by old wives' tales of the present day with which embarrassed parents brush off children's enquiries about the facts of life: I mean the explanation of new-born babies in the story of their being found under gooseberry bushes. This is indeed debased coinage but it comes from the same mint as the story in *Bundehesh* and the two *Eddas*.

As far as the later development of the northern version is concerned we shall need to discuss further the relationship between Vili, Vé and Hœnir, Lóðurr (see page 144ff).

5

NIGHT, DAY, SUN AND MOON

I have already quoted (page 60) the tradition recounted by Snorri of the creation of the heavenly lights from sparks and cinders blown up out of Muspellheim and of how from this labour of Odin, Vili and Vé came "the tally of nights and days and the measuring of the years".

Snorri unabashedly sets down other traditions about night and day, the sun and moon which plainly have no connection with that one just recalled. According to *Gylfaginning* X "Nörfi or Narfi was the name of the giant who first settled Jötunheim: he had a daughter called Night [*Nótt*] who was swarthy and dusky-haired, taking after her family. She was given in marriage to a person called Naglfari [or "Darkling"] and their son was Auðr [or "Space"]. Night was next married to Annarr [the "Second"] and Earth [Jörð] was their daughter. Last of all Dellingr or "Dayspring" [who was related to the gods] had her, and their son was Day [Dagr]: he took after his father's side being bright and fair." The next move is that the One called Allfather "took Night and her son Day and giving them each a pair of horses and a chariot, despatched them up the heavens to drive round the earth once in every twenty-four hours. Night was first with the horse known as Frostymane [*Hrímfaxi*] who each morning sprinkles the earth with dew from his bit. Day's horse, called Shiningmare [*Skinfaxi*], illumines all the earth and sky with the light from his hair."

This is a self-contained and satisfactory creation myth but it is quite distinct from the creation myth in which Ymir and the Sons of Bor figure. *There* the earth was made from the carcass of Ymir, *here* the earth is daughter of Night and Annarr (the "Second"); *there* Odin and his brothers created earth and the heavenly lights, *here* Allfather (**Tiwaz*, **Djevs*, the old Indo-European Sky Father) has a hand in the creation. It will simplify this myth of Night and her progeny if we set out the pedigree:

Nörfi ("the giant who first settled Jötunheim")

Night m. (1) Darkling (2) the "Second" (3) Dayspring

Space   Earth   Day

Attempts have been made to identify Nörfi with the dark moon. With regard to Annarr (the "Second") it is noteworthy that one of Odin's nicknames is Annarr and northern myth makes Odin not only Earth's (Jörð's) husband but her father too, as we shall see later: this tends to confirm the identification of Odin with "the Second". Other evidence to support this identity is found in Odin's identity in remote time with Vâta Lord of the Wind in the Hindu *Rigveda*, because in a Greek myth we learn that Night conceived of the Wind and brought forth the whole world. At the same time, Annarr might equally well stand for the Sky Father with Naglfari and Dellingr as manifestations of two of his aspects: Naglfari would be the evening sky (twilight) and Dellingr the morning sky (dawn). From the union of Night and Twilight comes Space, and from the union of Night and Dawn comes Day.

The evidence of the *Verse Edda* for the Night and Day myth just related is found in *Vafþrúðnismál* 24, 25, *Alvíssmál* 29, 30 and *Hávamál* 161 substantially as Snorri tells it; but it is obvious that Snorri was also drawing on other sources not now available for none of the three personages in the story, Auðr, Annarr or Naglfari is mentioned in the *Verse Edda*.

A third variant of the tale of how the "tally of nights and days" was begun must now be told. "There was once a man called Mundilfari who had two children so bright and handsome that he called the boy Moon (*Máni*) and the girl Sun (*Sól*); she was given in marriage to a certain Glenr (Gleam). But the gods paid him out for his presumption by snatching away the brother and sister and setting them to work in heaven. They made Sun postillion to the horses pulling the chariot of the sun, which to illumine the heavens, they had fashioned from the tongues of flame flashing up from Muspellheim. These two horses are called Early-wake (*Árvakr*) and Supreme-in-Strength (*Alsviðr*); and under their shoulders the gods hung a couple of bellows-bags to keep them cool (although according to the teachings of other people this is referred to as *iron-coolness*)." Allusions to this myth are found in three of the *Verse Edda* pieces, namely in *Vafþrúðnismál* 22, 23, *Grímnismál* 38, 39 and *Sigrdrífumál* 14. Before touching on these versions I might observe that nowhere except in Snorri's *Edda* is there reference to the creation of the heavenly bodies from sparks out of Muspellheim. Then both *Grímnismál* and *Sigrdrífumál* disagree with Snorri on the method used to protect the horses and the earth from the sun's blazing heat. *Grímnismál* 38, 39, says:

> Árvakr and Alsviðr
> hence drag up
>   wearily the Sun's weight,
> and under their collars
> the kindly gods set
>   in ancient time an iron cool.
>
> Svalin† it's called,
> in front of the Sun,
>
> † the Cooling.

a shield for the shining goddess;
mountain and sea
would set on fire
I know if it fell beneath.

Sigrdrífumál 14 mentions the shield Svalin by name as well as
the horses Árvakr and Alsviðr. The only ancient poem to
record Mundilfari is *Vafþrúðnismál* 23:

Mundilfari he's called
the father of Moon,
   he's also the sire of Sun;
a turn across heaven
they must take each day
   and tell the time for men.

No further direct information with regard to Mundilfari is
available. Indirectly we gather that he is a being connected with
the apparent diurnal turning of the heavens. *Mundil-* appears to
be cognate with *möndull*, a Norse word meaning the sweep or
handle of a mill; and *-fari* with the verb *fara*, to travel or move.
In *Skáldskaparmál* LVII Snorri repeats and adds to the information already given on the heavenly horses. He says "Árvakr
and Alsviðr pull the Sun (as is written before); Hrímfaxi and
Fjörsvartnir pull the Night; Skinfaxi and Glaðr are the Day's
horses".

We are dealing here (I suggest) with myths from different
levels of antiquity. The roots of the horse-and-chariot of the
Sun myth are deep in Indo-European soil, for we see the
flowers not only in northern myth but in Greek and Hindu
myth as well. We have written testimony to the provenance of
the northern version going back to A.D. 98 in Tacitus' *Germania* 45: "Passing the Suiones, we find yet another sea that is
sluggish and almost stagnant. The reason this sea is believed to
be the boundary that girdles the earth is that the last radiance of
the setting sun lingers here until dawn with a brightness that
makes the stars turn pale. Rumour adds that you can hear the

sound he makes as he rises from the waves and can see the shape of his horses and the rays on his head." But much further back in time than Tacitus even, we come across a northern Bronze Age image which depicts the sun not as a god or goddess but as a disc drawn by a horse. The whole is mounted on six wheels, two supporting the disc and four the horse (see plate 5). This image was found at Trundholm in Zealand and must date prior to 600 B.C. which is commonly supposed to be the terminus of the Bronze Age in these parts. The Dipylon style of the Trundholm sun image betrays connections with Greece: Schütte makes the suggestion in *Our Forefathers*, i, § 95 that its source may lie in Pharaoh Amenhotep IV's reformation of sun worship in Egypt *c.* 1400 B.C. If we come back to *Grímnismál* and *Sigrdrífumál* we may see a link between the sun disc drawn behind the horse and the shield called Svalin: originally the sun image was an impersonal representation of the sun, a golden disc. At some point in the myth's career the disc has ceased to be a symbol and has become what it was like in actuality, a circular shield. And to "explain" the shield, the poet has put forward the tale that it is there to protect the horse from the sun's rays.

In contrast with the sun chariot and disc myths, I personally believe that Snorri's explanation of the creation of the heavenly bodies from "tongues of flame flashing up from Muspellheim" is of comparatively modern origin. There appears to be no extant reference to such a myth except in Snorri's *Edda*. The nearest we get to it is the description in *Völuspá*† not of Creation but of Destruction, the Doom of the Gods when:

> fire and reek burl
> upwards and break
> with hazy heat
> against heaven itself!

I shall have to return to the closing stages of *Völuspá* later on: here, I must make the bald statement that I believe these

† *Völ.* 56.

stanzas owe much of their inspiration to Iceland's active volcano Hekla. Hekla has erupted on twenty-three occasions between 1104 and 1947: there is no reason to suppose that Hekla did not erupt many times before 1104 which is the year of the eruption in the first extant record of such an event. Snorri could have been influenced both by reading *Völuspá* and by actually having seen Hekla active.

We have not yet finished with myths concerning Night, Day, Sun and Moon. Snorri adds a story not found in the verses. He says, "Moon guides the moon and directs its waxing and waning: he himself carried off two human children named Bil and Hjúki as they were bearing on their backs the cask called Sægr and the pole named Simul from the well Byrgvi. Viðfinnr was their father's name. These children follow Moon as we may well see from the earth" (i.e. the shadows on the moon's face).

There can be little doubt but that this cryptic account, which Snorri makes no further attempt to expand presumably because he did not know how, has been remembered in nursery rhyme and folk lore. As the Rev. Baring Gould and others have pointed out[24] Hjúki and Bil are the Jack and Jill who "went up the hill to fetch a pail of water"; while their father Viðfinnr is the Man in the Moon who in Christian times was said to have been put there with a bundle of thorns on his back as a punishment for gathering sticks on a Sunday. Hjúki and Bil may be symbols for the waxing and waning aspects of the moon represented by the "well Byrgvi". At present, it seems to be anybody's guess.

Northern myth goes on to account for the motion across the sky of sun and moon otherwise than by means of horse and chariot. According to Snorri, "Swiftly flees the sun—almost as if she were afraid. She could go no faster if she were in fear of death. No wonder she scampers across the sky when the one who would hurt her dogs her close, for she has no bolt hole, but must needs run away." The cause of Sun's and Moon's flight is two wolves. "The one actually chasing Sun is called Skoll; it is he who is frightening her and in the end he will capture

her. The other, leaping ahead of her, is called Háti Hróðvitnisson (*Hate, son of the Mighty Wolf*) who intends to over-
take Moon: no one can doubt but that he will succeed." It is of
interest to know the origin of these wolves. At this point Snorri
says nothing directly of their father, although we gather from the
surname Hróðvitnisson (*son of the Mighty Wolf*) that Háti's
father was Fenrir son of Loki. And of both Fenrir and Loki
there will be much to say. Of the wolves' mother there is this
information: "there lived a witch in the forest called Ironwood
to the east of Midgard; in that same forest dwelt trollwives or
Ironwooders. The ancient Witch farrowed giants by the dozen
and all in the likeness of wolves: it's from them that these particular wolves come. Further, it is said a really frightful one in
line of descent called Moon-hound (*Mána-garmr*) shall throw
out. He shall be filled with the flesh of all men who die; he
shall swallow the moon; and he shall sprinkle with blood all
the sky and heavens at which the sun's light shall be put out
and winds shall rise up and howl hither and yon. Just as it says
in *The Spaewife's Prophecy*:†

> Eastward sat the crone
> in the Ironwood
>   who farrowed there
>   the brood of Fenrir.
> Of their get shall be seen
> a certain one
>   who shall shark up the moon
>   like a shadowy troll.
>
> He shall glut his maw
> with the flesh of men
>   and bloody with gore
>   the home of the gods;
> dark grows the sun,
> storms rage in summer
>   weather's a-widdershins . . .

> † *Völ.* 39, 40.

Völuspá, then, confirms that the progenitor of the wolves was Fenrir, the cruellest and most evil as well as the most famous of all the wolves of northern mythology. His father was Loki and he bit off Týr's hand; he was the brother of Hel and of Jörmungandr the World Serpent. The Ancient Witch who was covered by Fenrir to farrow these giants "by the dozen and all in the likeness of wolves" is nowhere directly named. Fenrir's parentage of Skoll and Háti is confirmed in *Grímnismál* 40, and it is certain that these are the two who will despoil the sky of sun and moon at the Ragnarök.†

6

GOTHONIC COSMOGRAPHY

Early research workers into the subject of the beliefs of the Gothonic nations assumed that our forefathers subscribed to a homogeneous religion which was reflected in such common Gothonic words (to give only a few examples) as Óðinn—Woden—Wotan, Thor—Thunor, Urð—Wyrd, Valkyrja—Waelcyrge, Miðgarðr—Middangeard—Mittilagart—Midjungards. The sacred books of the assumed common Gothonic religion were found in the Icelandic *Eddas*.

In our opening chapter and so far in our present chapter we have covered enough ground to show that the assumption of a shared homogeneous religion is not wholly confirmed; and the *Eddas* must be regarded as a special Scandinavian and particularly Norwegian-Icelandic exposition of myth. Two further points will be apparent: the records of myths in the two *Eddas* are, first, by no means always complete, but on the contrary often fragmentary, and second, there are different myths dealing with the same subject not only in the two *Eddas* but also in one and the same *Edda*; an example of this is Snorri's collection of myths on Night, Day, Sun and Moon.

There appear to be, however, certain fundamental ideas em-

† *Vaf.* 46, 47, suggests Fenrir himself as the Moon swallower.

FIG. 8 THE WORLDS IN THE TREE

Yggdrasill, the World Ash, with its three roots reaching Asgard, Midgard and Niflheim, supports all the nine worlds. Four dwarfs uphold the sky, two wolves chase the sun and moon, the World Serpent encircles the earth and the dragon Níðhöggr gnaws the root in Niflheim. The rivers all issue from the eternal spring Hvergelmir.

bodied in Gothonic words which go back to the primitive Indo-European level. This is especially noticeable where the cosmography is concerned. It is natural enough that there should be a number of shared synonyms for the world: we find "world" expressed by O.H.G. *weralt*, O.E. *weorold*, O. Fris. *wiarlt*, O.N. *veröld*; there is also "earth", O.E. *eormengrund*, O.N.

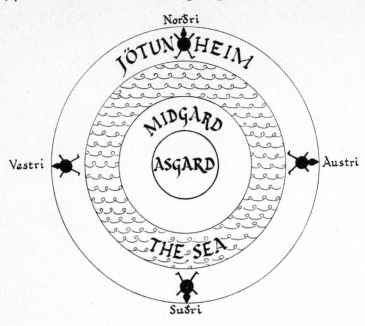

FIG. 9   THE NORTHERN COSMOS IN THE FORM OF A MANDALA

jörmungrund, and O.E. *eord,* O.N. *jörð.* With such serviceable names available it is obvious that the Gothonic nations wished to give expression to a definite idea when they also called the world "the middle enclosure", Goth. *midjungards,* O.H.G. *mittilagart,* O.E. *middangeard,* O.N. *miðgarðr.* Another common notion is that of "heaven", Gothonic **himinaz,* O.E. *heofon,* O.N. *himinn;* yet another is "hell", O. Fris. *helle, hille,* O.E. *hel,* O.N. *hel,* Goth. *halja,* Gothonic **halja;* and another O.H.G. *mûspilli,* O.L.G. *mûdspelli* "doomsday", O.N. *Muspellzheimr* "the home of the destroyers of the world". The conceptions embodied in such words are united into a satisfactory cosmography in the two *Eddas.* The earth is in the midst of the Yawning Gulf; it is in the middle of the sea which surrounds it; it is also in the middle of the worlds—Asgard centrally above, Niflheim (or Hel) together with Muspellheim below, and Jötunheim all around on the outer shores of the great sea. This is represented schematically in Fig. 8, while Fig. 9 shows us the view we might get if we were looking down on Midgard.

In either case we have a figure embodying the circle and the square, the sort of figure known as a "mandala". For a discussion of the mandala and its importance as a key to unlock the secrets of the myths we must wait until we arrive at our final chapter.

CHAPTER II
Cosmography

YGGDRASILL

WHEN King Gylfi visited Asgard and enquired† "Where is the headquarters—the holy of holies of the gods?" he was told "That's at the Ash Tree Yggdrasill: you'll find the gods giving judgment there every day."

Snorri Sturluson describes the Ash as follows: "That particular Ash is of all trees the hugest and most stately. Its branches overhang all the worlds and strike out above the heavens. The three roots of the tree, spreading far and wide, support it aloft: one root is with the gods, another with the Frost Giants (where formerly there used to be the Yawning Gulf), and the third stands over Niflheim: under that root is Hvergelmir with Níðhöggr [*the Dread Biter*] gnawing the root from below. But under the root which twists towards the Frost Giants there is Mímir's Well (for he is called Mímir who is warden of the well). Mímir is full of wisdom since he drinks at the well out of Gjallarhorn. . . . The third root of the Ash stands in heaven and beneath it is the spring (exceedingly sacred) called the Well of Urðr. That's where the gods have their judgment seat. Every day, over Bifröst Bridge [the Rainbow, lit. *Tremulous Way*] the Powers gallop to it; that's why it is also called Æsir's Bridge."

Snorri goes on to say "There's an eagle roosting in the boughs of the Ash Tree, wise beyond all knowing, and between his eyes sits the hawk called Veðrfölnir. A squirrel, by name Ratatoskr, darts up and down about the tree bearing spiteful tales between the eagle and Níðhöggr. Four stags browse over

† *Gylf.* XV.

the branches of the Ash and nibble at the bark. I'll tell you
their names: Dáinn, Dvalinn, Duneyrr and Duraþrórr. And
there's such a nest of serpents with Níðhöggr in Hvergelmir no
tongue could possibly tell their tale. Just as this verse says:†

> Yggdrasill Ash
> has troubles of its own
>   more than any man knows:
> the stag bites above,
> on the side it rots,
>   while Níðhöggr gnaws beneath.

And here's a bit more news:‡

> More wriggling worms
> writhe under Yggdrasill
>   than any stupid ape would suppose:
> Góinn and Móinn
> —they're Grafvitnir's sons—
>   Grábakr and Grafvölluðr
> Ófnir and Sváfnir
> shall always I think
>   tear at the twigs on the trunk.

It's said too, that the Norns who dwell round the Well of Urðr
every day take of the water of the well mixed together with the
gravel lying about the well and sprinkle it over the Ash to
prevent its limbs from withering or rotting. For that water is so
holy that all things which dip into the well become white as the
film which lies within the shell of an egg; just as this says:§

> There stands an Ash
> called Yggdrasill, I know,
>   a soaring tree with
>   white clay sprinkled;
> dews drip from it
> and fall in the dales:

† *Grím.* 36.   ‡ *Grím.* 35.   § *Völ.* 18.

> it stands ever green
> by the spring of Urðr.

This dew which drips on to the ground beneath is called honeydew by men, and bees are nourished on it. The Well of Urðr gives life to two birds named Swans, from whom are descended that kind of bird which is now so called."

Snorri has based his account of Yggdrasill squarely on *Grímnismál* stanzas 30–36 with a striking addition from *Völuspá* 18. But there are further references to the World Ash, allusive rather than descriptive in character, in three other poems of the *Verse Edda*, namely *Hávamál*, *Vafþrúðnismál* and *Svipdagsmál*. There is, too, an important reference in *Völuspá* 2 which Snorri omits probably because he regarded the information contained there as self-evident. The Spaewife says:

> Nine worlds I knew,
> the nine in the Tree
> with its mighty roots
> under the mould.

The "nine worlds" are those of the Æsir, Vanir, light elves, dark elves, men, giants, Muspell's sons, the dead and presumably of the dwarfs (though the ninth world is uncertain). At any rate, the information that the nine worlds are "in the Tree", coupled with Snorri's observation that of the three roots one is with the gods, one with the Frost Giants and the third stands over Niflheim, all goes to show that Yggdrasill is regarded as the agency by which the fabric of the universe is maintained. This conclusion is confirmed by the account in *Gylfaginning* LI of how, as a prelude to the destruction of the universe, "Yggdrasill the World Ash begins to tremble", or as *Völuspá* 46 says

> Yggdrasill wavers,
> the long-standing World Ash,
> the old tree judders. . . .

a sign that disintegration is at hand. Another conception to be noted is that of malevolent and benevolent forces both working on Yggdrasill, the destructive and restorative effects cancelling each other out until the Ragnarök. The malevolent forces (starting from the roots) are Níðhöggr, the Dread Biter, a dragon who continually gnaws the root over Niflheim; the serpents, also at this root; some agency causing the trunk to rot; and presumably the four stags who browse over the branches. To counteract the evil effects of these agencies the three Norns paste the sides of Yggdrasill with clay and water from the sacred Well of Urðr.

Neither *Edda* offers any mythological explanation of the origin of Yggdrasill, though there is a myth accounting for the tree's name. *Yggdrasill* means "the horse of Yggr", Yggr (the Terrible One) being a nickname of Odin. The story (which will be dealt with in detail later) tells how Odin discovered the secret of the runic wisdom by hanging himself on the World Ash and sacrificing himself to himself. The Ash Yggdrasill is thus shown to be a Tree of Knowledge also. The usual method of sacrificing a victim to Odin was by hanging: that is why Odin is also called Hangatýr (*God of the Hanged*) and Galgatýr (*Gallows God*); and the Northmen were wont to refer grimly to the gallows as the "horse of tree" or the "wooden horse". Yggdrasill then as a name must date from the cult of Odin, but the tree itself, the World Ash as a tree and as a symbol goes much farther back into antiquity.

Some authorities (e.g. Munch and Bugge) related Odin's hanging on the tree to Christ's Crucifixion: Bugge's theory was that Northmen in the ninth century on their viking raids to the Western Isles got acquainted with Christian doctrines, assimilated them and transferred them to Odin. Such a theory in connection with Yggdrasill is unnecessary. Many early Gothonic sources speak of a huge tree in proximity to a well and a hall or temple: a tree which is held in veneration and on which human sacrifices are made by hanging. Examples of such trees or poles are that standing by the temple at Uppsala and that of the Germans called Irminsul. These are actual objects round which ritual revolved but (as the following parallels will show) regarded as symbols of the World Tree. Part of Scholion 134 to Adam of Bremen describing the tree at Uppsala runs like this: *prope templum est arbor maxima late ramos extendens, aestate et hyeme semper uirens: cuius illa generis sit nemo scit* and further *ibi etiam est fons ubi sacrificia paganorum solent exerceri et homo uiuus immergi.* The sense of these passages is that a great tree with widely spreading branches and roots and whose leaves were green all the year round stood close by the temple. Nobody knew what kind of tree it was. There was also a well where sacrifices were made and living men drowned. The parallels between the description of the *actual* tree and well and the *mythical* World Ash and well are as follows:

(1) *prope templum est arbor maxima*
  Heiðrún heitir geit/es stendr höllu á/ok bítr af Læraðs limum.†
  "The goat is called Heiðrún who stands on the hall roof and browses Læraðr's branches."
  (i.e. the tree is so close to *Odin's hall* that its branches overhang the roof.)

(2) *late ramos extendens*
  es breiðask umb/lönd öll limar.‡
  "whose branches spread far and wide over every land."

(3) *aestate et hyeme semper uirens*
  (Yggdrasill) stendr æ of grœnn/Urðar brunni.§
  "(Yggdrasill) stands ever green by the Well of Urðr."

(4) *cuius illa generis sit nemo scit*
  es mangi veit/af hverjum rótum rinnr.‖
  "no man knows from what root it comes."

(5) *ibi etiam est fons ubi sacrificia paganorum solent exerceri et homo uiuus immergi*
  (Yggdrasill) stendr æ of grœnn/Urðar brunni.¶
  "(Yggdrasill) stands ever green by the Well of Urðr."

† *Grím.* 25.   ‡ *Fjölsv.* 19.
§ *Völ.* 18.   ‖ *Fjölsv.* 20.   ¶ *Völ.* 18.

These parallels make it clear that the tree as a World Tree and as a "steed of Yggr or Odin" are part of the pagan myth owing nothing to Christian influence.

Mannhardt (*Baumkultus*, p. 56) notes that the property of the world tree noted in *Fjölsvinnsmál* 22 ("Of its fruit some shall be carried out on to the fire for the sake of women sick with child") is identical with that popularly assigned to the "Vårdträd". So also the Vårdträd situated close to the family house corresponds not only to the tree at Uppsala beside the temple, but also to that of Læraðr (and Glasir—*Skáldskaparmál* 36) besides Valhalla.

The Ash has another proper name, Mímameiðr, that is to say the Tree of Mímir whose well is situated under one of the roots of the tree. This name *Mímameiðr* occurs twice and that only in the one poem, *Svipdagsmál*. The hero of the poem, Young Svipdagr, engages in riddles with one Fjölsviðr and asks, "What is the tree called—the one whose branches spread far and wide over every land?" Fjölsviðr answers, "It is called Mímameiðr, and no man knows from what root it comes: few men guess what shall fell that tree—neither fire nor iron will." Svipdagr's next question is, "What grows from the seed of the tree?" and Fjölsviðr replies, "Of its fruit some shall be carried out to the fire, then that which is within shall come out, and so is it mighty with men." These answers appear to leave us more mystified than if the questions prompting them had never been asked. The third mention of Mímameiðr in *Svipdagsmál* is simply as the perch for Víðófnir (*Tree Snake*) one of the cocks which will crow on the morning of Ragnarök to awaken either the gods or giants to battle.

The most important clue here seems to be that connecting Yggdrasill with childbirth, with the creation of life, especially when we remember that Yggdrasill is an ash and the first man (who came from a tree) was called Ash. Yggdrasill then is a symbol of generation: like the Hindu Lingam and other phallic symbols, Yggdrasill must be the macrocosm of the erect penis and all it stands for not only as regards the fulfilment of the individual but also as regards the procreation and continuance of the human race. "Few men guess what shall fell that tree—neither fire nor iron will" says Fjölsviðr; nor indeed does *Völuspá* tell us what will fell the tree. But that the tree must be felled we cannot doubt; and whatever finally felled it in the myth now presumed lost, whether the gnawing of Níðhöggr or the browsing of the four harts, or whether the agent came into the category of elemental substances like the fire and iron mentioned and so could be earth (quake), air (tempest) or water (flood); whatever it was we must suspect that the felling agent was an emblem of first, the loss of erection in the standing penis after ejaculation and second, the failing powers of the man due to the onset of old age. (See plate 6.)

What of the wells at the roots of Yggdrasill? Urðr's Well and Mímir's Well have this in common: they both supply to their respective roots the saps of life which preserve the tree and ensure its continuance as the maintainer of life and the universe. And the third well, Hvergelmir, the mighty Roaring Cauldron, the source of all rivers, whose resemblance to Okeanos "the origin of the gods" and "the origin of everything" we have already noted—Hvergelmir is in a different category to the wells of Urðr and Mímir. Hvergelmir as a generative force is more akin to Yggdrasill itself; and when we consider that the Hindu parallel to the Ash Tree, the Lingam, also had its counterpart in the female generative symbol, the Yoni, we might suspect that the Yoni too is the parallel to Hvergelmir.

Mythically, Yggdrasill as supporter of the nine worlds is akin to the four dwarfs who support the heavens; it is akin too to the various pillars and poles figuring in the myths of many unrelated peoples. South American Indians speak of the World Tree; while according to ancient Egyptian stories the sky was an iron roof supported by four pillars at the cardinal points, or again was the belly of the cosmic cow Hathor whose four legs were planted on the earth, or yet again was the body of the goddess Nut whom her father Shu held apart from her brother and husband Keb, the earth, by means of a number of pillars or according to another version a ladder; Eskimos tell of four posts supporting the firmament, and when these posts go rotten they have to be renewed by the angekok or wizards.[25] The myth of world or universal supports is a common one and so is the idea of a felling agent. Now it does not strain the reasonable to suppose that similarities between myths of the Indo-European peoples result from a common origin before the separation of the peoples; it is not unreasonable to suppose that myths from unrelated peoples have been adopted by the Indo-Europeans; but myths such as that of the Eskimos just mentioned which have features shared not only by Norse but by Hindu, Egyptian and Jewish tales can only have a common source in one place— the mind of man.

2

ASGARD

Snorri first mentions Asgard in *Gylfaginning* when he tells how Gylfi, a legendary king, set out from Sweden determined to find the gods and to discover the secret of their power:† "He walked up to their stronghold and saw a hall towering so high he could scarcely see above it. It was slated with shields of gold like a shingled roof, a fact alluded to by Þjóðólfr of Hvin who also implies that Valhalla was roofed with shields:

> Their backs were ablaze
> (though battered with stones)
>   with Odin's hall shingles
>   those stouthearted men."

If we are to believe Snorri, the order of creation was as follows: after Ymir had been slain, Odin, Vili and Vé created the earth, the seas, the sky, Giantland, Midgard, the clouds, human beings and lastly, Asgard. He says in *Gylfaginning* VIII, "towards the centre of the earth they built a fortress wall encircling

† Gylf. II.

the region against their giant enemies: and to make it they employed the brows of Ymir, and called their stronghold Midgard." In the next chapter we read "they set up their fortress (which is Asgard) in the middle of the world. There the gods and their descendants lived, and of that place came many notable events and matters for argument both in earth and heaven."

In this description of Asgard as a sort of mountainous eyrie rising abruptly from the plains of Midgard, Snorri has been accused of rationalizing the myth. His description in Chapter 2 of his historical work the *Ynglinga Saga* lends substance to the charge; there, he writes, "The country east of the Tanaquisl [the river Don] in Asia was called Ásaland, or Ásaheim, and the capital city in that land was called Asgard. In that city was a chief called Odin, and it was a great place for sacrifice." The Norse name for the gods was of course *æsir* (singular *áss*); and in *Ynglinga Saga* Snorri has rationalized Asgard into a city of Asia and Odin into a headman on the basis of a popular and false etymology. But this is not to say that he was rationalizing the position of Asgard in his description in the *Prose Edda* nor that there did not exist from ancient times a strong tradition of Asgard as a central abode of the gods running up on high from the midst of the earth.

In the *Verse Edda* the references to Asgard are allusive in character: the hearer is expected to know where and what Asgard is and there is no need to waste breath in giving unnecessary description. As a matter of fact, the name *Ásgarðr* occurs only twice in the thirty-five poems. Because of the allusive nature of the references to Asgard, because both gods and Valkyries have horses which move through the air, because gods and goddesses on occasion don birds' skins and fly down to the other worlds, because the rainbow (the gods' bridge) leads up to the heavens, because the river Þund (the stream of air) flows by Valhalla: for these and other reasons it has been supposed that Asgard is "up in the sky". But nowhere in the two *Eddas* is there any categorical statement that Asgard

is "up in the sky"; and so we cannot dismiss out of hand
Snorri's statements which make Asgard a high citadel running
up from the centre of Midgard, a citadel whose halls and towers
pierce the clouds, maybe, and protected by high battlements
and steep cliffs, but still with its roots in the earth. This notion
of a mountainous situation of the home of the gods is one
shared by other Indo-European races such as the Greeks who
settled their pantheon on Mount Olympus; it is surely behind
the Psalmist's, "I will lift up mine eyes unto the hills from
whence cometh my help. My help cometh from the Lord. . . ."

When Gylfi asks "which way does the road run from
heaven to earth?" he is told, " 'There's not much sense in a
question like that. Isn't it common knowledge that the gods
built a bridge from heaven to earth which is called Bifröst, the
Tremulous Way? You must surely have seen it. Could be that
it's called "Rainbow". It blends three colours, is very strong
and was made with more artifice and cunning than any other
handiwork. Strong as it is, yet shall it crumble when the Sons
of Múspell ride out and cross it, and swim their stallions
through swollen rivers; for over it lies their road.'

"Said Gylfi, 'I question whether the gods built the bridge
honestly seeing it's able to be broken—and they could have
built honestly had they wished.' "

His informant replied, " 'Don't blame the gods over the
head of this job. Bifröst is an excellent bridge, but no single
corner of the universe will remain unscathed when Múspell's
sons go a-plundering.' "

According to the *Prose Edda* all the gods except Thor ride
daily over Bifröst bridge to the Well of Urðr:† "The third root
of the Ash stands in heaven and beneath it is the spring which
is exceedingly holy called the Well of Urðr. That's where the
gods have their judgment seat. Every day, over Bifröst bridge
the Powers gallop to it—that's why it is also called the Æsir's
bridge . . . but when Thor goes to the Thing he walks and
wades those rivers called

† *Gylf.* XV.

Körmt and Örmt†
and the Kerlaugs twain;
   these shall Thor wade through
every day when
he walks to deem
   at the Yggdrasill Ash."

We are not told how the gods made Bifröst. Possibly a myth on the subject existed at one time and is now lost. From the hints given by Snorri about the bridge breaking under the Sons of Múspell and the suggestion of some sort of dishonesty in the making we may suspect a Bifröst-building myth similar to that recounting the building of Asgard walls (see below p. 216).

In reply to the question,‡ "What did the Allfather [i.e. in this case Odin] do when Asgard was built?" Snorri says, "In the beginning he appointed his chief helpers and bade them assist him in arranging the fates of men and the running of the fortress: this took place at Iðavöllr which lies in the middle of their stronghold. Their first task was to build that edifice in which stand their twelve thrones and one higher than the rest for The Father of All. That building is the best in the world and the vastiest: within and without it is like burning gold. Men call it Glaðsheim, 'Joyous Home'. A second hall which they built was a fane for the goddesses; it too was very fair: men call it Vingólf or Friendly Floor. Their next job was a workshop in which they set a forge and made besides a hammer, tongs and an anvil, and by means of these all other kinds of tools. Next thing they made metal, stone and wood, particularly that metal called gold, enough to have all their delf and dishes of gold. That's why this time was called the Golden Age."

Later Snorri mentions other abodes in Asgard:§ "There's the spot called Breiðablik or *Broad Gleaming,* than which none is fairer. There's Glitnir the shining, too, whose walls and every room and pillars are made of gold, while the thatch is

† *Grim.* 30   ‡ *Gylf.* XIV.   § *Gylf.* XVII.

solid silver. Or again, there's the corner called the Hill of Heaven, Himinbjörg: it stands at the far end of Paradise by the keystone of the Rainbow Bridge—you know, where Bifröst arches out from heaven. There's a very spacious abode (which is Odin's) called Valaskjálf, *the Shelf of the Slain.* The gods built that mansion and thatched it with sheer silver; inside is Gateshelf or Hliðskjálf (as the throne is called). And when the Allfather sits on this seat he is able to see out over the whole wide world. On the northern ridge of heaven stands that hall, fairer than any and brighter than the sun; it is called Gimlé. That edifice shall stand when heaven and earth have passed away. Righteous men, men of goodwill have built that place from time out of mind, as it says in *The Spaewife's Prophecy*:†

> A hall she sees stand
> fairer than the sun,
>   thatched with gold
>   in Gimlé;
> there shall they dwell
> the doers of right
>   and ever and ever
>   enjoy delight."

There are other palaces and natural features of Asgard mentioned by name. For instance, Thor's estate is known as Þrúðvangar, the *Paddocks of Power,* and his hall is called Bilskirnir, the *Flashing*:‡ "in it there are five hundred and forty rooms which makes it the most extensive known to men, as it says in *Grímnismál*:§

> Five hundred rooms
> and forty yet
>   are built in Bilskirnir;
> of all the mansions
> many-roofed
>   it seems my son's is greatest."

† *Völ.* 63.   ‡ *Gylf.* XXI.   § *Grím.* 24.

There is Nóatún which may be translated "Anchorage"; it is the god Njörðr's home, the "Ship Enclosure". Fólkvangar or Folk Plains is Freya's home where she has her palace called Sessrúmnir, the "Rich in Seats". Frigg, chief of the goddesses and consort of Odin resides in Fensalir, the "Sea Halls"; while the goddess Sága lives at "Sinking Beck" or Søkkvabekkr where, says _Grímnismál_ "cool waves flow and above their murmur it stands". Ýdalir or "Yew Dales" is the home of Ullr the archer among the gods.

There are two other spots which should be mentioned in connection with Asgard, and first Alfheimr the home of the Light Elves which appears to border on Asgard. It is plain that the Light Elves and the gods were regarded as having close and friendly ties: _Grímnismál_ 4 says:

> The land is holy
> that lies hard by
> the Æsir and the Elves;

while a phrase in _Völuspá_ (repeated in _Þrymskviða_), tolling like a knell before the Ragnarök, brackets the gods and Elves together:†

Hvat's með ásum?	How fare the gods?
hvat's með alfum?	How fare the elves?

The reply to this enquiry in _Þrymskviða_ brings out the closeness with which the fate of the elves is bound up with that of the gods, for Thor's hammer has been stolen by the giants and without it the gods are in imminent danger. This is emphasized in the reply:

Ilt's með ásum,	Ill fare the gods,
ilt's með alfum.	ill fare the elves.

In _Gylfaginning_ XVII Gylfi enquires, "Are there other sacred places besides this Well of Urðr?" and the answer is "many—many: lots of equally distinguished fanes. There's one called Alfheimr where the Light Elves live, while the Dark Elves in-

† _Völ._ 50 and _Þry._ 7.

habit the crannies of the earth beneath. Most unlike in appearance are these two, but even more unlike in their natures. The Light Elves are fairer than a glance of the sun, the Dark Elves blacker than pitch." There is a curious piece of information anent Alfheimr in *Grímnismál* 5 where we learn that "In days of yore the gods gave Alfheimr to the child Frey as a toothgift." A clue perhaps to the identification of the Elves with spirits of fertility, even as Frey was a fertility god.

The other heavenly place which needs mention here (but which must wait for fuller exposition) is Valhalla. Largely through the influence of Wagner's operas, Valhalla is commonly equated with the Norse heaven, Asgard. In the old traditions Valhalla is both more and less than that: *more* because in addition to the heroic, aristocratic "hall of the slain" connections it too has connections with the grave-mound, the perpetual battle and beliefs going much farther back than the Viking Age; *less* because Valhalla is only one of the many abodes in Asgard. This matter will be discussed later; here, in trying to get a general picture of Asgard, we may be content with a short description. The nominative form of the name in O. Icelandic is *Valhöll* meaning the "hall of the slain", the "slain" being those men who have met with a courageous death on the battlefield. Entrance to Valhalla is not easy: its approaches are guarded by the loudly roaring river Þund (*Grímnismál* 21) and by a gate most difficult to pass:†

> A barred gate stands
> (it's called Valgrind)
>   holy before the holy doors:
> that gate is old
> and few there are
>   will learn how tight it is locked.

As regards the hall itself, it is so huge as to accommodate "five hundred and forty doors" each able to take eight hundred champions shoulder to shoulder as they march out. Slain

† *Grím.* 22.

warriors have no difficulty in recognizing the hall for (as *Grímnismál* 9, 10 says) "its rafters are spears, its roof slates are shields and its benches are strewn with war-coats . . . and over the western door hangs a wolf with an eagle above it." When Gylfi himself got inside† he saw "many people, some playing games, some drinking steadily, others armed and fighting."

3

HEL

There was a common term among the Gothonic nations for the Underworld: it was **halja*, meaning "the place of concealment", a word which became *hel* in Old Norse. The Northmen looked upon hel as a region of fog and cold, traits which they emphasized in the alternative names Niflheim and Niflhel, where the first element of the words means fog, mist or murk.

It is doubtful whether any difference is intended when one of the three terms hel, Niflheim and Niflhel is used in preference to the others. Hel is the general name covering the infernal regions; Niflheim emphasizes the fog and cold and Niflhel does the same, though there is some suggestion in *Vafþrúð-nismál* that there are degrees of depth with Niflhel right at the bottom:‡

> to nine worlds I came
> to Niflhel beneath
>   where dead men drop from hel.

It is quite certain that hel is an Underworld, for all roads to it lead down; moreover it is dark, cold, bereft of joyful sound and inhabited by the dead who have some characteristics of what we know as "ghosts". All the dead in hel did not go there for the same reason, nor do all the dead go to hel—some, the Chosen Warriors, go to Valhalla in heaven. The tradition of the Viking Age is that those men not chosen for Valhalla go down to hel where they exist miserably until the Ragnarök; at

† *Gylf.* II.   ‡ *Vaf.* 43.

that momentous time of doom it appears that the dead in hel will march out in their legions and array themselves under Loki against the gods. But there are other traditions (already touched on) suggesting that hel is a region of punishment for the dead who have sinned in this life; and particularly for the punishment of those two sins abhorrent to the northern code, namely the forswearing of oaths and murder. There can hardly be any doubt but that Christian thought has affected these traditions (see page 96 ff).

Hel is an amorphous region about which there is little definite description in the sources. The entrance to hel, or at least the beginning of the road to hel, appears to be a grim black cave set among precipitous cliffs and ravines. In some accounts the dark cavern is guarded by a fearsome hound with bloody chest, Garmr, who is said to be chained there until the Ragnarök. It is to be presumed that the blood on the hound's chest is not his own and that his coat has become beslobbered through his eating. If the Greek Kerberos is a parallel then the blood on Garmr's chest is from the men who have tried to escape from hel. Naturally, at the Ragnarök when Garmr is set free, the way out of hel will be open. Further on the helway, at the confines of hel proper, the river Gjöll (that is to say Howling or Echoing) forms a boundary. This river (according to Snorri) is only to be crossed by a bridge roofed with gold. On guard at the Gjöll Bridge stands the mysterious maiden called Móðguðr. Beyond the bridge, the way is barred by Hel Gate: within is the hall of the queen of hel whose name is Hel also.

Snorri's story of the god Hermóðr's ride from heaven to hel brings out many of the points just made. Hermóðr mounted Odin's horse Sleipnir and galloping from Asgard† "he rode nine days and nights down ravines ever darker and deeper, meeting no one, until he came to the banks of the river Gjöll which he followed as far as the Gjöll Bridge: this bridge is roofed with burning gold. The maiden is called Móðguðr who

† *Gylf.* XLIX.

guards the bridge. She asked him his name or lineage, saying only the day before five droves of dead men had padded over the bridge 'but the bridge echoed less under them than under thee. Anyway, you haven't the pallor of a dead man: why are you riding down the helway?'

"He replied, 'I ride to hel to seek out Balder. You don't happen to have set eyes on Balder on the road to hel?'

"She said Balder had already ridden over Gjöll Bridge 'and the road to hel lies down still and to the north.'

"Hermóðr galloped on until he came to Hel Gate Bars, where he slid off his horse and tightened the girths. He mounted again and raked his spurs along the animal's ribs. The stallion lept so high there was plenty of twilight between him and the bars. And Hermóðr rode on to the hall of Hel where he got down and went in to see his brother Balder sitting on a throne. Hermóðr stayed with him that night. . . ."

It is, of course, impossible for one not to notice the parallels in Greek myth: the descent and the darkness; the boundary river—Gjöll in the one case, Styx in the other; the mysterious bridge warden Móðguðr and the ferryman Charon; and (in the next account) the hound Garmr and the hound Kerberos.

The story goes that when the beautiful god Balder had dreamed ominous dreams, Odin threw a saddle over Sleipnir's back and rode down to hel to consult a dead *völva* there. The account is contained in the eddaic verses entitled *Baldrs Draumar*, thought to have been composed about A.D. 950:†

> Up rose Odin
> the old enchanter,
>   and flung a saddle
>   on Sleipnir's back;
> he galloped thence down
> to deep Niflhel;
>   he met the hound
>   that came from hel;

† *Baldrs Draumar*, 2, 3.

he was blood be-streaked
on his breast before:
  he howled and growled
  at the god from afar;
forward rode Odin,
the earth re-echoed,
  till he reached the hall
  of Hel so high.

When, by means of spells which raise the dead, Odin had forced the *völva* to rise from her grave, she spoke of the cold and rain in hel:

I was drifted with snow
and drenched with rain,
  I was dank with dew:
  long was I dead.

A little more light is shed on this darkest of worlds in the refrain stanza from *Völuspá* where we learn:

Garmr bellows loud
before Gnipahellir,

Gnipahellir being the entrance to the underworld and meaning the "Cliff Cave", suggesting as I have already said "a cave set among precipitous cliffs and ravines." Although Snorri does not mention Garmr in his description of Hermóðr's ride, he does say in another place (*Gylf.* LI) that before the Ragnarök "the hound Garmr, who was chained by the Bottomless Pit, at last breaks free, a fearsome monster. . . ." With the watchdog away, the road *out* of hel lies open: then "the rust-red cock at the bars of hel" crows loud. This cock, whose name is nowhere mentioned, is paralleled in Asgard by the bird Gullinkambi and in Giantland by Fjalarr. The function of Gullinkambi is to crow on the morning of Ragnarök to wake the gods for the final fray; similarly Fjalarr is to crow the giants from their beds to rise and arm; but "the rust red cock at the bars of hel"— whom is he to arouse? The answer can only be the wraith-like

dead. Allusions in *Völuspá* tend to confirm this conclusion, for
we read *troða halir helveg* which Vigfusson and Powell translated "the Dead are marching up the road of Hell";[26] while
Snorri† says that Loki's followers at the last battle are "the sons
of hel" who (by implication) voyage part of the way to the
Plain Vígríðr aboard the vessel called Naglfar made from dead
men's nails. If this is so then Naglfar must be building in hel,
and at what better wharf than Náströnd, the Corpse Strand?
But *Völuspá‡* puts a hall on Náströnd and makes it a horrid
place of punishment. This hall stands far from the sun and
even then its doors face north; serpents make a wickerwork of
the walls and roof while their venom drips and dribbles
through the smoke-hole. Here (according to *Völuspá*) congregate the oath-breakers, murderers and adulterers; before they
reach the hall they appear to be punished on the way for they
must wade through the river Slíðr (*Fearful*),§ a river of knives
and sharp swords, which drops from the east and rattles
through Venom Vales.

Other names indicating the mysterious topography of hel
are Niðafjöll ("the hills of darkness"), Nágrindr ("the corpse
gate") and possibly Ámsvartnir. In the last lines of *Völuspá* the
old dragon Níðhöggr is described as flying upwards from
Niðafjöll bearing corpses on his wings; Nágrindr is mentioned
only once in *Lokasenna* and once in *Skírnismál*: in both cases it
occurs in the same phrase *fyr Nágrindr neðan* "down underneath
the Corpse Gate", and in both cases it occurs in a threat by
one person to send another down to hel. In the *Skírnismál* allusion a monster called Hrímgrímnir (*Rime-hooded*), evidently
a Frost Giant, is spoken of as living below Nágrindr. Here-
abouts too are "the roots of the tree" and beings called *víl-
megir* who seem to be minions of punishment; for as the Valkyries carry round mead from the udders of the goat Heiðrún
in Valhalla, these are said to administer goat's urine to the un-
willing guest. Ámsvartnir is a lake mentioned only by Snorri
(*Gylf*. XXXIV). It is the water over which the gods rowed the

† *Gylf*. LI.   ‡ *Völ*. 36, 37.   § *Völ*. 34

wolf Fenrir to the island Lyngvi when they were desperately
minded to fetter him. The name Ámsvartnir suggests the darkness of hel, and on the island is a crag Gjöll (a name also connected with hel) at the foot of which Fenrir is eventually
bound.

Hel is pre-eminently the abode of prisoners who are to break
out and wreak destruction at the Ragnarök. Apart from the
dead, the chained Garmr, the fettered Fenrir, the snakes and
Níðhöggr, we must conclude that the prime-mover of evil,
Loki, is also bound there; for an obscure passage in *Völuspá*†
speaks of a captive tied hand and foot under Hvergelmir in hel,
and that this captive is Loki is made obvious by the remarks
that Sigyn (Loki's wife) "sits near by, sad at heart, over her
husband". Snorri describes the binding of Loki in the following words:‡ "Loki was captured unconditionally and lugged
off to a cavern. The gods got hold of three rocks, set them on
end and split a wedge out of each. They then captured Loki's
sons Váli and Nari (or Narfi); Váli they charmed into the
shape of a wolf and he ripped his own brother Nari to pieces;
whereupon the gods drew out his entrails to bind Loki with
over the three rocks standing on edge: one stood under his
shoulders, the second under his loins and the third under the
hollow of his knees. He was then bolted in with iron. Lastly,
Skaði got a poisonous snake and knotted it above him in such
a way as to let the venom drip from the snake into his open face.
But Sigyn, Loki's wife, always stands beside him holding a
basin under the drops. When the basin is full to overflowing
she hurries to pour away the poison, and meanwhile the venom
drips on to his face, which throws him into a convulsion so
terrific that all the earth trembles (that's what we call earthquakes). And there he lies in bonds until the Doom of the
Gods."

One other denizen of the underworld needs to be mentioned, namely its queen called Hel. Snorri's tale of her descent
is well authenticated; he says, "To tell you the truth, Loki has

† 106 ff. ‡ *Gylf.* L.

an awful brood of children. There's an ogress in Giantland called Angrboða: upon her body Loki got three offspring. The first was Fenriswulf, the second Jörmungandr (*the World Serpent*), and lastly Hel. When the gods saw that these three nephews and nieces of theirs (so to speak) were being bred up in Giantland of all places, they did a bit of private table-rapping and found they had to expect a heap of unpleasantness from these brothers and their sister: for they could have inherited nothing but evil (so everyone thought) judging by their mother—and still more so by their father. So the Allfather sent word to the gods to kidnap the whelps and lead them to him, and when they did come before him he cast the serpent into the deep sea, where it now lies completely ringing-in the world. For the old dragon increased so in length and girth that he came full circle and now grips his tail-end in his jaws. Hel, the Allfather tumbled down into Niflheim and gave her the rule of nine worlds with absolute power over all who are once sent into her charge, namely those who breathe their last on the sick bed or who die of old age. She is queen of a far-flung land of weeping and wailing; her courts are exceedingly vast and her portal wide as death. Her palace is called Sleetcold; her platter is Hunger; her knife and fork Famine; Senility her house-slave and Dotage her bondmaid; at the entering-in her doorstep is Pitfall; Bedridden is her pallet and Woeful Wan its curtains. Her complexion is half livid, half normal; and so she is easy to recognize and what you might call stern of looks, and even hideous."

It is obvious that part of this tale ("her palace is called Sleet-cold; her platter is Hunger," etc.) is not myth at all, but literary personification; it is fairly certain that Hel took her name from the region she ruled and not the other way about; but it is sure that the idea of an evil goddess connected with death, and who may or may not have been queen of the underworld, goes far back into antiquity.

Many different subconscious symbols and ideas, and much

conscious working on these symbols and ideas at different times have gone to make up the northern hel. What we have *not* got is a consistent body of myth. Some of the accretions appear to stand out from the original story; for instance, doubts have been expressed as to whether hel was originally regarded as a place of retribution for crimes committed on earth.[27] It is significant that the conceptions of reward in Valhalla and punishment in hel are closely connected with the comparatively late development of the viking faith. We may say that hel is older than Valhalla, for Valhalla by its very name "the hall of the slain" was built in Odinic times to house the warriors chosen for or by Odin; but hel "the place of concealment" is probably as old as the grave. When Northmen came into contact with Christians, but long before they were converted to Christianity themselves, their hel no doubt attracted some of the positive attributes of the Christian place of punishment: this must have happened easily for there were already striking similarities—the deep, dark abode and the old dragon, the chained monster Loki—once a lord of light in heaven and now cast down into the bottomless pit—among them. The pictures of the hall of venomous serpents on Náströnd, and of the wriggling snakes at the root of Yggdrasill are almost certainly late: they have more than a passing resemblance to the snake-pit of Norse and Anglo-Saxon legend and even history. The *Old English Chronicle* under anno 1137 asserts that there were snake-pits in England in the twelfth century; in the O. Norse poem *Krákumál* there is an allusion to the half-historical half-legendary death of the viking Ragnarr Loðbrók in king Ælla of Northumbria's snake-pit: Ragnarr in the poem, when at the point of death, says "Góinn has housed himself in my heart!" Góinn being the name of one of the snakes (according to *Völuspá*) at the root of Yggdrasill.

If we can brush away the legendary material we shall find that the ancient myth of hel was of an underground place, dark and mysterious, the prison of monsters; but, only towards the end of the mythic development, of monsters who were eventually to rise and overthrow established order in the shape of the gods. This Ragnarök, this Götterdämmerung, this Twilight of the Gods, more accurately "Doom of the Divine Powers" is possibly the most significant development of Gothonic myth and will need to be discussed later at length.

4

JÖTUNHEIM

All sources do not locate Jötunheim consistently in the one place, though by viking times two situations are holding the field: one is "in the east", the other is on the outer shores of the ocean.

Jötunheim is one of the "nine worlds in the Tree" mentioned by the *völva* (*Völuspá* 2); but the eddaic poems, in their usual allusive way, give no cut and dried description of Giantland or exactly where it is. According to the verses, Jötunheim lies "to the east": for instance, Hrymr, leader of the giants at the Ragnarök is said to "sweep from the east",† while in *Hárbarðs-ljóð* 23 Thor says "I was out east killing giants. . . ." In the same poem (stanza 29) Thor also declares that while he was in the east he guarded a river where "the sons of Svarangr" (evidently giants) hurled rocks unavailingly at him. Mention of a river called Ífing is made in *Vafþrúðnismál* 16: this river is said to separate the realms of the gods and giants; it never freezes over but remains open, presumably to prevent the giants from crossing on foot to attack Asgard in a body.

Although Snorri quite often echoes the verses by saying that Thor is "off in the east"‡ killing trolls or giants, he is definite in asserting that "the earth is round, and about it lies the deep blue sea; along the outward shores of the ocean [the gods] gave to the race of giants a grant of land to settle in." Snorri also tells how Jörmungandr or Miðgarðsormr (both names mean "the World Serpent") lies in this ocean completely encircling the

† *Völ.* 48.   ‡ *Gylf.* VIII.

earth with his tail in his mouth; and both Snorri (*Gylf·* XLVIII) and the eddaic poem *Hymiskviða* tell how Thor and the giant Hymir rowed out from Jötunheim "along the outward shores of the ocean" and fished for the World Serpent. Many references to Jötunheim's being north and south as well as east seem to bear out the truth of this outward circular situation: Gefjun took four oxen "from the north out of Jötunheim",† Surtr (a fire giant) is said at the Ragnarök to come "from the south",‡ and so on. But most convincing of all is the alternative name for Jötunheim which is *Útgarðr*, Outgard, the Outer Enclosure, whose king is Útgarða-Loki, *Loki of Outgard* (Snorri *passim*, Saxo Grammaticus Bk. 8).

Jötunheim was looked upon as a land of towering forests, strong rivers, vast caverns, mighty mountains and tremendous distances: in other words, an exaggeration of the topography well known to the Northmen of the Scandinavian peninsula. Snorri describes a famous jaunt into Giantland made by Thor, Loki and two human children (Thor's servants) Þjálfi and Röskva:§ the god Thor "left his two billy-goats and went on foot eastward in the direction of Giantland as far as the coast where he put out over the deep sea. When he made landfall he disembarked—he and Loki and Þjálfi and Röskva. Having trudged a little way they found a great forest rise before them, and they tramped through it all that day until nightfall. . . ." Eventually, the party arrived at the stronghold of king Loki of Outgard.‖ "Thor and his companions saw soaring high above them a burg set in the middle of an open plain. Even though they pressed back the crowns of their heads on to the napes of their necks they still couldn't see its battlements. They walked round to the main gate and found it blocked by a great grille. They went up to the grille but couldn't budge it. They were determined to get in and did so by sidling between the bars. Next, their eyes were caught by a vast edifice towards which they went. The door was open so they entered and saw there crowds of men sitting up to two trestle-tables. Men? They were

† *Gylf.* I.   ‡ *Völ.* 51.   § *Gylf.* XLV.   ‖ *Gylf.* XLVI.

giants! Almost at once they found themselves in front of king
Loki of Outgard saying 'How do you do?' to him. But he
was slow to notice them and when he did, his upper lip drew
back from his teeth and he sneered, 'Of course, news travels
slowly to us here at the Back-of-Beyond and I may be quite
wrong in what I'm thinking; but is it—can this young bully-
boy be Two-Goat Thor . . .?' "

This is not the time to continue *that* particular story, its
recital will come later; here we can glean further information
about the topography of Jötunheim by drawing attention to an
encounter of Thor's with another giant, Hrungnir.† In this
case, the rocky, mountainous aspect of Jötunheim is emphasized, for Hrungnir's home is called Grjótúnagarðr, Rock
Town Enclosure; and Hrungnir's links with rocks and stones
are brought out in such of his members and organs (his head
and heart) as are made of stone. Hrungnir's shield was also
stone and his weapon in the duel with Thor was a flint hone
such as might be used to sharpen a gigantic scythe. There are
strong connections here between giants and rocky caves in the
mountains. This is the hill-giant stock remembered in such
Middle English literature as *Sir Gawayne and the Greene Knighte*:

> Sumwhyle wyth wormeȝ he werreȝ, and with wolues als,
> Sumwhyle wyth wodwos, þat woned in þe knarreȝ,
> Boþe wyth bulleȝ and bereȝ, and boreȝ oþer-quyle,
> *And etayneȝ, þat hym anelede of þe heȝe felle;*
> Nade he ben duȝty and dryȝe, and dryȝtyn had serued,
> Douteles he hade ben ded and dreped ful ofte.

stock which has links with the cave-dwelling, rock-hurling
Polyphemus and his tribe of Greek myth.

In Northern myth giants are divided into two kinds, Hill
Giants and Frost Giants which are distinctly chthonic beings,
and a third kind, Fire Giants which represent the destructive
power of fire. The generic term *jötunn* (O.E. *eoten*, Mod. Eng.
ettin) appears to be connected with the Indo-European root

† *Skáld.* XVII.

meaning "to eat", and suggests that our forefathers had come up against a neighbouring people with cannibalistic tendencies whom they dubbed "eaters". And just as in modern times the words "Hun" and "Turk" achieved a half-mythic meaning, so in ancient times the word which gave rise to *jötunn* achieved a full mythic significance. The strength of the original meaning of *jötunn* can be judged by the viability of the trait of cannibalism which we still find in our own nursery giants:

> Fee Fie Fo Fum!
> I smell the blood of an Englishman!
> Be he alive or be he dead
> I'll grind his bones to make my bread!

Northern giants then, are a mongrel breed, although they mainly owe their existence to the animistic interpretation of natural phenomena. Rockfalls, landslips and earthquakes were the work of hill giants; flaring volcanoes, destructive lightning, and the frightening northern lights were caused by fire giants; and avalanches, glaciers, ice-caps, freezing seas and rivers by frost giants—now sadly diminished to Jack Frost.

Apart from the fundamental mythic concepts of giants there are later conscious literary embroideries. For instance, two of the eddaic poems (*Þrymskviða* and *Hymiskviða*) present the giants' houses and social set-up as a reflection of aristocratic halls and society of the viking period, and Snorri often does the same. This is not to say, however, that in the tales themselves the true mythic basis is not present: it is. An example of such literary embroidery on the groundwork of true myth is to be found in *Þrymskviða*: in fact, two myths have been skilfully joined, one dealing with the theft of the gods' only infallible weapon in their constant struggle with the giants, and the other with the theft by the frost giants of Freya the goddess of fertility. A quotation from *Þrymskviða* will illustrate what I mean by literary embroidery. The giant king Þrymr begins preparations

to receive his hoped-for bride Freya into his home and he
shouts to his servants like any viking *jarl*:†

Spring to it, giants
and spread the benches—
    now they're bringing Freya
    to be my bride,
Njörðr's only daughter
out of Nóatún.

Gold-horned cattle
collect in my paddocks,
    jet-black oxen
    a giant's joy;
many are my trinkets
many are my treasures,
    Freya alone
    did I seem to lack.

Oh, a crowd of people
came by early evening;
    beer was broached
    and borne before the giants;
Thor ate an ox;
he ate eight salmon;
    he gobbled all the cakes
    got in for the ladies,
and then tossed off
three tuns of mead!

This story derives its humour, of course, from the central situation of Thor's being disguised by a bride's veil and Þrymr's
thinking he is Freya. In the other poem mentioned, *Hymiskviða*, the giant Hymir is represented as living the kind of combined farming and fishing life enjoyed (or endured) by most of
the Icelandic settlers and many of the Scandinavian coastal
dwellers.

†*Þrym.* 23–25.

5

MIDGARD

Midgard does not figure largely in either of the *Eddas*. Its place in the Norse cosmography is definite and important, but it is safe to assume that neither the poets nor Snorri intended wasting time dilating on a subject of which their audience had a personal knowledge. Most of the relevant information about Midgard has already been given, but it will be useful here to summarize it.

Miðgarðr means the "Middle Enclosure", the World, the Earth; it is one of the "nine worlds in the tree" and according to *Völuspá* 4 the three sons of Bor (Odin, Vili and Vé) "lifted up the level land and created Midgard the Mighty" in the midst of the Yawning Void. The materials of which Midgard was made were the remains of the giant Ymir, and more particularly the "enclosure" was created from his eyebrows. "The earth is round", says Snorri,† "and about it lies the deep blue sea. Along the outward shores of the ocean [the gods] gave to the race of giants a grant of land to settle in. But towards the centre of the earth they built a fortress wall encircling the region against their giant enemies: and to make it they employed the brows of Ymir, and called their stronghold Midgard. They took his brains too and flung them to the winds and so created the clouds. . . ." The sons of Bor also created humankind,‡ "the man Askr and the woman Embla. These two brought to birth all Mankind who were given a dwelling-place on Midgard."

The giants were regarded as being near enough to Midgard to be a menace to men. There was always the possibility of giants "coming in over Midgard" (*Gylf.* XLII) and that is why the gods fortified it and their own abodes. In addition, the god Thor is especially regarded as the giants' enemy and as "Midgard's defender" which is one of his nicknames. Snorri

† *Gylf.* VIII.   ‡ *Gylf.* IX.

says in *Skáldskaparmál* IV "what synonyms are we to use for Thor? . . . Defender of Asgard and of Midgard, Adversary and slayer of Giants and Troll-wives."

The road from earth to heaven lay over the Rainbow, variously known as Ásbrú "the gods' bridge" and Bifröst or Bilröst, both meaning "the tremulous or wavering way". Only the Æsir may pass this bridge and of the Æsir it is now time to speak.

FIG. 10 WALRUS IVORY CHESSMAN
One of a set found at Uig, Isle of Lewis. Twelfth century English or Scandinavian. (British Museum)

CHAPTER III

Æsir and Vanir

ENOUGH has been written to indicate that Northern Mythology is no simple homogeneous system with a pantheon which came into existence complete and full-grown. If we may take a geological metaphor then there are at least three main strata of myths: at bedrock there is Allfather the old Indo-European Sky Father; resting closely above him there are the cosmogonic beings Ymir, Norfi[28] the father of Night (whose various marriages produced Space, Earth and Day), Mundilfari and his son and daughter the Moon and the Sun, Ægir and his wife Rán (god and goddess of the sea), Hœnir, Mímir and the three Norns; at the surface lies what is today commonly accepted as *the* Northern Mythology, namely, Odin and the rest of the Æsir and Ásynjur, and inter-marrying with them the originally alien Vanir.

None of the sub-strata of myth is completely covered though much is now lost to sight. Outcrops from the two main sub-strata rise to the surface where (unless he knows the geology of the section) they confuse and frequently quite baffle the observer. Examples of such outcrops are the name and some of the qualities of the ancient Allfather which have been applied to Odin; the co-existence of the ancient god of the sea Ægir and the new-comer Njörðr.

We have so far looked more closely at what remains to be seen of the lower strata; it is now convenient to examine the upper stratum.

The Northmen of the Migration Age called the race of their gods *Æsir* from a singular form *áss* meaning (for them) "god". In the rationalizing *Prologue* to his *Prose Edda* Snorri Sturluson seeks to derive the word Æsir from the word Asia. This etymology is a popular and unscientific one, although apart from the superficial similarity of the two words, Snorri's derivation may have been founded on a tradition according to which the cult of certain gods migrated to Scandinavia from the south and ultimately from Asia Minor.

It seems extremely likely that gods *did* come from the direction of Asia Minor: they were not Æsir but members of another race of gods called in both *Eddas* by the name Vanir. The advent of the new gods is represented in the mythology by a war between Æsir and Vanir in which neither party gains complete victory. In other words, that rather unusual result of a struggle between warring gods had come about, a draw: neither team was demoted *in toto* as demons, elves or fairies, though certain insecure members were dropped from the Æsir's side (Mímir, Hœnir); and Vanir deities (Njörðr, Frey, Freya) were accepted into the northern pantheon alongside the Æsir.

If we examine some of the later gods separately we shall get a better idea of the stratification and faulting of Northern Mythology. The obvious starting point is the chief of the Æsir, Odin.

I

ODIN

According to Snorri,† "The gods of unbroken divine descent are twelve in number. . . . Odin is supreme as well as being the oldest of the gods. He has his way in all things. Mighty as the other gods may be, nevertheless they all serve him as children obey their father. . . . Odin is called Allfather because he is father of all the gods; he's called, too, Valfather or Father of the Slain, because all those are his sons by adoption who fall in battle; he billets them in Valhalla and Vingólf, and they are called Einherjar or Champions. Odin has other names such as Gallows-god, Gaolbird-god and God of Cargoes; and he declared himself owner of much more distinguished names when he went to see king Geirröðr:‡

† *Gylf.* XX.   ‡ *Grím.* 47 ff.

My name is Grímr	Hooded
also Gangleri,	Wayweary
Herjan and Hjálmberi,	*Ruler: Helmet bearer*
Þekkr and Þriði	*Much loved: Third*
Þuðr and Uðr	*? ?*
Helblindi and Hárr;	*Hel blinder: High*
Saðr, Svipall	*Truthful: Changing*
and Sanngetall,	*Truthful*
Herteitr and Hnikarr,	*Host glad: Overthrower*
Bileygr, Báleygr,	*Shifty-eyed: Flaming-eyed*
Bölverkr, Fjölnir	*Ill-doer: Many-shaped*
Grímnir, Glapsviðr and	*Hooded: Swift in deceit: Wide*
Fjölsviðr;	*in wisdom*
Síðhöttr, Síðskeggr,	*Broad hat: Long beard*
Sigföðr, Hnikuðr,	*Father of Victory: Overthrower*
Alföðr, Atríðr, Farmatýr,	*Allfather: Rider: God of*
	Cargoes
Óski, Ómi	*God of wishes: Shouter*
Jafnhárr, Biflindi	*Even as high: ?*
Göndlir and Hárbarðr;	*Wand bearer: Greybeard*
Sviðurr, Sviðrir,	*Changing(?) Changing(?)*[29]
Jálkr, Kjalarr, Viðurr,	*Gelding: Keel: ?*
Þrór, Yggr, Þundr,	*? : Terrible: Thunderer*
Vakr, Skilfingr,	*Wakeful: Shaker*
Váfuðr, Hroptatýr,	*Wanderer: Crier of the gods*
Gautr and Veratýr."	*Father: Lord of men.*

Snorri goes on to say that these "ekenames", nicknames, were given to Odin "for something he did" and that "some events in his wanderings which are well worth relating have given rise to these names."

Before I remark on any of these bye-names, it will be best to consider the chief name *Óðinn*, Odin. In the Prologue to his *Edda* Snorri calls the god "Vóden" as well as Odin. A characteristic of the Norse language was its loss of the initial

w-sound (written "v") in certain cases; this loss did not occur
in West Gothonic where we find O.H.G. Wuotan, O.L.G.
Wodan and O.E. Woden. The English form of the name,
Woden, would appear to be connected with the old adjective
wood meaning "furious", "wild", "mad", well known to
Chaucer but becoming archaic by Shakespeare's time when in
A Midsummer Night's Dream he diverts his listeners with a pun
making the angry Demetrius say that he is "wood within this
wood".[30] Adam of Bremen, IV, 26, says, "Wodan, id est
furor" (*Wodan, that is, fury*); and the primitive conception of
Odin is the German storm giant Wode leading his "wild
army", O.H.G. *Wuotis-her*, the procession of the homeless dead
through the air.

A vivid memory of the Wild Hunt is to be found in the
Old English Chronicle Anno 1127: "Let no one be surprised at
what we are about to relate, for it was general knowledge
throughout the whole country that immediately after [Abbot
Henry of Poitou's] arrival [on 6th February 1127] . . . many
men both saw and heard a great number of huntsmen hunting.
The huntsmen were black, huge, and hideous, and rode on
black horses and on black he-goats, and their hounds were jet
black, with eyes like saucers, and horrible. This was seen in the
very deer park of the town of Peterborough, and in all the
woods that stretch from that same town to Stamford, and all
through the night the monks heard them sounding and winding their horns. Reliable witnesses who kept watch in the night
declared that there might well have been as many as twenty or
thirty of them winding their horns as near as they could tell."†

The conception of a furious host of beings rushing through
the sky led by a wild rider or flyer is not defunct among present-
day descendants of the Indo-European races. In English folklore the wild hunt has become the yapping, yelling pack of
Gabriel's hounds; while as recently as 1949 the myth has re-
appeared in a popular American cowboy song the *Riders in the*

† *The Anglo-Saxon Chronicle*, translated by G. N. Garmonsway, page 258,
Dent 1953.

Sky[31] in which the homeless dead are a ghostly "devil's herd" of cattle whose "brands wuz still on fire" and whose "hooves wuz made of steel" while Odin is represented as ghostly cowboys condemned to a terrible eternity of rounding-up "across these endless skies".

If we extract the main ideas from this pastiche we find a god whose ancient name gave the various forms Óðin—Vóden—Wuotan—Woden, a name meaning wild or furious; and that this god is made manifest in a noisy, bellowing movement across the sky. Such another is to be found in Vâta, Lord of the Wind of the Hindu *Rigveda*, and it becomes obvious that the names Odin and Vâta are doublets; and the inference is that both personages are descended from an Indo-European god of the wind.

The ancient **Djevs*, the Indo-European Sky Father, retained his pre-eminence among others of the related tribes as for instance Dyaus among the Hindus, Zeus among the Greeks and Jupiter with the Romans; but among the Gothonic tribes *Djevs in the person of *Tiwaz was ousted by the one who in Indo-European times had been Lord of the Wind and whom the Northmen knew as Odin. *Djevs himself lived on among the Gothonic nations in a sort of dichotomy: as *Tiwaz, who gave rise to O.N. Týr and O.E. Tíw, he was nominally the god of war, but with few if any of the attributes of a true wargod; and as Allfather, who became assimilated to Odin.

It would be interesting and possibly enlightening to find out when Odin usurped Týr's place. The Romans equated Odin not with Jupiter (as would now seem natural—both being fathers of the gods) but with Mercury. The reason for this identification is undoubtedly that both Odin and Mercury were regarded as the Psychopompos "the leader of souls". Odin and Týr are linked together by Tacitus under the names of Mercury and Mars in *Ann.* XIII 57. He notes that in the war between Chatti and Ermunduri both sides had dedicated the whole of their enemy—men and booty—to Odin and Týr: "by this vow men and horses, in fact everything belonging to the vanquished, is given over to destruction." This annihilation of the Chatti (who lost the fight) took place in A.D. 58. An early example of this custom of dedicating an enemy to total destruction is given by Orosius (V 16). He tells of the defeat of Caepio and Mallius by the Cimbri in 105 B.C. and says "the enemy captured both camps and a huge booty. They went on to destroy everything they had got their hands on in fulfilment of a novel and unusual vow: all clothing was ripped in pieces and thrown away; gold and silver were flung into the river; the war coats of the men were hacked to bits; the horses' harness destroyed; the horses themselves were drowned under; the men were strung up on trees with nooses round their necks, so that no booty remained for the victor nor was any pity shown to the vanquished." This particular battle took place in the lower Rhône valley, but the Cimbri had started their wanderings from Jutland about 113 B.C. and remnants of the tribe remained in Jutland from where, in A.D. 5 they sent ambassadors to Augustus. It was in central Jutland that "Tollund Man" was dug up in May 1950. This Man of the North, although some 2000 years old, had been very well preserved in the Tollund bog. His appearance and the conditions under which he was found afford striking parallels to those mentioned of the sacrificed prisoners described by Orosius in the passage just quoted. Tollund Man had been *hanged*: the rope of two plaited leather thongs was still round his neck. Then, except for a leather cap and a leather belt about his waist, he was stark *naked*. Many other such bodies have been found in the Tollund bog, many are naked, many have the rope which hanged them round their necks and many are *wounded*. Professor P. V. Glob of Aarhus University, Denmark, wrote of the discovery that "the general belief is that such naked hangings were ritual sacrifices in connection with the great spring fertility festival of antiquity." I contend that in the case of Tollund Man the evidence is conclusively in favour of a sacrifice of prisoners after a battle. He was discovered hanged, naked, along with many others some of whom were wounded, in Central Jutland, the home of the Cimbri. Some ten years after the Cimbri left their home we hear of them dedicating their prisoners to a ritual destruction by hanging: it is unreasonable to suppose that the Cimbri at home, fifteen years earlier, did not observe such traditional customs. Then we know from Tacitus (*Ann*. XIII 57) that two Gothonic tribes were well able to vow each other's destruction through sacrifice to "Odin and Týr": the enemy did not need to be Roman or some other non-Gothonic people.

Now while we are not told that the Cimbri sacrificed their prisoners and booty to Odin and Týr, the circumstantial evidence points to their having done so. We may conclude then that by the first century B.C. Odin was already challenging Týr for precedence. (See plate 1.)

Tacitus in *Germania* 9 (A.D. 98) says of the "Germani", "Above all gods they worship Mercury and count it no sin to win his favour on certain days with human sacrifices." But this observation proves to have been lifted from Caesar's *de Bello Gallico* where it refers to the Gauls. In any case Tacitus' personal knowledge of the "Germani" was of the Western Group alone, and we are justified in accepting Odin as chief god by A.D. 98 only among those tribes. We can say that the northern boundary of Woden—Odin's kingdom at this time would be roughly the 52nd parallel running from the Rhine mouth to the middle Elbe.[32]

Odin's influence reached its height in the Migration Age. Because his adherents were making their way in the world primarily by force of arms, Odin's warlike aspect is emphasized; but his earlier character as a Psychopompos, a leader of souls, is still of equal importance but with a new twist: the souls he leads are those of warriors for whom he has prepared a special heaven, Valhalla.

Snorri gives an account of the spread of the cult of Odin in the *Prologue* to his *Edda*; and in Chapter V of *Ynglinga Saga* he makes Odin travel northwards from Saxony to Fyn and then on to Sigtuna on the Uppsala fiord whence the cult travelled west and south-west. It is not to be supposed that Odin was finally accepted as chief god at any one time by all North-men: he is usually found as one of a trinity; and another member of the three may be favoured some time in some district more than he. In the first century of the Christian era the West Gothonic tribes (according to Tacitus *Germania* 9) worshipped "Mercury, Mars and Hercules", that is Odin, Týr and Fjör-gyn; the Saxons of the eighth and ninth centuries revered Woden, Thor and Saxnot, and the Northmen of the same age Odin, Thor and Frey. Many Northmen of the Migration Age put Thor before Odin in their estimation; this was particularly the case among the farmers of Denmark and Norway. Odin was especially the god of professional warriors and aristocrats and as such the snobbish could regard him as higher in the social scale than the rest: this opinion is put into words in *Hárbarðsljóð* 24:

> To Odin come
> the battle-slain earls,
>   but Thor has the tribe of thralls.

Of all the Norse pantheon Odin has the longest list of bye-names: there can be little doubt that this resulted from his adoption as the upper-class warrior god, for the poets were protégés of jarls and kings, and what more natural than that the skald should sing the praises of his master's deity? It was but a step for the skald to honour his own profession by making Odin himself the chief poet, *Fimbulðul*, the mighty counsellor, fount of all wisdom, who " spoke everything in rhyme, such as now composed, which we call skald-craft".† It is possible to group those of Odin's names of which we know the meaning accord-ing to attributes and activities. Odin as war-god has several names, perhaps first *Sigföðr* Father of Victory, then *Hjálmberi* Helmet bearer, *Herblindi* Host blinder, *Herteitr* Host glad, *Hnikuðr* Overthrower, *Hnikarr* Overthrower, and *Valföðr* Father of the slain. This last name, *Valföðr*, is a reflection of Odin as the leader of the souls of the dead, a manifestation

† *Yng. Saga* VI.

which is developed until in Migration times he is represented as the Lord of Valhalla (the hall of the slain) to whom those who die on the battlefield are brought by Valkyries (the choosers of the slain). This conception will need further explanation later on. *Báleygr* the Flaming-eyed seems to fit into this category too: Snorri says† when Odin was sitting "among his friends his countenance was so beautiful and dignified that the spirits of all were exhilarated by it; but when he was in war he appeared dreadful to all his foes." Whether this assumption of a terrible aspect in war was an attribute borrowed from Celtic myth we shall probably never know,[33] but we can be fairly sure that Snorri is wrong in identifying such an attribute with plain shape-changing.‡ Odin was indeed a shape-changer as we might gather from *Fjölnir*, Many-shaped and *Svipall*, Changing, while Snorri says he was "able to change his skin and form in any way he liked." Apart from shape-shifting, Odin frequently wandered through the worlds in disguise, particularly in the disguise of an old man with a staff, one-eyed, grey-beared and wearing a wide-brimmed hat; such a person as is described in *Bandamanna saga*, "somebody getting on in years, an old fellow wearing a black sleeved-cape which had seen better days, in fact with only one sleeve left and that dangling down at the back. He had an iron-tipped staff in his fist and he was wearing a floppy-brimmed hat." This manifestation is remembered in Odin's ekenames *Grímr* and *Grímnir* Hooded, *Gangleri* Wayweary, *Síðhöttr* Broad hat, *Síðskeggr* Longbeard, *Hárbarðr* Greybeard, *Göndlir* Staffbearer and *Váfuðr* Wanderer. Other names emphasize special characteristics of Odin as for example *Saðr* and *Sanngetall* Truthful, *Bileygr* Shifty-eyed, *Glapsviðr* Swift in deceit, *Fjölsviðr* Wide in wisdom, *Yggr* Terrible, *Þundr* Thunderer, *Vakr* Wakeful and *Jálkr* Gelding. As a specialized deity we find him called *Farmatýr* God of cargoes and *Óski* God of wishes. An interesting group of titles are those which appear to show Odin as a trinity—*Hárr* High, *Jafnhárr* Even-as-High and *Þriði* Third.

† *Yng. Saga* VI.   ‡ *Yng. Saga* VI.

Of these names, Fjölsviðr recalls the ancient Sky Father and a half-forgotten myth telling how he got his wisdom and why the sky has only one eye. This tale is alluded to in *Völuspá* 28, its details now forgotten:

> I know it all, Odin,
> where you hid your eye
>   deep in the wide-famed
>   well of Mímir;
> every morning
>   does Mímir drink
>   mead from Valföðr's pledge. . . .

Mímir is a puzzling being who will need to be discussed later; here we may advance on trust that he is connected with the Underworld and his well under the root of Yggdrasill which reaches towards the Frost Giants is an emblem of the sea. The eye of Odin (really *Djevs) is an emblem of the sun and Mímir's drinking mead from it *every morning* a representation of the sun's rising just as the hiding of the eye is the sun's setting. Mímir's name appears to be connected with Latin *memor*, "memory" and hence with wisdom: the myth then develops into a tale of a Sky God who pledged one eye in return for the gift of wisdom.

This is only one of a number of myths connected with Odin's winning of wisdom: it is of the type involving suffering or privation. Another of the same type is the story told about Odin's hanging himself upon the Ash Tree in order to learn the secret of the runes of wisdom: but whereas the hidden eye story reaches back into Indo-European myth, the hanging story is affected by Christian myth. In the old pagan ritual, sacrifices to Odin were made by hanging and the ⊓-shaped gallows was frequently referred to as "the horse of wood". It is a possibility that because of its connection with sacrifice to Odin this kind of gallows got the name *Yggdrasill* "the horse of Yggr" where Yggr=Terrible, a bye-name for Odin. This theory is given support by the very name Yggr, for to the victim such a god must indeed have seemed terrible. On the other hand, there is no reason why the Odin who hanged himself on the Ash Tree should be called "the terrible". The conclusion is then, that Yggdrasill as a name for the sacrificial gallows was transferred to the World Ash after the making of the myth of Odin's winning wisdom by self-sacrifice. The myth is told in *Hávamál* stanzas 138, 139 and 141. *Hávamál* is a *Verse Edda* piece; its title means "the words of the High One [Odin]"; it is a conglomeration of proverbs, charms and fragmentary narrative in different verse forms badly bundled together. The three stanzas run as follows:†

> I'm aware that I hung
> on the windy tree,
>   swung there nights all of nine;
> gashed with a blade
> bloodied for Odin,
>   myself an offering to myself
> knotted to that tree
> no man knows
>   whither the root of it runs.
>
> None gave me bread,
> none gave me drink,
>   down to the depths I peered
> to snatch up runes
> with a roaring screech
>   and fall in a dizzied faint!
>
> Wellbeing I won
> and wisdom too,
>   I grew and joyed in my growth;
> from a word to a word
> I was led to a word
>   from a deed to another deed.[34]

> † *Háv.* 138, 139, 141.

Other versions of the wisdom-winning myth (e.g. the stealing of the mead of poetry from Suttungr's sons) show Odin's cunning, patience and willingness to commit perjury to bring enlightenment to the sons of men.

Another nickname, Atríðr, meaning *Rider* links Odin with the original wind god galloping across the sky. A rider needs a horse, and as befits the Father of All, Odin's horse is said to be "the best among gods and men";† it is a gray, has eight legs and is called Sleipnir or Slippery. Sleipnir's sire was a famous stallion by name Svaðilfari, but strangest of all, Sleipnir's dam was the god Loki. The later Odin, patron of vikings, wore a golden helmet such as that discovered in the Sutton Hoo burial mound as recently as 1939 (see plate 4). The symbol of this Odin's power as the arbiter of battles was the spear Gungnir whose marvellous property lay in its never ceasing in its thrust once started.[35] This weapon was created by two dwarfs Brokkr and Sindri the sons of Ívaldi at the instigation of Loki (as will be related). With Gungnir Odin started the "first war in the world" and he carried Gungnir in the last battle at the Ragnarök. Another famous possession of his was Draupnir, a gold ring, forged by Brokkr and Sindri on the same occasion as the making of Gungnir. Every ninth night eight similar rings dropped from Draupnir. It was the ring Odin placed on his son Balder's breast as the bright god lay on the funeral pyre aboard his long-ship Hringhorni. And Hermóðr saw Balder wearing Draupnir on his finger afterwards down in hel.

Odin as Allfather, brooding over the nine worlds, was used to sit in the watch-tower Hliðskjálf (*Gate Shelf*). Snorri says (*Gylf.* XVII) "There's a very spacious abode (which is Odin's) called Valaskjálf, *the Shelf of the Slain*. The gods built that mansion and thatched it with sheer silver; inside is Gate Shelf or Hliðskjálf (as the throne is called). And when the All-father sits on this seat he is able to see out over the whole wide world." Further, Snorri says of Hliðskjálf‡ that "Odin used to sit on his high seat to look across all the worlds and see every

† *Gylf.* XLII.   ‡ *Gylf.* IX.

man's behaviour, knowing full well all the things he sees
there". Upon this brooding Odin's shoulders perch the two
ravens Huginn and Muninn;† they "whisper into his ears
every scrap of news which they see or hear tell of. . . . At crack
of dawn he pushes them off to flap all around the world and
they return in time for second breakfast. This is the source of
much of his information, and the reason why men call him the
Raven god, just as this says:‡

> Huginn and Muninn§
> every day fly
>   over the big wide world;
> I worry after Huginn
> when he harks not back,
>   though I watch much more for Muninn."

Ravens and wolves were naturally associated with battlefields
in the minds of the Gothonic peoples and are appropriate to
Odin as Valföðr, Father of the Slain. Snorri tells of two wolves
attendant on Odin:‖ "The food which stands on his table he
gives to two wolves which he has, called Geri Greediguts and
Freki Gobble-up; he himself needs not a crumb. Wine is to
him both meat and drink, as it says here:¶

> Geri and Freki
> the Host Father feeds
>   (that Person proud in arms);
> but on wine alone
> does the weapon-decked god
>   Odin, live for aye."

Odin's wife in Asgard is Frigg, and they are the father and
mother of the gods. In Chapter IX of *Gylfaginning* Snorri says
that Odin's "wife is called Frigg Fjörgyn's daughter and from
their union sprang the race whom we call the Æsir." In the
same chapter he says Odin "may well be called Allfather

† *Gylf.* XXXVIII.   ‡ *Grím.* 20.   § Thought and Memory.
‖ *Gylf.* XXXVIII.   ¶ *Grím.* 19.

because he is father of all the gods and men and all those sprung
from them. His strength was full grown. Jörð was his daughter
and his wife also; he begat his first son upon her, who is Thor
of the Gods." We conclude from this that either Odin had (at
least) two wives, Jörð and Frigg, or that Jörð and Frigg are one
and the same goddess.

Jörð is our "earth", "Mother Earth", and a synonym for
Jörð in *Völuspá* 55 and *Hárbarðsljóð* 55 is Fjörgyn; but Odin
too is called Fjörgyn as for instance in *Lokasenna* 26:

> Shut you up, Frigg,
> you are Fjörgyn's wife . . .!

It is confusing (to say the least) to find both husband and wife,
i.e. Odin and Jörð, called Fjörgyn: and the complication is
increased when Frigg, as Odin's wife, is referred to as Frigg
Fjörgyn's daughter. The explanation seems to be as follows:
the word Fjörgyn as applied to Odin was not originally the
same word as Fjörgyn applied to Jörð. Fjörgyn as a synonym
for Jörð appears to me to be most closely connected with
Gothic *fairgúni* and the cognate O.E. *fyrgen* meaning "mountain": this Fjörgyn is used in *Skáldskaparmál* LVI as a synonym
for Jörð-Earth along with such others as Field, Ground, Land
and Country. Fjörgyn in this sense also occurs in the *Þulor* or
Rhymed Glossaries.[36] The other Fjörgyn meaning Odin could
have developed from a Gothonic *Ferguniz or *Furguniz
which is not far from Percunis the Prussian thunder god[37], a
doublet of Odin under his bye-name Þundr.

The upshot of all this seems to be that Jörð and Frigg are to
be identified as one and the same—the Earth Mother and
goddess of Fertility. Jörð is probably the earlier name; she is the
spouse of Odin under his earlier avatar the Indo-European Sky
Father and their parallels in Greek myth are Gaia and Ouranos.

It will be necessary later on to recount myths in which Odin
plays a chief part; perhaps here it will be useful to summarize
the important events which shape and are shaped by Odin. It
must always be remembered that the gods of the north are

frequently bi-valent, often multi-valent, and Odin is no exception: the Óðinn of the Migration Age is the son of two fathers, namely the Indo-European *Djevs and the Lord of the Wind. From *Djevs he inherits his attributes of Allfather and Creator of heaven and earth and all within, or as the myth says, he is father and husband of Earth and of all sprung from their union. As the resplendent Sky Father he is the enemy of darkness in all its manifestations; later he is the preserver of mankind and the sacrifice for mankind's benefit as for example when he puts his eye in pawn. As the descendant of the Wind God, Óðinn is the Psychopompos, the leader of souls, and this side of his divine character is amplified with attributes of war until he becomes lord of Valhalla. Those who live by the sword shall perish by the sword, and in accepting the traits of a war god Óðinn must needs accept the qualities of a finite being: as such he is given a genealogy which represents him as the son of Bor son of Búri who was licked from the primeval ice by the cow Auðumla; and his mother is the giantess Bestla. His brothers are Vili and Vé. Another creation myth is attached to these three brothers: they are said to have brought into being the world, the sea and the clouds from the body, bones and blood of Ymir; they created the dwarfs. Vili and Vé disappear from the myth (at least, under those names), Óðinn has Frigg to wife and begets the Æsir race. Then ensues the period of the Golden Age, an age which is brought to an end by the mysterious female Gullveig whom the gods slay thrice, only to have her thrice come to life. Óðinn precipitates a war with the rival god-clan, the Vanir: this war ("the first in the world") appears to be a direct result of Gullveig's murder. Neither side wins but hostages are exchanged. Evil enters the scheme of things. Óðinn purchases wisdom in a draught from Mímir's Well and the purchase price is one of his eyes. Afterwards, he foresees the doom of the divine powers and takes measures such as the collection of the Champions in Asgard to help at the last fight, the chaining of the wolf Fenrir and of Loki, the casting of Hel into Niflheim, and of the World Serpent into the sea.

No measure can withstand the Fates and Óðinn leads his
battalions against the forces of destruction at the Ragnarök.
Óðinn himself is swallowed by the wolf and so completes his
course as Óðinn—Vóden—*Djevs when (as *Völuspá* fittingly
says)†

> The sun grows dark,
> earth sinks under sea;
>   from their steadings in heaven
>   the bright stars turn. . . .

*Djevs is dead and there is no more sky. At least, for the time
being.

2

THOR

Snorri relates‡ how after Odin among the gods "Thor tops the
rest—sometimes called Thor-of-the-gods and Whip-it-up-
Thor. He is the strongest of gods and men. He rules that region
called Þrúðvangar or the Paddocks of Power and his castle hall
is Bilskirnir or Lightning; in it there are five hundred and forty
rooms which makes it the most extensive mansion known to
men, as it says in *Grímnismál*:§

> Five hundred rooms
> and forty yet
>   are built I know in Bilskirnir;
> of all the homes
> hall-roofed I've seen
>   it seems my son's is greatest.

Thor has two goats (Toothgnasher and Toothgrinder)‖ and
a chariot which they draw and he drives: that's why he's called
Whip-it-up-Thor. He has in addition three wonderful pos-
sessions. One of them is called Mjölnir or Mullicrusher (his

---

† *Völ.* 56.   ‡ *Gylf.* XXI.
§ *Grím.* 24.   ‖ *Tanngnjóstr* and *Tanngrisnir.*

hammer), which is well known to the frost giants and hill-ogres when it rockets up the sky—nothing wonderful about that. His second treasure (and best) is the Strength-increasing-belt, for when it buckles about him his brawn is added to by half. His third possession, in which is vested inestimable worth, is his iron gauntlets: without them he would be unable to grasp his hammer-shaft. But nobody has a memory long enough to be able to tell all his wonderful works—though I myself could recount enough to keep you occupied for hours before I had told you all I know."

There are two things so obvious about Thor that Snorri has thought it hardly worth while to mention them: one is his appearance—he had red hair, a red beard and beetling red eyebrows; the other is his association with thunder. The name I have translated "Whip-it-up-Thor" is in the original *Öku-Þórr* or "Driver Thor" according to Snorri's derivation; Cleasby and Vigfusson dispute this as another popular etymology and I believe they are right. They say that *Öku* is not a derivative of the verb *aka* "to drive" but comes rather from a Finnish *Ukko*, the Thunder God of the Chudic tribes.[38]

Further information on Thor may be gained from the per-missible poetic paraphrases of his name given by Snorri in *Skáldskaparmál* IV: "One should call him son of Odin and Jörð, father of Magni and Móði and Þrúðr, husband of Sif, stepfather of Ullr, Wielder and Possessor of Mjölnir and of the Girdle of Strength, and of Bilskirnir; Defender of Asgard and Midgard, Adversary and Slayer of Giants and Troll-women, Smiter of Hrungnir, of Geirröðr and of Þrívaldi, Master of Þjálfi and Röskva, Foe of the Midgard Serpent, Foster-father of Vingnir and Hlóra."

Thor, then, is pre-eminently the god of thunder. His hammer Mjölnir is the thunderbolt, the lightning flash and the claps of thunder: these may be also the sparkles and rumblings of his chariot drawn by the two goats across the sky. After being thrown, Mjölnir has the boomerang quality of returning to his hand. This hammer (according to Schütte) is probably derived from the double axe or "labrys" of the Cretan and Hittite thunder god. The *attributes* of Thor as a thunderer and a strong god no doubt go back to Indo-European times: Odin himself has been a thunderer as we can guess from his bye-name Þundr "Thunderer",† and indeed as we should expect from one who was a sky god. As for the *name* Thor (O.N. *Þórr*, O.E. *Þunor*, O.H.G. *Thonar*), it is equivalent to the Celtic Jupiter *Tanarus*, the Thundering Jupiter; and to say that Thor is the first-born of Odin is a way of indicating the birth of a new god from an attribute of an older one. Neither the name "Thor" nor the usual Latin rendering "Jupiter" is exemplified among the Gothonic nations of antiquity.[39] Still, the name Thor must have been adopted in a West Gothonic dialect from the period before the Gothonic Sound Shift, i.e. before A.D. 1, and gradually the god's cult under his name Thor extended to the uttermost north and west through Iceland as far as Greenland.

Thor also attends to agriculture and in this way becomes a patron of farmers and thralls (cf. *Hárbarðsljóð* 24, quoted on p. 112). He is depicted as being very close to earth. According to both *Eddas* Thor is the son of Jörð or Mother Earth; and he is the husband of Sif the golden haired fertility goddess, the emblem of the ripe cornfield, the northern Ceres. A remembrance of the union of Thor and Sif has (I contend) lived on in the folklore of the north of England. I am referring to the tale heard at my grandmother's knee that the beneficent sheet lightning of summer flashed over the swollen ears of corn in order to ripen them. Thor has other wives including the giantess Járnsaxa, and he became the father of sons and at least one daughter. If we accept the doctrine "by their fruits ye shall know them" then Thor is compact of fierce courage, colossal might and strength; for these qualities are implicit in the names of his three children Móði=fierce courage, Magni=colossal might, and Þrúðr=strength. Of Thor's stepson Ullr there will be something to say later on; here we may set out his family tree:

† *Grím.* 54.

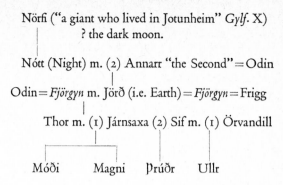

Nörfi ("a giant who lived in Jotunheim" *Gylf.* X)
? the dark moon.

Nótt (Night) m. (2) Annarr "the Second" = Odin

Odin = *Fjörgyn* m. Jörð (i.e. Earth) = *Fjörgyn* = Frigg

Thor m. (1) Járnsaxa (2) Sif m. (1) Örvandill

Móði   Magni   Þrúðr   Ullr

Thor's great role is that of the adversary of giants and of the protector of both Asgard and Midgard from attacks by giants as we shall see in the stories. Later on he becomes something of a comic character, rather simple, a great eater and drinker, a shock-headed, red-bearded giant himself. And indeed, although the deadly enemy of giants, he has giant blood on both father's and mother's side, as we can see from his pedigree. At the Ragnarök he dies alongside Odin when he and Jörmungandr succeed in killing each other.

3

BALDER

"Balder—Odin's second son is Balder—a personage of very good report indeed," says Snorri.† "He is pre-eminent; he loves all things great and small. He is so blonde and fair of face that a power of light beams from him and a certain grass is so white that they liken it to Balder's brows. It is the whitest of all grasses and from that you may well remark his beauty, both as regards his hair and his body. He is the wisest of the gods, the fairest spoken and most gracious and physically the most shapely; and so fully endowed by nature that nobody can gainsay his judgments. He lives at the place called Breiðablik (*Broad Gleaming*):

† *Gylf.* XXII.

it is, of course, in heaven, a place where nothing impure may come, as it says here:†

> It's called Breiðablik
> where Balder has
>   a hall set for himself,
> in that land
> where I know lie
>   the fewest evil fates."

In addition, we learn from *Skáldskaparmál* V that Balder is the "Son of Odin and Frigg, Husband of Nanna, Father of Forseti, Possessor of Hringhorni and Draupnir, Adversary of Höðr, Companion of Hel, God of Tears." Five of these periphrases owe their origin to the myth of Balder's death: Hringhorni is the name of Balder's ship on which his funeral pyre was laid and his body burnt; Draupnir is Odin's ring placed by the Allfather on Balder's breast before the pyre was lighted; Höðr is the blind god who, used as a catspaw by Loki, flung the mistletoe shaft which killed Balder; Hel is the daughter of Loki and ruler of hel or Niflheim where Balder went after his death; and Balder is called the "God of Tears" because the condition of his release from hel was that everybody and everything should weep for him—as they did, all except Loki disguised as the old witch Þökk.

Balder is a most interesting god and the myth of his life and death is one of the most beautiful and moving. There are two supremely significant references to Balder in *Völuspá*: one is stanza 31's "Balder the bleeding god" and the other is contained in stanza 61 which tells of the return of Balder to the new heaven after the Doom of the Gods:

> unsown fields
> will wax with fruit,
>   all ills grow better,
>   Balder will return;

† *Grím.* 12.

> both Höðr and Balder
> live in Hroptr's† hall
> along with the mighty gods.

If we consider the characteristic attributes of Balder, namely his surpassing brightness and beauty, that a plant is called after him, his bloody wound and death, the fact that tears are shed in an attempt to resurrect him, and his eventual return in close connection with "unsown fields" which "will wax with fruit", then we are forced to enquire what connection there is between him and the oriental-Mediterranean Tammuz-Adonis.

The Syrian Tammuz was called by the Greeks "Adonis" from a Semitic vocative form of his name, Adoni, "My Lord". The original meaning of Norse *Baldr* and its cognate O.E. *bealdor* was also "lord". We have to remember, too, that Jesus is "Our Lord".

As a child Adonis the son of Myrrha was surpassingly beautiful and was hidden in a chest by the goddess Aphrodite. She gave the chest to the Queen of the Underworld for safe-keeping, but Persephone opened it and seeing how beautiful Adonis was, she did not want to give him back. Zeus was asked to arbitrate between the two goddesses and decided that Adonis should live a third part of the year by himself, a third with Persephone and a third with Aphrodite. Every year Adonis was killed by a wild boar while on a hunting expedition and so descended to the Underworld and Persephone. Where his blood dripped to the earth red anemones sprang up and the brook Adonis in Lebanon ran red. Aphrodite was compelled to shed bitter tears before ever Adonis came back to her. Women who worshipped Adonis brought him little "gardens" symbolizing their own private parts, their own femininity: this certainly in Greece: further east in some oriental shrines Adonis' worshippers gave their bodies to strangers It is clear that here is a fertility cult with Adonis' death and return to life mirroring the seasonal death and revival of nature.

† *Odin.*

The parallels between Balder and Adonis are apparent. There is the name, in both cases meaning "Lord"; there is the beauty, the sudden death from a bloody wound, the connection with flowers or plants, the descent to the Underworld and finally the resurrection. Many of these conceptions were common property to the peoples of the Middle East. Another eastern god, Baal, is also a "lord". Balder's wife or lover has the same name as Baal's wife, Nanna. Like the eastern Nanna's son, the Lydian hero Atys, Balder is killed by a stray shot. Balder's garden, the name of a locality west of Veile in Denmark (Dan. Baldershave, seventeenth century) is reminiscent of the "gardens of Adonis" symbolizing fertility and the rebirth of vegetation. The religious prostitution of some eastern shrines is paralleled in Scandinavia too: there are evidences of such practices at Uppsala in Saxo's *Danish History*, IX, 301. Saxo's account points to religious prostitution not in connection with Balder but with Frey. This practice may at first appear fortuitous until we learn that the name Frey also means "lord".

The parallels between the attributes of Balder and Adonis are so strong as to make it certain that Balder is no native of the Gothonic cosmogony but an immigrant from Asia Minor and Greece. Balder shares attributes also with Jesus Christ and it may be objected that something of Balder is borrowed from Christian myth. I personally am quite certain that this is not so, and that the evidence given above is more than ample to prove the existence in the countries about the eastern end of the Mediterranean of a fertility cult connected with a "lord" who was killed and who came to life again; and that the Northern myth of Balder is a direct offshoot of this cult. Nay, as far as Christianity is concerned, the boot is on the other foot: there is strong evidence that the myth of Balder affected the early northern Christian conception of the story of Christ. The Northmen called Jesus "the *white* Christ" even as Balder was represented as being blond and with brows so white that "the whitest of all grasses" was called after them. But the most striking example of Balder's melting into Christ is to be found

KRIST • WÆS • ON •

MI		RO
Th'S		DI·
TRE		HW
LU		E Th
M'G		RÆ·
I W		ThE
UN		R'F
DAD·		USÆ·
ALE		
GDU		FEAR
NHIÆ		RAN·
HINÆ·		KWO
		MUÆ
LIMW		ThThIL
ÆRIG		ÆTIL
NÆGI		ANU
STO		MIC·
DDU		ThÆTA
NHIM·		L·BIH

FIG. II RUTHWELL CROSS, DUMFRIESSHIRE
The runic inscription on the left recalls the myth of Balder's death.
(For translation see page 128.)

in an old English devoutly Christian poem attributed to Cynewulf who flourished in Northumbria in the seventh century. The poem is *The Dream of the Rood*, part of which was first discovered carved in runes on the Ruthwell Cross in what is now Dumfriesshire. There are three references in *The Dream of the Rood* which have their origin in heathen myth and which certainly have no roots in Canonical or Apocryphal scriptures. These references are to three of the main situations of the Balder myth: Balder (by the planning of his mother Frigg) is impervious to hurt from all missiles except one—the mistletoe; therefore his brother gods often take their sport in throwing darts and spears at him and he remains uninjured until a mistletoe wand thrown by blind Höðr deals him a bloody wound and death; and the condition of his release from hel is that all created things should weep for him. The references in the poem are as follows: first, there is the memory of the gods' sport in throwing weapons at Balder, for the rood says:

> *Eall ic wæs mid strælum forwundod*
> I was all wounded with missiles;

next comes a remembrance of the "bleeding god":

> *Forleton me þa hilderincas*
> *standan steame bedrifenne*
> The warriors then left me
> to stand steaming with blood-drops;

and thirdly, a memory of the tears demanded from all created things for Balder's release from hel:

> *Weop eal gesceaft*
> *cwiðdon cyninges fyll*
> wept all Creation,
> wailed the fall of their king.

The tenacity of the pagan story and its power to colour Christian writ is shown well into the Middle Ages in the disguising of Höðr as the Roman soldier who pierced Christ's side. In Middle Age Christian accounts the soldier is called Longinus or Longius or Longeus and he is represented as being *blind*. When Christ's blood runs down the spear and is transferred from Longeus' hand to his eyes his blindness is cured: "Whanne oure Lord was don on the crosse thanne come Longeus thedyr [thither] and smot hym with a spere in hys syde. Blod and water ther come owte at the wounde and he wyppyd hys eyne and anon he sawgh kyth [saw clearly]."[40]

An even more surprising parallel is the Jewish legend found in the thirteenth century *Toledoth Jeschu*.[41] According to this version Christ is again the central figure, filling the place of Balder. All trees take an oath not to injure him, but Judas, playing a role similar to Loki's, contrives that a cabbage stalk shall be overlooked, and Christ's death ensues when he is struck with it.

Balder and Frey have this in common, that both their names mean "lord" and that both names are used by Christian writers as synonyms for Jesus. In *The Dream of the Rood*, for instance, "Christ Almighty" is rendered *Frea Ælmightig*. Balder in fact is more closely connected with that group of gods called the Vanir (Njörðr, Frey and Freya), who also came from Asia Minor, than with the gods of pure Indo-European descent. But Balder must have come north earlier for he is accepted as a son of Odin whereas the Vanir claim no family relationship with the "Allfather". Again, Balder is not represented as fighting with the Vanir in the great war.

4

NJÖRÐR, FREY AND FREYA

Snorri says,† "The third god is he who is named Njörðr. He lives in heaven at Nóatún (or the Anchorage); he has power over the wind, he will smooth the sea and dowse fire. Mariners call on him in their voyages and deep sea fishing, for he is so wealthy and well-stocked he may give them either land or booty, and they are to ask him for these things. Njörðr is not of the same family tree as the Æsir but was born and bred in Vanaheim the home of the Vanir. The Vanir delivered him up to the gods as a hostage taking in exchange the *áss* called Hœnir: so Njörðr is on good terms with both Æsir and Vanir.

"Njörðr took to wife Skaði, daughter of the giant Þjazzi. Skaði was determined to set up house at a back-of-beyond called Þrymheim (*Home of Clamour*): but Njörðr just had to be near the sea. So they came to terms: they would be one week at Þrymheim and the next at Nóatún, turn and turn about. When Njörðr came back from his first week on the fells he cried:

> How I hate those hills!
> Not long was I there,
> † *Gylf.* XXIII.

> only nine single nights;
> the howling of wolves
>   seemed evil to me
> against the cry of the gannet,

and Skaði rejoined:

> I couldn't sleep a wink
> on the bed of the sea
>   for the miauling of gulls and mews;
> not a dawn went by
> but flying from the deep
>   the whistling widgeon woke me.

Then Skaði left for the mountains and made her home at Þrymheim. She was forever off out on snowshoes, hunting animals which she shot with her bow and arrows, and so she's referred to as the Showshoe Goddess or the Goddess on Skis, as it says here:

> It's called Þrymheim
> where Þjazzi lives,
>   the giant of wicked ways;
> now Skaði bides there
> bright bride of the god
>   in her father's ancient home."

How Skaði came to be married to Njörðr will be told later but here I may indicate the outlines of the story. The gods killed Skaði's father and she came seeking restitution at Asgard gates. Part of her *wergild* was that she was to be given one of the gods in marriage but she had to make her choice without seeing her prospective husband's face. The Æsir arranged what must be the first ankle-competition for Skaði was compelled to choose her mate by his feet. She picked out the best and cleanest pair of feet believing that she was choosing Balder; but Njörðr, god of the sea, whose limbs presumably were constantly laved with salt water, turned out to be her victim.

FIG. 12   WAGON FROM THE OSEBERG SHIP (*c*. A.D. 850)
No doubt Tacitus had in mind some such ornamental wagon when he wrote of
the goddess being drawn from place to place. (Oslo)

Snorri tends to emphasize Njörðr's position as god of the sea;
he is Njörðr of Nóatún (literally "the Enclosure of Ships", i.e.
the sea), he has power over wind and water, and is a patron of
fishermen and deep-sea sailors. But there is good reason for believing that the old Gothonic god of the sea was one Ægir
whose wife was Rán. Ægir does indeed figure in both *Eddas*,
but Njörðr has pushed him from the foreground. On
the other hand, there is the strongest suspicion that the original
Njörðr is closely related to Tacitus' *Nerthus* "Mother Earth".
In *Germania* 40 Tacitus writes of the cult of Nerthus among
Angli and other tribes along the west coast of the Baltic:
"There is nothing particularly noteworthy about these people
in detail, but they are distinguished by a common worship of
Nerthus or Mother Earth. They believe that she interests herself in human affairs and rides through their peoples. In an
island of Ocean stands a sacred grove, and in the grove stands
a car draped with a cloth which none but the priest may touch.
The priest can feel the presence of the goddess in this holy of
holies, and attends her, in deepest reverence, as her car is
drawn by kine. Then follow days of rejoicing and merry-

making in every place that she honours with her advent and stay. No one goes to war, no one takes up arms; every object of iron is locked away; then, and then only, are peace and quiet known and prized, until the goddess is again restored to her temple by the priest, when she has had her fill of the society of men. After that, the cloth and, believe it if you will, the goddess herself are washed clean in a secluded lake. This service is performed by slaves who are immediately afterwards drowned in the lake. Thus mystery begets terror and a pious reluctance to ask what that sight can be which is allowed only to dying eyes."[42]

The procession of the float and cows, and the immersion of the goddess are reminiscent of Asia Minor's divine mother Cybele whose cult Tacitus found again in the Baltic region: "[The Æstii] worship the Mother of the gods. They wear, as emblem of this cult, the masks of boars" (*Germania* 45). In this connection it is significant that Njörðr's children, Frey and Freya, are associated with swine: both Frey and Freya are said to possess the golden boar Gullinbursti or Hildisvín, and one of Freya's nicknames is Sýr (*Sow*). The boar is a symbol of fertility as the sow is of fecundity: Njörðr is a fertility god— "the Swedes believed Njörðr ruled over the growth of seasons" (*Ynglinga saga* XI). The weeping at Njörðr's grave mentioned in *Ynglinga saga* XI is also an Asiatic rite, and this and other Asiatic features of Nerthus-Njörðr worship betray an old cultural stream from the south-east with the Dacians as the intermediate link. The name *Nerthus* must have completed its travels before the Gothonic Sound Shift.

Snorri says,† "Njörðr of Nóatún begat in the fulness of time two children. He called the son Frey and the daughter Freya." According to *Ynglinga Saga* IV these two children were the fruit of Njörðr's union with his sister whose name is not mentioned. This marriage took place in Vanaheim before Njörðr became a hostage and (of course) before his marriage to Skaði. Snorri goes on, "Both the children were fair to look upon and mighty.

† *Gylf.* XXIV.

Frey is the most beautiful of the gods, having power over the rain and sunshine together with the natural increase of the earth: it is sensible to call on him for fruitful seasons and for peace. He is the one who directs the good fortunes of men. Likewise, Freya is the most beautiful of the goddesses. Her home in heaven is called Fólkvangr or the People's Plain. When she rides to battle she takes one half of the corpses and Odin the other half, as it says here:†

> It's called Fólkvangr
> Where Freya rules
>   who shall have seats in the hall;
> half of the dead
> she chooses each day
>   and Odin rakes up the rest.

Her palace, which is spacious and airy, is called the Rich-in-seats (*Sessrúmnir*). On her journeys she sits in a trap driving a pair of cats. She is by far the most favourable for men to call on, and from her name comes that title of high rank given to notable women, namely *Freya* or Lady. She is well pleased with songs of Love; and on her it is fitting to call in affairs of the heart." Later, Snorri gives further information on Freya and couples her name with that of Frigg:‡ "Freya is exalted with Frigg: she is married to the one called Óðr and their daughter is Hnoss (or *Gem*) who is so sparkling that precious and beautiful gems are called after her name. Óðr was accustomed to going away on long journeys and Freya used to weep for him and her tears were all red gold. Freya has many names, and the reason for this is that she called herself now this, now that, when she travelled among strange races looking for Óðr: she's called Mardöll and Hörn and Gefn and Sýr. Freya owns Brísingamen, the Necklace of the Brísings. Oh, and she has one other name: Vanadis."

Freya (as Snorri says in the passage just quoted) is the "lady" as her brother Frey is the "lord". There is a memory of Frey in

† *Grím.* 14.   ‡ *Gylf.* XXXV.

the Old English poems, in *The Dream of the Rood*, for instance, where Frey is used as a title of Christ:

> *Geseah ic þa Frean mancynnes*
> I saw there the Frey of mankind;

and quite frequently in *Beowulf* (17 times) where "frea" means "lord" and nothing more. In the same poem "bealdor" (Balder) occurs twice and means simply "lord". Frey is a "lord" like Baal and Adonis and, nearer home, Balder; Frey, like his father Njörðr has "power over the natural increase of the earth", he is a fertility god. He has an attribute of Tacitus' Nerthus, namely the "Fróði Peace": Tacitus remarks on this, in the passage already quoted, in these words "then, and only then, are peace and quiet prized"; Snorri in the following, "Frey built a great temple at Uppsala and made it his chief seat . . . then began in his days the Fróði-peace," (*Ynglinga Saga* XII). Because of this he is nicknamed Frið-fróði or Frode Fredegod in Zealand. The Fróði-peace is mentioned by Snorri,† significantly, coupled with the name of Christ, for world peace associated with the birth of the Messiah is a Christian belief too: "Caesar Augustus imposed peace on all the world. At that time Christ was born. But because Fróði was mightiest of all kings in the Northern lands, the peace was called after him wherever the Danish tongue is spoken, and men call it the Fróði-peace." Frey is drawn in the same sort of waggon procession as Nerthus.[43] In Uppsala Frey is depicted "cum ingenti priapo"[44] and is called Fricco "lover", a name which appears to derive from an Indo-European root *prij* "love", the same to which the names Freya, Frigg and Priapus are related. Frey's love-sickness is the start and finish of *Skírnismál*. His disappearance underground is an echo of the myth about the Thracian god Zalmoxis[45]—and of course Tammuz, Adonis and other similar deities. His worship is celebrated with orgies[46] and religious prostitution; in fact, his cult is typically Asiatic.

Freya is her brother Frey's double and might well be treated

† *Skáldsk* XLII.

here; since, however, she forms a link through Frigg between Vanir and Æsir, I shall deal with her in the next chapter along with the other goddesses.

5

TÝR

Of Týr, the account in *Gylfaginning* XXV runs as follows: "There is one god called Týr, without doubt the most daring and courageous. He has a great deal of say in the ordering of victory in battle. Warriors ought to remember to call on him in their prayers. There's a saying that a man is 'brave as Týr' when he surpasses others nor sits quietly by. He is wise too, so it's a common saying when a man is most wise that he is 'learned as Týr'. There was a striking example of his audacity when the gods enticed away the Wolf Fenrir to clap the shackle Gleipnir on him. Fenrir put no trust in their ever letting him go again until they laid the hand of Týr in his jaws as a token of good faith. When the gods wouldn't loose him he snapped the hand right off (it's now called the Wolf's Limb); and so the god is one-handed and not called a Peacemaker."

In *Skáldskaparmál* IX Snorri says, "How should one peri-phrase Týr? By calling him the One-handed God, and Fosterer of the Wolf, God of Battles, Son of Odin." Týr is called Fosterer of the Wolf because (as will be told) among all the gods Týr was "the only one sufficiently courageous to go and feed him" (*Gylf.* XXXIII).

Týr is the oldest of the Gothonic gods; his name goes back to the Indo-European Sky Father *Djevs* the Shining One; and he is the double of Dyaus, Zeus and Jove. Týr lost his position as Allfather in the Northern pantheon to Odin, as has already been related; and Odin seems to have begun his climb in the social scale round about the first century A.D. and to have completed it by the end of the Migration Age. While Týr as the Sky Father or Allfather seems to be meant by Tacitus'

regnator omnium deus "the god who rules over all" of the Sem-
nones (*Germ.* 39), certainly other tribes had developed Týr in
Tacitus' time into a war god equated with Mars. In A.D. 58
the Ermunduri defeated the Chatti and sacrificed all their
prisoners and captured horses to Mars and Mercury, that is Týr
and Odin (Tacitus, *Ann.* XIII, 57). The strength and spread
of Týr's worship at one time are indicated by his name in
place-names: in Bavaria there is Zierberg; in Hesse, Diensberg
and Zierenberg; in Saxe-Weimar, Tisdorf and Zeisberg; in
Jutland, Tystathe and Tuslunde; in Zealand, Tisvelae; in
Sweden, Tistad, Tisby, Tisjö and Tyved; while in England
we have Tuesley (Surrey), Tifield (a district in Sussex mentioned in Domesday Book), Great Tew and Duns Tew
(Oxfordshire), Tewin (Herts) and Dewerstone cliff on Dart-
moor. There are no place-names in Iceland of which the name
Týr is part; and in Norway he is remembered in only one
sanctuary, the island of Tysnes in South Hordaland.

Can we safely deduce anything about Týr's fall from these
place-names? Starting at the end we may say that Odin had
ousted Týr and become chief god by A.D. 874, when Iceland
was settled for there are no place-names in Iceland featuring Týr;
Týr was, however, remembered enough to have places named
for him in England after A.D. 450, though he is evidently (from
a comparison of the number of place-names) subsidiary to
Odin and Thor. The decision between Odin and Týr was
probably forced round the beginning of the Christian era; for
by A.D. 98 Tacitus in *Germania* 9 is identifying Týr (Tiw) with
the Roman war god Mars: this indentification was general some
time after A.D. 300 for it was then that the Romans adopted the
seven day week and the Gothonic tribes equated Mars' day,
dies Martis, with Týr's day, Tuesday. We can deduce however
from the widespread places including Týr's name, that before
and at the very beginning of the Christian era Týr was still the
Allfather, chief of the Gothonic gods.

6

HEIMDALLR

Snorri says,† "There's one named Heimdallr: people call him the White God and he is mighty and holy. Nine damsels—all sisters—in common gave him birth. His other names are Hallin-skíði (*Ram*) and Gullintanni (*Golden-teeth*) for his teeth are living gold; his horse also is called Golden topping (*Gull-toppr*). He lives at Heaven's Edge close by Bifröst Bridge where he stands sentinel at the end of heaven watching out for the assault of the Hill Giants on the bridge. He has to sleep like a bird with one eye open. And talking of eyes, he can see equally well night or day one hundred leagues away from him. More than that, he can hear the noise the blades of grass make as they grow, or the hairs getting longer on the sheep's back, and of course, everything that makes a louder noise. He has a bugle called Gjallarhorn or *Clangorous Horn* whose blasts can reach every nook and cranny of all the worlds. Heimdallr's sword is called Head. It says here:‡

> It's known as Heaven's Edge
> where Heimdallr, they say,
>   is master of all men there;
> there the gods' sentry
> sups in his hall
>   with gladness the good honey mead.

And he himself sings in the *Heimdalargaldr*:

> I am son of the nine maidens,
> the child of the sisters nine."

Further, in *Skáldskaparmál* VIII Snorri goes on, "How should one periphrase Heimdallr? By calling him Son of Nine Mothers, or Watchman of the Gods, as has been written already; or White God, Foe of Loki, Seeker of Freya's Necklace. A sword is called Heimdallr's Head: for it is said that he

† *Gylf.* XXVII.   ‡ *Grím.* 13.

was pierced by a man's head. The tale thereof is told in *Heim-dalargaldr*; and ever since a head is called Heimdallr's Measure while a sword is called Man's Measure. Heimdallr is Owner of Gulltoppr [his horse]; he is also Frequenter of Vágasker and Singasteinn where he fought Loki for possession of the Neck-lace Brísingamen; he is also called Vindlér. Ulfr Uggason composed a long passage in the *Húsdrápa* on that legend, and there it is written that they [i.e. Heimdallr and Loki] were in the shapes of seals. Heimdallr is also a son of Odin."

The first conclusion we may come to about Heimdallr is that we no longer have his real name: Heimdallr (like Hallinskíði, Gullintanni and Vindlér) is a nickname. If we did have Heim-dallr's real name, no doubt we could identify him at once.

There are traits about Heimdallr that have caused scholars to wonder whether or not he should be classed with the Vanir; indeed, Vigfusson and Powell translated stanza 15 of *Þryms-kviða* in such a way as to make him a Vanr: "Then Heimdall spake, the whitest of the Anses; he had great foresight, as all the other Wanes have."[48] There is a contradiction in terms here of which the *Þrymskviða* poet could not have been guilty he could not have called Heimdallr "whitest of the Æsir" in one breath and one of the Vanir in the next. In fact, the word which Vigfusson and Powell translated "other" is best read as "even" and the sense of the passage becomes "Then Heim-dallr spoke up, the whitest of the Æsir: he was well able to see into the future even as could the Vanir."

For my own part, I have not the least hesitation in asserting that Heimdallr is no Vanr but is one of the ancient Gothonic gods, as I hope to be able to prove.

In his latest manifestation Heimdallr is closely associated with the Doom of the Gods: he is the guardian of the Rainbow Bridge over which in the end the Children of Múspell will ride to destroy the universe. He has in his keeping the Gjallarhorn on which he is to blow the "stand to" when he sees the forces of destruction approach. It is in connection with his function of sentinel at the bridge Bifröst that we must interpret his latest nickname, Heimdallr, which can mean only "World Bow". In other words, because he has been made sentinel of the Rainbow he has been nicknamed Heimdallr. Why should he have been associated with the bow in the first place? Perhaps there is a clue in *Gylfaginning* XV where Hárr quotes from *Grímnismál* 29

> for the Æsir's bridge
> burns all with flame . . .

and Gylfi asks "Do you mean to say fire burns over Bifröst?" To which Hárr replies, "Certainly. What you see red in the Rainbow is burning fire. You can bet your boots the Hill Giants would swarm over heaven's walls if every Tom, Dick and Harry were free to pass across Bifröst." So we are told variously that fire guards the Rainbow Bridge and that Heimdallr guards it. Is Heimdallr fire? There can be no doubt but that he is.

Heimdallr is the double of Agni, the fire-god of the ancient Hindu *Rigveda*. The resemblances between Heimdallr and Agni are too many and too close to be coincidental: Heimdallr is "The white god, mighty and holy" and "his teeth are living gold"; Agni is the pure, white god (*Rigveda*, iv, 1, 7; iii, 7, 1), young, strong and with golden teeth (v, 2, 2); Heimdallr "can see equally well night or day one hundred leagues away from him", he can hear grass or the wool on the sheep's back grow; Agni has searching eyes (iv, 2, 12) which penetrate night's darkness (i, 94, 7) and as the guard of order (i, 11, 8) he is always attentive (i, 31, 12); Heimdallr is the watchman of the gods with a bugle "whose blasts can reach every nook and cranny of all the worlds"; Agni protects the world night and day from dangers (i, 98, 1) and can make himself heard like thunder so that both halves of the world re-echo his voice (x, 8, 1); Heimdallr was the son of nine mothers; Agni is variously the son of two, seven, nine and ten mothers.

This multiplicity of mothers teases the curiosity. Its explanation starts from Agni's name which is cognate with Latin *ignis* meaning "fire", and from Heimdallr's nickname Vindlér, a word which is related to O.N. *vinda*=to wind, twist or turn. Agni's two mothers are figuratively the two pieces of wood anciently rubbed together to produce fire; his ten mothers, "twice five sisters dwelling together", are the ten fingers and thumbs of the person producing friction fire with a bore-stick. And Heimdallr's name Vindlér, the *Turner* or *Borer* shows him as the producer of domestic fire by friction. Both Agni and Heimdallr represent beneficial fire. In *The Short Völuspá*, Heimdallr's nine mothers are called Gjalp, Greip, Eistla, Eyrgjafa, Ulfrún, Angeyja, Imdr, Atla and Járnsaxa, names which have been variously explained as having connections with the sea, fire or the "world mill". These nine mothers, "giant maids", are said to have borne Heimdallr "at the world's edge", that is, by the ocean shore; and there is an echo of the threefold quality of Agni in the threefold strength of Heimdallr's origin:†

> he was made with
> the might of earth,
>   of the ice-cold sea
> and the blood of swine.

It might seem strange that Heimdallr should be born of the "ice-cold sea", but Agni too in his manifestation as Apam Napat is the Son of the Waters: Hymn II, 35, 4, of the *Rigveda* says of this Agni, "He with clear flames unfed with wood, shines in the waters."

Agni became "the husband of wives" (i, 66, 4), fathered human descendants (i, 96, 2) through whom he founded the classes or castes of men (vi, 48, 8). Now in *Völuspá* 1 mankind are referred to as "Heimdallr's sons *both high and low*"—an immediate suggestion of class or caste; again, the thirteenth century prose annotater of another eddaic poem, *Rígsþula*, identifies Rígr of the poem with Heimdallr. Rígr (a name said to be almost certainly based on the O. Irish word "ri" or "rig" meaning "king")[49] is depicted as a god in disguise who wanders

† *Short Völuspá* 9.

FIG. 13 HORNED FIGURES

Left: The "little sorcerer", after Breuil, from a painting in les Trois-Frères caves, Ariège, perhaps 16,000 years old; *centre:* a stamp for embossing bronze plaques on Vendel helmets, Sweden; *right:* a figure from a panel of the Sutton Hoo helmet.

over the world and fathers the thralls, peasant farmers and warriors—the three castes of early society. But modern scholars tend to identify Rígr with Odin and claim that the reference to mankind as "Heimdallr's sons" has "caused much perplexity".[50] It may be possible to resolve this perplexity.

Rígr's founding of the thralls, karls (yeomen) and jarls (nobles) of Northern society is directly parallel with Agni's founding of the castes of men. Agni is sometimes depicted as being horned like a bull, while Heimdallr's nickname Hallinskíði according to the *Þulor* is a synonym for "ram"[51] as, for that matter, "Heimdali" is said to be too. Like the bull, the ram is a horned animal, and a horned figure embossed on the Sutton Hoo helmet could be intended to represent Heimdallr. If we take all these evidences into account we may be led to suggest a different derivation for the name Rígr from that which connects the word with O. Irish "ri" or "rig" meaning king. There is a Northern English word, i.e. a word from the Danelaw, "rig" or "rigg" (according to *N.E.D.* of uncertain origin) commonly used to this day by shepherds and farmers for a ram which has been imperfectly castrated. It is a well-known phenomenon in philology that words can change their significance and take on a specialized meaning of their original. It is arguable that "rig" meant simply "ram" before it came to mean a ram that was half-castrated. Rígr, like Hallinskíði, may well be "ram", a meaning singularly appropriate to the exploits of the god with the wives of Ái, Afi and Faðir as related in *Rigsþula*.

As a fire-being Heimdallr is the opposite or complement of another fire-being, an evil one, Loki; and so Heimdallr is called "Foe of Loki". Other periphrases of Heimdallr arise from his enmity with Loki and the myth of the necklace Brísingamen which must be unravelled later: these periphrases include "Seeker of Freya's Necklace" and "Frequenter of Vágasker and Singasteinn".

By the close of the pagan period Heimdallr's main function is that of the gods' watchman who will summon them to fight at the Ragnarök. Yet to the end he maintains his attribute of the beneficent fire, fire that is the good servant, for at the Doom of the Gods he destroys (and is destroyed by) the evil manifestation of fire, fire that is the bad master, Loki.

But I have not suggested what Heimdallr's real name—not a nickname—was: later I may be able to do so (see p. 147).

7

OTHER GODS

Snorri says,† "There's another god called Bragi: he is celebrated for his wisdom and especially for his eloquence and skill with words. He, more than any other, knows the secrets of poesy; in fact Poetry is sometimes called after him 'Bragi's Breath', just as they are named Bragi's men (or women) who surpass ordinary folk in writing poetry. His wife is Iðunn who guards within her ashwood casket the apples which the gods have to nibble at as they age and fail—then all at once they are young again: this goes on right up to the Ragnarök."

† *Gylf.* XXVI.

In *Skáldskaparmál* X Snorri asks, "How should one peri-phrase Bragi?" and replies, "By calling him Husband of Iðunn, First Maker of Poetry, and the Long-bearded God (after his name, a man who has a great beard is called Beard-Bragi) and Son of Odin."

Bragi is a late and little characterized god of poetry. He is mentioned only three times in the poems of the *Verse Edda*: in *Grímnismál* 45 where he is said to be "the best of skalds", in *Lokasenna* where, along with the other gods and goddesses he engages in a "flyting" with Loki, and in *Sigrdrífumál* 14, an obscure passage where a person referred to only as "he" bids write runes on various mythical and other objects, from Sleip-nir's teeth to Bragi's tongue.

Snorri summarizes what information he has about five other gods in *Gylfaginning* XXVIII–XXXII: "Blind Höðr is another of the Æsir: a god of adequate powers but the others never wish the need to arise of his being named on account of that bit of handiwork† which will rankle long in the minds of both gods and men.

"There's Víðarr, a silent god who has charge of the Thick-most Shoe. He is strongest next to Thor and the gods put quite a deal of trust in him for any tight corner.

"Then comes Áli (some call him Váli), son of Odin and Rindr, very brave in battle and an exceedingly good shot.

"Ullr is Sif's son and Thor's stepson. He is so accomplished an archer and so expert on skis nobody can come up to him; what's more he's fair of face and has great powers as a warrior. You should pray for his help in single combat.

"Forseti is the name of the son of Balder and Nanna Nep's daughter: his is the hall in heaven known as Glitnir the Shin-ing. Everyone without fail who brings to him a seemingly in-soluble problem or suit will go away with peace of mind. His is the finest place for sound judgments among gods or men. It says here:‡

† His slaying of Balder with the mistletoe.   ‡ *Grím.* 15.

The hall is called Glitnir
with pillars of gold
and seemlily thatched with silver;
there does Forseti
feast on most days
and puts to sleep all suits."

Of these five gods there is not much more news to be gained from the *Verse Edda*. Höðr, Víðarr and Váli each have one main dramatic function to perform: Höðr unwittingly to slay Balder, Váli to avenge the crime by slaying Höðr, and Víðarr to avenge his father Odin by killing the Fenris Wolf. But after the Ragnarök these four gods Höðr, Váli, Víðarr and Balder live in peace and goodwill in the new heaven.

Three mysterious figures among the gods are Hœnir, Lóðurr and Mímir. Hœnir and Lóðurr (together with Odin) figure in the myth of the creation of the first human beings, Askr and Embla. In actual fact, Lóðurr is mentioned only in connection with this one work, and in only one place, *Völuspá* 17. Hœnir lasts a little longer but is finally dismissed from the tale by being handed over as a hostage to the Vanir after the war in heaven. Njörðr replaces Hœnir in Asgard, but after the Ragnarök Hœnir goes to the new heaven where he is imbued with the gift of prophecy—in direct contrast to his "dumbness" among the Vanir which is said to have led to Mímir's beheading.

If we try to unravel matters chronologically, then in *Völuspá* 16, 17 we read:

Then came three
out of the throng
of the mighty and gracious
gods at home;
they found on the land,
empty of force,
Askr and Embla
empty of fate.

> They had no spirit
> and no five senses,
>   no heat, no motion
>   no healthy hue;
> spirit gave Odin,
> sense gave Hœnir,
>   heat gave Lóðurr
>   and healthy hue.

When Snorri tells the tale of the creation of Askr and Embla in *Gylfaginning* IX, the trilogy of gods who take part are named Odin, Vili and Vé. We must believe then, that Vili and Vé are the same as Hœnir and Lóðurr. But Snorri also tells how Odin, Vili and Vé took part in the creation of the world from the carcass of the giant Ymir; and if the two trilogies are the same, then Hœnir and Lóðurr should have played a part in a world creation myth. There is evidence that Hœnir did so.†

In *Skáldskaparmál* XV Snorri mentions two strange kennings (culled from lost verses) which may be employed to denote Hœnir. They are *langifótr* "Longleg" and *aurkonungr* "Mud king". Vigfusson and Powell offered what appears to be the only explanation of these curious epithets:[52] "Longleg" and "Mud king" make sense if they are applied, for instance, to such a bird of the ooze as the stork. It so happens that the name Hœnir (related to Eng. *hen* and Germ. *hahn* "cock") is cognate with Sanskrit *sakunas* and Greek κύκνος which means "white bird". In Vigfusson and Powell's words, "It is now easy to see that this bird is the Creator walking in Chaos, brooding over the primitive mish-mash or tohu-bohu, and finally hatching the egg of the world."[53] Hœnir must be one of the ancient gods going back to Indo-European times, a being who corresponds to the great black bird of Greek myth, Nyx or Night, who conceived of the Wind and laid her silver egg

† And a memory of the identification of Lóðurr with Heimdallr-Rígr in the creation by both of humankind?

in the lap of Darkness. From this egg came the whole world. But Hœnir is only dimly remembered in Northern myth: he is still coupled with the ancient Lord of the Wind (in the shape of Odin) in a creation myth in one poem (*Völuspá*); but apart from that, and what even to Snorri must have appeared the strange epithets "Longleg" and "Mud king", his original function as a world-creator has been forgotten and so he is dismissed (ironically) to Vanaheim. Hœnir is, of course, really being displaced by eddaic times by the assimilating Odin who blew his divine wind, the breath of *spirit* into men, and who assimilated not only the qualities of his ancient relatives but of the gods of newer, warlike cults.

A similar trilogy of gods to that just discussed (Odin, Hœnir and Lóðurr), but this time Odin, Hœnir and Loki, plays a part in two tales (1) the stealing of Iðunn's apples (*Skáldskaparmál* I), and (2) the stealing of Andvari's treasure (*Skáldsk.* XXXIX). Editors in the past have identified Lóðurr with Loki,[54] an identification which is obviously shaky, for all Loki's works are evil and all Lóðurr's recorded works are good. Lóðurr is a beneficent being who gives to Man and Woman the gift of *heat* and *healthy hue*, a gift which Loki would never make. Such a gift is quite within the powers of a fire-being; and the assumption that Lóðurr is a fire-being is bolstered up by Jacob Grimm's comparison of the god's name with German *lodern* "to blaze". The assumption becomes a conviction when we consider how some of the skaldic verse calls Loki (another fire-being, but a maleficent one) "companion of Hœnir", "staunch friend of Hœnir"[55] and when *Skáldskaparmál* I and XXXIX makes the trinity Odin, Hœnir and Loki. Because the two were fire-beings they were able to be confused. Really it was Lóðurr the giver of heat to mankind who merited the kennings "companion of Hœnir" and "staunch friend of Hœnir"; but the malevolent Loki was a "living shame to everyone whether mortal or divine"† and certainly not to be identified with Lóðurr. By the time of the

† *Gylf.* XXXIII.

eddaic poems, say *c.* A.D. 950, Loki has usurped Lóðurr's place and driven him (under the name of Lóðurr) almost out of existence; so that Loki now has some "good" qualities as well as all his own bad ones—the good from Lóðurr. And that is why Snorri found Loki so bewildering a personage: about him there lingered a memory of Lóðurr's goodness which was so difficult to reconcile with Loki's evil. Lóðurr is, in fact, the complement, the opposite of the fire-being Loki, and as such is rather to be identified with that other beneficent fire-being Heimdallr. My own contention and firm belief is that Lóðurr is the earlier name of the Northern god corresponding to the Hindu Agni and that Heimdallr is the "ekename".† (See p. 142.)

I have already touched on the tale of the dismissal of Hœnir from Asgard, a dismissal which according to *Ynglinga Saga* is shared by Mímir. In some ways Mímir is more mysterious than either Hœnir or Lóðurr, although his main attribute is clear enough: Mímir is the fount of all wisdom. As far as we know at present, the name Mímir is cognate with Latin *memor* (*mindful, remembering*), with the Sanskrit root *smar-* of *smarti* (*memory*) and indeed with English *memory*.

Ynglinga Saga IV says that after the war between Æsir and Vanir "both sides appointed a meeting place for a peace conference, agreed on an armistice and exchanged hostages. The Vanir sent their best men, Njörðr the Rich and his son Frey. The Æsir sent a man called Hœnir, whom they thought perfectly suited to be a chief because he was a well-set-up and handsome man; and together with him they sent a man of great wisdom called Mímir. On the other side, the Vanir sent the wisest man in their community, a man called Kvasir. Now, immediately Hœnir came to Vanaheim he was made a chief, and Mímir backed him up with sound advice on all occasions. But when Hœnir was present at Things or other conferences and any difficult subject was debated, if Mímir was not near

† See note on p. 145. Another reason for identifying Lóðurr with Heimdallr.

him he always answered in the one way. 'Let somebody else advise on this matter.' So the Vanir began to suspect that the Æsir had deceived them in the exchange of men. Therefore, they took Mímir and cut off his head and sent it to the Æsir. Odin received the head, smeared it with herbs to keep it from rotting, and sang spells over it. In this way he gave it the power of being able to speak to him whereby it discovered many secrets to him."

This account bears the marks of being cobbled, but all the rationalizing in the world will hardly make an everyday matter of a head which can be treated with herbs and forced to speak. This is the stuff of dream—or myth. Whether the speaking head is from the reservoir of original Gothonic myth remains open to doubt.

Skáldskaparmál I tells a different tale about Kvasir: "The gods had a quarrel with the people called Vanir and they held a peace conference and arranged an armistice this way: they each went up to a pot and spat their spittle into it. When they parted, the gods took that peace token and rather than let it perish they made of it a man. This man is called Kvasir, so wise that nobody could question him about anything at all without his knowing the answer." The story goes on to tell how Kvasir was killed by two dwarfs who caught his blood and mixing it with honey made a drink which conferred on the consumer wisdom and the power to compose poetry.

This story bears the marks of late composition: it is a poet's work to explain and extol the inspiration of the craft of poesy. In any case, Kvasir is nowhere mentioned in the *Verse Edda*: Bragi (himself a late creation) is the god of poetry there. Then again, the myth with which Kvasir is connected, that of the war between Æsir and Vanir, is also comparatively late; that is to say it is a Gothonic rather than an Indo-European myth. All of which suggests that the myth of the severing of Mímir's head (so closely connected with Kvasir) is a late addition to Northern story. Yet the name Mímir does go back to Indo-European times. How are we to explain this?

The severed head uttering words of wisdom is remembered in the *Verse Edda*. *Völuspá* 45 says that at the Ragnarök:

> Shrilly shrieks Heimdallr's
> horn across the sky;
> Odin whispers
> with the head of Mímir . . .

Völuspá has already been suspected of showing Celtic influences and this story of the cut-off talking head may well be one of them. It is essentially the same story found in the ancient Irish and Welsh cycles of tales. The speaking head of Bran was called in the *Mabinogion* 'Uther Benn' Wonderful Head and 'Urddawl Benn' Venerable Head. Speaking heads from the Irish cycle are those of Lomna, Finn mac Cumaill, Donn Bó and Fergal mac Maile Dúin. (See T. F. O'Rahilly *Early Irish History and Mythology*, pp. 282–3). And it is remembered in the Middle English romance *Sir Gawayne and the Greene Knighte* (*c*. 1400) which owes so much of its story to Celtic sources. One is inevitably reminded of head-hunting by this version of the Mímir myth, and head-hunting is and was a far more widespread practice than is commonly supposed. For instance, heads buried separated from their bodies found in Azilian deposits at Ofnet in Bavaria appear to indicate a mesolithic belief in the importance of such a practice. Strange as it may seem, head-hunting persisted among peoples of Celtic descent in Ireland and the Scottish marshes until medieval times and there were Montenegrin head-hunters as late as 1912![56] This rite seems based on a primitive belief in a quasi-material soul matter which pervades the whole body and which may be concentrated in certain portions of the anatomy, particularly in the head. This soul-matter is thought to maintain all life and the taking of a head (or among some peoples, limbs and other extremities) brings also the effectiveness of the soul-matter to the taker or his people. This is in effect what happens when Odin takes Mímir's head and uses its wisdom for his and the Æsir's good.

But there is a quite different version of the Mímir story alluded to in the very same source (namely *Völuspá*) as that mentioning the severed head myth. Snorri paraphrases and quotes from *Völuspá* as follows:† "Under the root [of Yggdrasill] which twists towards the Frost Giants there is Mímir's Well (for he is called Mímir who is warden of the well). He is full of wisdom since he drinks at the well out of Gjallarhorn. The Allfather came there looking for a draught from the well, but he didn't get it until he had put one of his eyes in pawn: as it says in *Völuspá*:‡

> I know all, including
> where Odin lost his eye
>   deep in the wide-famed
>   well of Mímir;
> every morning
> does Mímir drink
>   mead from Valföðr's pledge . . ."

It is obvious that these two versions of the Mímir myth are irreconcilable. The severed head version (though springing from primitive sources) is connected with later material in Northern myth (the coming of the Vanir) and gives indication of being borrowed from Celtic story; but Mímir as a being guarding the well of wisdom under Yggdrasill goes back directly to Indo-European times. This Mímir has dealings (as Snorri so rightly says) with Allfather, the original **Djevs*. It is not Odin the wind god who loses his eye, but the old Sky Father. As I have already written, the eye of the Sky Father is an emblem of the sun; Mímir's drinking mead from it every morning is a representation of the sun's rising, just as the hiding of the eye is the sun's setting.

One must suppose that a good deal of information about Mímir is now irretrievably lost and that the fragments which remain serve only to confuse. It is puzzling to be told by Snorri that Mímir drinks from his well out of Gjallarhorn, though

† *Gylf.* XV.   ‡ *Völ.* 28.

there may be a clue in the nicknames Hodd-Mímir *Treasure-Mímir* (*Vafþrúðnismál* 45) and Hoddrofnir *Treasure-opener* (*Sigrdrífumál* 12): Mímir may have been the smith or guardian of ancient mystic treasures. The name Hodd-Mímir occurs in the reply to Odin's question put to the giant Vafþrúðnir as to who of mankind shall be saved after the Monstrous Winter which precedes Ragnarök. Vafþrúðnir says: †

> Líf and Lífþrasir
> lie and hide
>   in the holt of Hodd-Mímir;
> they have for their meat
> the morning dews;
>   from them the new race shall arise.

Hodd-Mímir's holt, wood or grove has been variously interpreted as the Ash Tree Yggdrasill (also called *Mímameiðr*, *Mímir's Tree*, and said to transpire life-giving dews such as Líf and Lífþrasir feed on); and as a subterranean paradise.

Mímir has evidently been a being of supreme power. He can be classed with the Norns as originally one over whom Odin held no sway and to whom even Allfather had to appear as a petitioner. It was only to be expected that the fosterers of the later Northern myth should diminish or forget the exploits of Mímir in favour of the new and rising star, Odin.

† *Vaf.* 45.

CHAPTER IV

Asynjur

THE oldest divinity of the Gothonic tribes is the one corresponding to the Indo-European Sky Father; the oldest of the female deities would seem to be the Earth Mother. Night (O.N. *Nótt*) is ancient too; according to some accounts she is older than Earth (Jörð) and in fact Earth's mother by the old Sky Father. Night herself is said to be the daughter of the Dark Moon Nörfi. There are (literally) one or two other goddesses who may claim to be contemporaries of the Earth Mother, for instance the sun goddess (called Sunna by the Germans, Sól by the Northmen), and the sea goddess (O.N. Gefjun, O.E. Geofon). There may have been, too, a goddess of the Underworld whom we come to know later as Hel.

But whichever came earliest into being, by the start of the Christian era the Earth Mother is taking up first place: we have documentary evidence for her worship among the Æstii as "Mother Earth"[57] and among the Anglian group of Gothonic tribes as "Nerthus"[58] in the first century A.D. By the Migration Age the Earth Mother is established as chief goddess whether under the title of Jörð or Fjörgyn (cf. Gothic *fairguni*, O.E. *fyrgen*= mountain). Later she takes the name of Frigg as wife of Odin, but "Frigg" is only a thin disguise for "Jörð". In fact, Frigg and her double Freya are the fertile, beautiful Earth Mother; and the remaining goddesses of the Northern pantheon little more than specialized aspects of the Earth Mother's attributes or literary personifications of qualities such as wisdom (Snotra) and justice (Syn).

I

A LIST OF THE ÁSYNJUR

Ásynjur is the O. Norse feminine of Æsir and may be taken as equivalent to "goddesses". Snorri says† that of the Ásynjur "Frigg comes before any: hers is the palace called Fensalir Sea-Halls—a magnificent spot! Next we have Sága who lives at Sökkvabekkr or Sinking Beck—that's a most extensive abode. Third is Eir, the best of all physicians. Fourth, Gefjun, the virgin goddess: they who die in maidenhood serve her. The fifth is Fulla, also a virgin, who walks with floating hair and a fillet about her brow. She looks after Frigg's ashwood casket and keeps her shoes and knows all her secrets. The sixth, Freya, is exalted with Frigg. . . . Seventh is Sjöfn who is much occupied with turning people's thoughts to love (both men and women); and from her name love-longing is called *sjafni*. The eighth is Lofn: she is so gracious and kindly to those that call upon her, that she wins Allfather's or Frigg's permission for the coming together of mankind in marriage, of women and of men, even though before they asked her blessing the course of their love was not running smooth; from her name such permission is called 'leave' and so also she is much 'loved' of men. The ninth is Vár: she gives an ear to the oaths and vows of men and so they call solemn oaths Vár's pledges. In addition, she metes out condign punishment to those who break faith. Tenth—Vör: she is wise and always searching after knowledge so that ultimately nothing is hidden from her. It's a proverb that *A woman becomes wise when she sees with Vör's eyes.* The eleventh is Syn, who has watch and ward over the doors of halls and prevents unauthorised entry. She is, moreover, well employed at trials as a defence against such suits as she wishes to refute. From her comes the expression '*Syn (denial)* is my plea' when a man pleads 'not guilty'. Twelfth is Hlín who is always on the look-out to succour people whom Frigg wishes to save

† *Gylf.* XXXV.

from any peril: and from this we get the saying about one who escapes a danger that 'he's under Hlín's wing'. Snotra is thirteenth, wise and gentle in her ways: from her name, wise men and women are called Snotra's kin. Fourteenth is Gná: Frigg sends her to the various worlds to do her errands. She has a horse called Hófvarpnir, *Hoofwalloper* which skelps over the sky and sea. Once upon a time some of the Vanir saw her riding through the air and one cried:

> Hey! what flew there?
> What fizzed away
>   clearing the tops of the clouds?

She replied:

> I'm not flying
> though I fizz away
>   clearing the tops of the clouds;
> Hófvarpnir's my mount
> by Hamskerpir
>   got out of Garðrofa.

From Gná's name it's said of anything which goes high that it 'soars like Gná'. Sól and Bil are counted among the goddesses (it is said) rather because of the work they do." Later, in *Gylfaginning* XXXVI Snorri adds, "Jörð (Thor's mother) and Rindr (Váli's mother) are reckoned to be goddesses." Again, in spite of the seeming exhaustiveness of his list of Ásynjur, Snorri has for the moment forgotten Nanna (Balder's wife), Sif (Thor's wife) and Iðunn (Bragi's wife) who are among the more conventional goddesses; to say nothing of such slightly unorthodox characters as Skaði the patron goddess of Scandinavia.

It is significant that Snorri's account of the goddesses fits into one chapter as compared with his account of the gods which runs to thirteen chapters. Admittedly five of his chapters on the minor gods are just about as short as his single or double sentence references to most of the goddesses; but it is

clear that there was not much more Snorri *could* say about the
goddesses, and one might pause to ask why.

A reasonable answer would be that some of the goddesses
are not separate entities at all, but names covering special
attributes of another goddess (as I have already remarked). For
instance, Snorri mentions in his list "Gefjun the virgin
goddess: they who die in maidenhood serve her"; but that
Snorri was prepared to equate Gefjun with Frigg is suggested
by his treatment of a quotation (in *Gylfaginning* XX) of a
stanza which appears—and only *appears*—to come from
Lokasenna. The stanza runs:

1. You're mad now Loki
2. and out of your mind
3.   why don't you, Loki, leave off?
4. Frigg, I know is
5. wise in all fates
6.   though herself will say no fortunes.

No such stanza is to be found in *Lokasenna*, although two
stanzas very much like it (21 and 29) do occur; the main difference between them is that in 21 it is Gefjun and in 29 Frigg
who can foretell the future. Snorri's quotation is, in fact, a con-
coction from three of *Lokasenna's* stanzas: lines 1–2 come from
Lokasenna 21, line 3 from *Lokasenna* 47 and lines 4–6 from
Lokasenna 29. Whether Snorri carpentered his quotation consciously or unconsciously, it is obvious that he found no difficulty in equating Gefjun and Frigg, nor did he expect his
contemporary readers to find any. Gefjun's supposed virginity
need be no stumbling block to her indentification with Frigg,
for there are plain statements in other works (including
Gylfaginning itself—Ch. I) to the effect that Gefjun was no maid
though she might be a patron of maids. *Lokasenna* 20 goes like
this:

Hold your noise, you, Gefjun!
For now I shall say
   who led you into evil life:

the lily-white boy
gave a necklace bright
and you threw your thigh over him;

a stanza which impugns Gefjun's virginity and by mentioning
the necklace (of the Brísings?) suggests an identification not
only between Gefjun and Frigg, but also between Gefjun and
Frigg's *alter ego* Freya.

That Gefjun originally had an existence of her own is indis-
putable, as is the fact of her connection with the sea: in
Beowulf for instance, her name occurs four times as a synonym
for "sea"; there is, moreover, a remembrance of Gefjun as a sea
goddess in *Gylfaginning* I where she is said to have harnessed
four oxen (giants in disguise and own sons to her by a giant) to
a monstrous plough with which she gouged out of Sweden a
ploughgate of land huge enough to accommodate Lake
Mälaren. This land she dragged into her own domain, the sea,
where it remains to this day as Zealand.

But Frigg's abode was said to be Sea-Halls (Fensalir) and
another of her shadows, Sága, has a sea-home. Sága is mentioned once in the *Verse Edda* when the skald of *Grímnismál* is
describing the heavenly abodes:†

It is called Sökkvabekkr‡
where cool waves flow
re-echoing over all;
there Odin and Sága
sit each day drinking
gaily from cups of gold.

It is almost certain that this stanza was Snorri's source for his
remarks on Sága; but the stanza does not suggest she was a
separate goddess. In fact, all the clues point to Sága being an
ekename for Frigg: Sökkvabekkr, the Sinking Beck or Stream
where cool waves flow and re-echo is undoubtedly the same
place as Frigg's dwelling called Fensalir Sea-Halls; and the one

† *Grím. 7.*   ‡ *Sinking Beck.*

person with whom Odin could "sit each day drinking gaily from cups of gold" is Frigg.

Another of Snorri's goddesses, Hlín, is mentioned (apart from his list) in only one other place, namely *Völuspá* 52 where it is plain that Hlín is a pseudonym of Frigg. Eir, the third in Snorri's list of goddesses, is he says "the best of all physicians". He mentions her but once; and once only does she figure in the *Verse Edda* when she is listed as one of the nine handmaidens of Menglöð in *Fjölsvinnsmál* 38. The name Menglöð means "Necklace glad" and suggests identity with Frigg-Freya, the necklace in question being Brísingamen. Apart from the association of Menglöð and Eir as mistress and maid in *Fjölsvinnsmál*, there is a connection between Menglöð on her mountain and Snorri's assertion that Eir is "the best of all physicians". Menglöð is said to be on Lyfjaberg, that is the "hill of healing" which, says stanza 36, has long been a joy to the sick and sore and which will cure sick women who climb it. The implication is that Menglöð is (like Eir) a goddess of healing, and in fact that Eir is simply a hypostasis of Menglöð who in turn is a hypostasis of Frigg-Freya. One of the characters in *Oddrúnar-grátr*, namely Borgný, after bringing forth twins, names Frigg and Freya as goddesses of healing.†

So far then, out of Snorri's list of goddesses, it seems that, by Migration Times, Freya, Gefjun, Hlín, Sága and Eir are identifiable with Frigg who in turn is to be identified with Jörð-Fjörgyn. This does not mean that a number of deities of a similar nature have not coalesced—in fact, they have; and as we shall see, the name Frigg is probably a fairly late importation from the south-east. The goddess Fulla (virgin) is nowhere mentioned in the poems of the *Verse Edda*, but Snorri puts her in the closest association with Frigg; she is Frigg's shadow, the shadow of her former virginity. As for Sjöfn, Lofn, Vár, Vör, Syn, Snotra and Gná (Hlín and Fulla come into this category too), these are plainly personifications of ideas or attributes from which their names are derived (Sjöfn, O.N. *sjafni*=love-

† *Odd.* 8.

longing, Snotra, O.N. *snotr*=wise, prudent, etc.); and all these attributes may be easily referred to Frigg.

2

FRIGG

Snorri says† Odin's "wife is called Frigg Fjörgyn's daughter and from their union sprang the race whom we call the Æsir who settled the Ancient Asgard and the parts running up to it: they are the gods." He says further of Odin that "Jörð was his daughter and his wife also; he begot his first son upon her, who is Thor of the gods." A characteristic of Frigg is‡ that "though she will tell no fortunes, yet well she knows the fates of men: you can see that from these words uttered by Odin himself to the god called Loki:

> You're mad now Loki
> and out of your mind!
>   why don't you, Loki, leave off?
> Frigg I know is
> wise in all fates
>   though herself will say no fortunes."[59]

Skáldskaparmál XVIII mentions a sort of feather coat, a hawk-plumage, owned by Frigg which gave her (or anyone who wore it) the power of flying like a bird.

In later Northern Myth Frigg can be said to play hardly more than a passive role: as Frigg-Jörð-Fjörgyn she is Mother of the gods. But whereas Jörð and Fjörgyn were from the first chthonic deities, Frigg in her own right was a goddess of love and fertility, and because of that easily assimilable to Mother Earth. Frigg's name gives her away: apart from such modern English connections as the vulgarisms *frigg*=to commit the sexual act upon, and *prick*=the penis, the name Frigg goes back to the Indo-European language. O.N. Frigg corresponds to

† *Gylf.* IX.   ‡ *Gylf.* XX.

O.H.G. Friia of the *Origo Langobardorum*. It is a doublet of the name Fricco applied to the Priapic god Frey;[60] and Fricco may be referred to an Indo-European root **prij* "love" from which Priapus' name is derived too. It is more than probable that Frigg-Frey-Freya are directly derived from Priapus the god of Asia Minor.

In the two *Eddas* Frigg is first the mother of the gods. But the removal north has affected her blood which has become cold and chaste—except that there is a memory of lustiness in her shadow Freya. Frigg's activities are mainly confined to a Cassandra-like quality of knowing the future without the will or power to affect its course: this, except in the one case of Balder's death. When Balder dreamed bad dreams of impending harm, Frigg extracted a promise from all creation (except one small plant, the mistletoe) not to harm Balder. This fatal omission led, of course, to Balder's death.

Frigg must have come north before the Vanir for she is identified as Odin's wife in both *Eddas* and as mother of the Æsir.

3

FREYA

Of Freya, Snorri gives this information:† "She is exalted with Frigg; she is married to the man called Óðr and their daughter is Hnoss (or Gem): she is so sparkling that precious and beautiful gems are called after her name. Óðr was used to going away on long journeys and Freya used to weep for him and her tears were all red gold. Freya has many names, and the reason for this is that she called herself now this, now that, when she travelled among strange races looking for Óðr: she's called Mardöll and Hörn and Gefn and Sýr. Freya owns Brísingamen the Necklace of the Brísings. Oh, and she has one other name: Vanadis."

† *Gylf.* XXXV.

In another place (*Gylf.* XXIV) Snorri adds "Freya is the most beautiful of the goddesses. Her home in heaven is called Fólkvangr or the People's Plain. When she rides to battle she takes one half of the corpses and Odin the other half, as it says here:†

> It is called Fólkvangr
> where Freya rules
>   who shall have seats in the hall;
> half of the dead
> she chooses each day
>   and Odin rakes up the rest.

Her palace, which is spacious and airy, is called the Rich-in-seats (*Sessrúmnir*). On her journeys she sits in a trap driving a pair of cats. She is by far the most favourable for men to call on, and from her name comes that title of high rank given to notable women, namely *Freya* (*Lady*). She is well pleased with songs of love; and on her it is fitting to call in affairs of the heart."

We gather from these two extracts that Freya is the *Lady* as her brother Frey is the *Lord* and so linked to the Asiatic "Lord" cult exemplified by Adonis, Tammuz and Baal, and nearer home by Balder. Freya's husband Óðr has a name which is a doublet of Óðinn and which is connected with Vâta the Hindu Lord of the Wind. Freya's weeping for Óðr is undoubtedly the mourning for the lost Lord, the bleeding god; but Freya is a multi-valent goddess holding the attributes of many. For instance, the tears shed for Óðr may also be represented as Hnoss or Gem their child, a mythic way of showing the association of Dawn, Wind and Dew. Yet again Freya's actual identification with the lost Lord is indicated by the hinting in Northern myth of her former captivity in Giantland (as Menglöð) and by the attempts made by giants to carry her off (e.g. in the story of the mason who built Asgard walls and wanted Freya as part of his payment; and of Þrymr the giant king who in *Þrymskviða* is not prepared to return Thor's stolen

† *Grim.* 14.

FIG. 14   DECORATIVE MOTIFS FROM SUTTON HOO

Above: Interlaced boars from a buckle. The boar (a symbol of fertility) was connected with Frey and Freya

Below: Design from a purse. There seems little doubt that the original designer was remembering the myth of Odin being swallowed by the wolf.

(British Museum)

hammer unless Freya is sent to Giantland as his wife; and of the giant Hrungnir who in *Skáldskaparmál* XVII threatened to abduct both Freya and Sif). Again Freya's connection with Tacitus' Nerthus or Mother Earth is suggested by her names Hörn and Sýr and by her carriage and team of cats. In Hörn, Rydberg sees a connection with German *harn* meaning liquid manure; Sýr meaning "sow" is an emblem of fecundity just as the boar connected with Frey is an emblem of prepotent fertility; and the carriage drawn by cats is strongly reminiscent of Tacitus' "Mother Earth or Nerthus" and her "car drawn by kine" (*Germ.* 40) as well as the Phrygian Matar Kubile, in Greek Kybele, the Mother of the Gods who plays with a lion or drives a chariot pulled by lions.

That there is, or was, a darker side to Freya seems to be

proved by two things: first her identification as a psychopomp (like Odin she is represented as a leader of souls, a leader of the dead) and her connection with sorcery. As the wife of Óðr, who was always away on long journeys, that is to say Odin in his manifestation as the wind god, it is perhaps natural that Freya should share the choosing of the slain with her husband. There is a link here, too, between Freya as a sorceress or witch and the Valkyries who chose the slain for Odin.

As one of the Vanir, Freya came north from Asia Minor along with Njörðr, her father, and Frey, her brother. In *Lokasenna* 36, Loki accuses Njörðr of incest with his sister who gives birth to Frey; *Ynglinga Saga* IV says that both Freya and Frey were the fruit of Njörðr's union with his sister. Then in *Lokasenna* 32 Loki accuses Freya of incest with Frey her brother. This "incest" appears to be a mythic way of indicating the identity originally of Njörðr, Frey and Freya. Frigg enters into it too, for in *Ynglinga Saga* III and *Lokasenna* 26 she is accused of cohabitation with her brothers-in-law. The basic qualities of these gods and goddesses were those of the mother (Nerthus), especially the quality of fertility, to which were added those of the lover (Priapus) and his power of fertilisation.

4

OTHER GODDESSES

Other goddesses appear in myth and are mentioned elsewhere by Snorri although not included in his list already quoted from *Gylfaginning* XXXV. These goddesses are the wives of gods and they pair off as follows: Sif with Thor, Nanna with Balder, Skaði with Njörðr, Gerðr with Frey, Iðunn with Bragi, and Sigyn with Loki.

Each of these six, Sif, Nanna, Skaði, Gerðr, Iðunn and Sigyn appears to have one main contribution to make to the mythology. Sif is yet another aspect of the Earth Mother, she is the northern Ceres, the goddess of the waving golden tresses, the goddess of the cornfield; Sif's hair was stolen by Loki but Thor forced the mischief maker to replace his wife's locks with others of pure spun gold fabricated underground by the dwarfs. Nanna is the wife of the "Lord", she has the same name as the wife of Baal one of the "Lords" of Asia Minor, and her chief function in Northern Myth is to accompany her husband Balder to hel. Skaði married Njörðr but separated from him; she was a giantess and so equipped to assist in the binding of Loki; she appears to have consorted with Odin when she became the eponymous founder of Scandinavia and as such she is more at home in legend than in myth. Gerðr, although a giantess, is a person of surpassing beauty: when she lifted her hand to the door latch a light was reflected over all the northern sky; Gerðr is (like Menglöð) a maiden difficult of attainment and the cause of Frey's love-sickness. The golden Iðunn is still one more manifestation of the bounteous Earth Mother, this time bearing the gift of youthfulness: she has a casket of precious fruit, apples of gold they are said to be, at which the gods nibble to prevent their growing old. Like all the others who represent earth's seasonal fruition, her waxing and waning, like Freya, Frey, Balder and Sif, who are taken away themselves or robbed of their informing attribute, Iðunn is carried off temporarily by the giants. Sigyn as the wife of Loki bears him two sons one of whom kills the other so that the dead one's entrails may be used to bind the father; but Sigyn portrays the prized northern attribute of faithfulness: she stays by her bound husband's side until the Ragnarök, holding a basin and catching venom dripping from two snakes above his face.

Four of these goddesses then, Sif, Nanna, Gerðr and Iðunn can be connected in some way or another with fertility myths and their adventures are a reflection of some aspect of the seasonal increase and decrease of fertility.

Skaði seems otherwise, although she is linked with the fertility myth in that she marries Njörðr. Of all the goddesses Skaði is the most nordic. Snorri says† "she was forever off out

† *Gylf.* XXIII.

on snowshoes, hunting animals which she shot with her bow and arrows, and so she's often referred to as the Snowshoe Goddess or the Goddess on Skis." Her home, of course, was in the mountains, in Þrymheim the Home of Clamour. She is the eponymous goddess of Scadin-auja, Scandinavia, and in her marriage to Njörðr it is tempting to see a reflection of the acceptance wholeheartedly for a time in Scandinavia of the fertility religion of the Vanir which came from the south; likewise, with Skaði's divorce from Njörðr, her return home to the mountains and the rumour of her becoming one of Odin's wives, we have a reflection of the Northmen's return to the Æsir religion.[61]

CHAPTER V

Loki and His Brood

I

LOKI

SNORRI says in an uneasy sort of way† "There is also counted among the heavenly powers one whom some call the Mischief Maker of the gods and the first father of lies: he's a living shame to everyone whether mortal or divine. His true name is Loki or Loptr, son of Fárbauti (that is Danger-Dunts) the giant, his mother being Leafy Island (*Laufey*) or Needle Nál. His brothers are Býleistr and Helblindi. Loki is handsome, easy on the eyes, but inside, the soul of spite and completely fickle. He has a talent and skill in slyness which leaves everybody else far behind, knowing a trick for all occasions. He is eternally plunging the gods into hot water, and quite often he gets them out again with his crafty advice. His wife's name is Sigyn, and their son's name Nari or Narfi."

In addition, the periphrases in *Skáldskaparmál*‡ say that the god Heimdallr is called "Foe of Loki . . . he is also Frequenter of Vágasker and Singasteinn, where he contended with Loki for the necklace Brísingamen"; and that Loki himself may be periphrased§ by calling him "Son of Fárbauti and Laufey (or Nál), Brother of Býleistr and of Helblindi, Father of the Monster of Ván (that is, Fenriswulf), and of the Vast Monster (that is, the Midgard Serpent), and of Hel, and Nari, and Áli; Kinsman, Uncle, Evil Companion and Benchmate of Odin and the Æsir, Visitor and Chest-Trapping of Geirröðr, Thief of the Giants, of the Goat, of Brísingamen, and of Iðunn's apples, Kinsman of Sleipnir, Husband of Sigyn, Foe of the Gods, Harmer of Sif's Hair, Forger of Evil, the Sly God,

† *Gylf.* XXXIII.   ‡ *Skáld.* VIII.   § *Skáld.* XVI.

165

Slanderer and Cheat of the Gods, Contriver of Balder's Death, the Bound God, Wrangling Foe of Heimdallr and of Skaði".

These periphrases (or most of them, whose meaning is known) will be explained in the stories that follow. But first, we should start with Loki's own name: it appears to be cognate with Lat. *lux* "light" and Lucifer "the light bearer". But Loki was not the bearer of beneficent fire or light; that was the function of Heimdallr-Vindlér the bore-stick producer of useful domestic fire. Loki was the bringer of destructive fire, and so Heimdallr and Loki are opposites, antitheses, and therefore represented mythologically as constant and bitter enemies, and in fact each other's destroyer at the Ragnarök.

Loki's family relationships bear out his character of uncontrollable, destructive fire: his father Fárbauti's name means Dangerous Smiter and his mother Laufey's name is best explained as a kenning for "tree", the "leafy island". Loki is brought to birth when the Dangerous Smiter and the tree come together; and his brothers are Býleistr and Helblindi. Býleistr has been variously explained as the "Trampler of Towns" or "Whirlwind from the east". Helblindi means (it seems) Helblinder: a reference in *Ynglinga Saga* 51 from the skald Þjóðólfr equates him with a water spout. Taking this evidence into account it seems reasonable to accept Fárbauti as a thunderstorm giant whose children are the whirlwind and the waterspout and, in the case of Loki, the destructive forest fire born of the lightning flash and the tree. A forest fire was one of the most destructive agencies known to the ancients, and it is perhaps significant that at the Ragnarök the fire-giant Surtr, who destroys everything with fire and who comes at the same time as Loki, is said to bear in his hand "the bane of branches". The "bane of branches" (*með sviga lævi*) is of course a kenning for destructive fire; and any one who has seen the aftermath of a certain type of swift forest fire—the bare and barren parade ground with its ranks of charred poles which were once trees—will agree with the aptness of this figure of speech.

But there is an awful beauty about fire, no matter how destructive it may be. Fire is a friend and a foe, a good servant and a bad master. Our forefathers were well aware of these things and so they represented the beneficent aspect of fire as a Heimdallr and the maleficent aspect as a Loki. But although destructive fire is maleficent to man, man can still see its beauty, and so we get this confusion expressed in the myth: nobody knows whether Loki, "handsome" yet "completely fickle", should be classed as a god or not. He is said to be a "kinsman of the Æsir" but also the "Foe of the gods"; yet he is not the son of Odin nor Frigg; nor is he a relative of Odin except perhaps by the rite of blood-brotherhood, for in *Lokasenna* he says:†

> Don't forget, Odin,
> in olden days
> we blent our blood together. . . .

It was by this relationship of blood-brotherhood with Odin that the myth was able to reconcile the idea of evil being able to exist in heaven. The confusion has penetrated to the *accounts* of some of the myths, so that where we should expect a beneficent god to take part, we find a maleficent one, a Loki instead of a Heimdallr. The truth is that from earliest times, from before the creation of the world and mankind there has existed a fire-spirit who has been confused with Loki (cf. p. 142 and p. 146). This is Lóðurr, a brother of Odin and Hœnir. As has already been related, Lóðurr makes a present of heat to the newly created mankind: it is inconceivable that the evil Loki should have been present at the creation of mankind as it is related in the *Eddas*. Lóðurr is wholly beneficent and (as I have argued) is to be equated with Heimdallr, Loki's antithesis. Although Loki is accepted in Asgard, he is not one of the Æsir, nor of the Vanir, nor is he a friend to either; on the contrary his sole and ultimate aim is the annihilation of the gods and the universe: long does he prepare the conflagration of the world, working

† *Lok.* 9.

like a serpent in their midst. And the supreme irony is that the gods know well that evil is among them and of their inadequacy to deal with it. The myth is dualistic. And to explain the dualism, Loki is made by some stratagem to prevail on Odin to accept him as a blood-brother and so gain protection and hospitality in Asgard. The power of the blood-brotherhood is indicated in Odin's reply to Loki's reminder already quoted:†

> Don't forget, Odin,
> in olden days
>   we blent our blood together. . . .

Up to this point, the gods have barred Loki from what is to be his last banquet with them; but at this reminder of blood-brotherhood, Odin says shortly to his son Víðarr:‡

> Rise you, Víðarr,
> let the Wolf's father
>   push to a place at table. . . .

The Wolf, Loki's son, is of course Fenrir; and at the Ragnarök the Wolf swallows Odin. The poet of *Lokasenna* has thus shown a fine irony in relating that Odin (remembering the blood-brotherhood) orders the son who *he knows* is to avenge him, to make a place for the father of the Wolf who is to be his slayer: and Odin's perception of the whole situation is made crystal clear in his use of the phrase "the Wolf's father" instead of the name Loki.

Loki's wife, but not the mother of Fenrir, is Sigyn whom Snorri places among the goddesses in *Skáldskaparmál* I. By Sigyn Loki had two sons called Narfi (or Nari) and Váli. When, after Balder's death, the gods finally bound Loki they used the entrails of his son Nari who had just been torn to pieces by his brother Váli in the guise of a wolf. It is obvious from the story that no ordinary bonds would hold Loki. As he lay prostrate, fettered to rocks underground, venom dripped over his face from serpents fastened there by Skaði (in revenge for her father Þjazzi's death which had been encompassed by

† *Lok. 9.*   ‡ *Lok. 10.*

Loki). The faithful wife, Sigyn, continually shielded her husband by catching the serpents' venom in a dish. When the dish got full and Sigyn had to turn away to empty it, the venom dripped on to Loki's face and induced such spasms in his frame as to cause earthquakes. And there, says Snorri, lies Loki bound until the Doom of the Gods. Such a captivity is quite consonant with an evil fire-spirit: no doubt Loki was regarded as being beneath a volcano such as the Icelanders knew in Hekla, and when he writhed in anguish the volcano erupted and the earth quaked.

2

LOKI'S BROOD

"To tell the truth" (says Snorri)† "Loki has an awful brood of children. There's an ogress in Giantland called Angrboða: upon her body Loki got three offspring. The first was Fenris-wulf, the second Jörmungandr (*the World Serpent*), and lastly Hel. When the gods saw that these three nephews and nieces of theirs (so to speak) were being bred up in Giantland of all places, they did a bit of private table-rapping and found they had to expect a heap of unpleasantness from these brothers and their sister: for they could have inherited nothing but evil (so everyone thought) judging by their mother—and still more so by their father.

"So the Allfather sent word to the gods to kidnap the whelps and lead them to him, and when they did come before him he cast the serpent into the deep sea, where it now lies completely ringing-in the world. For the old dragon so increased in length and girth that he came full circle and now grips his tail-end in his jaws. Hel, the Allfather tumbled down into Niflheim and gave her the rule of nine worlds with absolute power over all who are once sent into her charge, namely those who breathe their last on the sick bed or who die

† *Gylf.* XXXIII.

of old age. She is queen of a far-flung land of weeping and wailing; her courts are exceedingly vast and her portal wide as death. Her palace is called Sleetcold; her platter is Hunger; her knife and fork Famine; Senility her house-slave and Dotage her bondmaid; at the entering-in her doorstep is Pitfall; Bedridden is her pallet and Woeful Wan its curtains. Her complexion is half-livid, half-normal; and so she is easy to recognize and what you might call stern of looks, and even hideous.

"The Wolf, the gods reared at home, Týr being the one sufficiently courageous to go and feed him. But when they saw how tremendously he put on weight every day, and knowing that all prophesies foretold his intention to do them serious damage, the gods made an adamantine fetter (which they called Lœðingr) and took it to the Wolf. They suggested he might like to try his weight on the fetter, and because it didn't seem to the Wolf to be beyond his strength he let them do as they were minded to.

"The very first kick the Wolf gave, he snapped the fetter.

"So the gods manufactured another fetter half as strong again which they called Drómi and asked the Wolf to test it. They flattered him about his strength being pretty wonderful if such a bond were unable to hold him prisoner. The Wolf thought to himself that this fetter was much stronger, but he believed at the same time that his own powers had increased since he broke Lœðingr and in any case he would need to risk it if he were to enhance his reputation: he let the gods shackle him. When the gods said they were ready, the Wolf shook himself and ran the fetter down his leg to the ground, then he struggled a little, kicked out and shattered it to bits.

"That's how he rid himself of Drómi. And since that time it has been a proverb to *Light out of Lœðingr* or to *Dodge out of Drómi* when anybody manages to escape from a really tight corner.

"Well, the Allfather sent him who is called Skírnir (Frey's man) over into Svartálfaheim to a certain dwarf and had him forge the fetter known as Gleipnir. It was compounded of six ingredients: the noise of a cat's footfall, the beard of a woman, the roots of a mountain, the nerves of a bear, a fish's breath and the spittle of a bird: and although you may not have heard this news before, you can quickly get certain proof that nobody has lied to you. Of course, you've noticed that women don't have beards and there's no *clip-clop* when the cat walks, nor are there roots under mountains; but I myself know perfectly well that all the authorities agree completely with the account as I have given it to you, even though in some details you may find it difficult to prove. . . .

"Now, this fetter Gleipnir was soft and smooth as silk, yet at the same time so firm and tough as you shall hear in a moment.

"When the fetter was brought back to the gods they thanked their messenger heartily for his errand. Then the divine powers rowed out on the lake known as Ámsvartnir, as far as the island called Lyngvi (*or Heather*) and intreated the Wolf with them. They showed him the silk-like bond and told him to snap it. They said it was in all likelihood a little stronger than appeared from its thickness and they passed it from one to the other and tested it with their hands, but it didn't break; 'Hm,' they said, 'the Wolf ought to snap this.'

"But the Wolf made answer, 'I don't exactly see how I'm to make a name for myself by breaking this bootlace—by shattering so frail a rope of sand. But if, on the other hand, a deal of craft and cunning have gone into the making of the bond, then let it seem as soft as it likes—it doesn't come near *my* legs.'

"The gods protested he couldn't help but tear it apart in a moment—snip-snap—so feeble a ribbon as it was; especially when on former occasions he had flung asunder great fetters of iron and so on; 'and in fact,' they said, 'if you find you can't slit it then you'll no longer be in a position to scare the gods and we shall, of course, set you free.'

"The Wolf observed, 'If you bind me in such a way that I'm unable to break out, you'll be a bit backward in coming forward to help me. I am not over eager to let that bond bind me. But if you really are determined to try my mettle, well, let one of you lay his hand between my fangs as a guarantee that you don't intend to double-cross me.'

"At this, all the gods glanced at each other and felt themselves properly cornered; certainly not one of them intended losing his hand, until Týr thrust out his right fist and laid it within the Wolf's jaws.

"But when the Wolf kicked out, the noose tightened round him, and the more violently he tried to break away, the fiercer bit the bond. Then everybody guffawed except Týr: he lost his hand.

"When the gods saw the Wolf was bound for good, they grabbed the chain attached to the fetter (it's called Gelgja) and fastened him to the foot of a lofty crag called Gjöll which has its foundations miles below in the earth. Then they took an enormous boulder (called Þviti or Thwacker) and pile-drove the crag still deeper into the ground, using the boulder afterwards to weight down the crag. The Wolf gaped terrifically, struggled madly and tried to bite; so they wedged a sword between his chops, the pommel at his bottom jaw and the point transfixing his palate: that gagged him somewhat. He bellowed hideously and bloody slaver roped down from his gob: that's the river called Ván. And there he lies till the Ragnarök."

In reply to the question "Why didn't the gods finish the Wolf off instead of living in hourly expectation of something evil from him?" Snorri reports that the High One replied, "The gods so valued their mansions and their fanes that they were loath to pollute them with the blood of the Wolf, even though the prophesies said he would prove Odin's bane."†

† The myth, of course, needed the Wolf to swallow Odin who originally was delivered from the "jaws of death" by his son Víðarr.

3

LOKI AND ANGRBOÐA

The identity of Angrboða and the details of Loki's mating with her are confusing to a degree; nevertheless we have to make some attempt to sort them out from the allusive, broken and often mistaken relics now remaining.

The *Short Völuspá* (10) says:

> Loki got the Wolf
> with Angrboða . . .

and in the next stanza:

> Loki ate the heart
> which lay in the coals,
>   half-burnt he found
>   the heart of the woman;
> Loptr was fertilised
> by the foul woman:
>   thence in the world
>   came all the wolves.

From this it appears that an evil woman, presumably Angrboða, had for some reason been burnt by persons not mentioned; her heart remained undestroyed; Loki found it and ate it; was fertilised by it and gave birth to the monster Fenrir from whom sprang the race of wolves. Loki's androgynous nature is made manifest elsewhere in the myth which tells how he transformed himself into a mare, lured away a stallion and afterwards gave birth to the most famous of all horses, Sleipnir, who had eight legs and whom Odin claimed.

The puzzle now is how did Angrboða come to be burnt and who were the burners? We may begin from Loki's enmity with the gods and his continual working against them. From Loki and Angrboða sprang the Fenriswulf who was at last to kill Odin, so it is reasonable to suppose that Angrboða was herself evil and an enemy of the gods. Is there any record of an "evil woman" an enemy of the gods being burnt? As it happens, there is. It occurs in *Völuspá*, in one of the most allusive and puzzling parts of that great poem, namely stanzas 20 to 25. The völva says first:†

> I mind the folk war—
> the first in the world—
>   when they pierced Gollveig
>   with their pointed spears,
> and her they burnt
> in the High One's hall;
>   she was three times burnt
>   and three times born,
> over and over
> yet ever she lives.
>
> They call her Heiðr
> who came to their home,
>   a far-seeing witch
>   cunning in sorcery. . . .

It appears then that Gollveig (*Gold Might*) otherwise called Heiðr (*Shining*), a cunning sorceress, was slain by spears in Valhalla (the "High One's hall", i.e. Odin's Hall) presumably by the Æsir. She was burnt and reborn three times and still lived on. This murder was connected with the "folk war—the first in the world", the war between Æsir and Vanir.

A memory of this is contained in a heroic lay of the *Verse Edda* called *Völsungakviða*.‡ Considering the fact that *Völsungakviða* dates from after the year A.D. 1000, that is, after the introduction of Christianity to Iceland, the memory it contains of the incident under discussion, despite the allusiveness of the passage, can hardly be disputed. *Völsungakviða* 40 runs:

> Thou wast a Valkyrie
> thou loathsome witch
>   evil and base

---

† *Völ.* 20. 21.   ‡ Also called *Helgakviða Hundingsbana* I.

in Allfather's hall;
the Champions all
were forced to fight
for thy sake
thou subtle woman.

This stanza surely confirms the interpretations of *Völuspá* 20 that it was the murder of Gollveig which precipitated the war between Æsir and Vanir. There is a reference to Gollveig under her name Heiðr in the *Shorter Völuspá* 4 where she is said to be one of Hrímnir's two children, the other being a son called Hrossþjófr (*Horse Thief*). No other daughter of the frost giant Hrímnir is mentioned in the *Eddas* and so it is reasonable to suppose that Heiðr-Gollveig is referred to in the verse from *Þórsdrápa* which calls fire "the lifting drink of Hrímnir's daughter" *lypti-sylgr . . . Hrímnis . . . drósar*.[62] This elaborate kenning refers to fire as the drink which Heiðr-Gollveig was forced to consume when she was raised on an arch of spears over the flames of the long fire running down the middle of Valhalla.

After the murder of Gollveig (according to the *Codex Regius* version of *Völuspá*), the Celestial Powers took counsel together to decide whether the Æsir should pay a "wergild" for Gollveig. Since this discussion was brought abruptly to an end by Odin flinging his spear (a Gothonic signal for the start of a battle) and since a war between Æsir and Vanir followed, it seems evident that the "wergild" was to have been paid to the Vanir. If that is the case then Gollveig must have been a relation of the Vanir. Rydberg argued in his *Teutonic Mythology* that Gollveig-Heiðr-Angrboða was also known in Giantland as Aurboða. This Aurboða was the mother of Gerðr who married the Vanr Frey. If Frey's mother-in-law was indeed murdered by the Æsir, then by the Gothonic code Frey would be morally bound to avenge her death and to call on his near relatives to help him: and so we should arrive at a satisfactory cause for the war between Æsir and Vanir. Such a cause would be supremely ironic for Aurboða is suspected of having been the cause of Frey's sister Freya being abducted by the giants; and the price of her daughter Gerðr's hand was the famous sword belonging to Frey which fought of itself and for lack of which he was killed at the Ragnarök. However, the fragments of myth remaining are so badly broken as to resist the piecing together of a reliable picture. We can be certain of one thing, that Loki, the root of all evil, has played some part in it.

CHAPTER VI

Choosing the Slain

IT will be as well to begin with Snorri's account of Valkyries and Champions for there is no doubt but that what he wrote has become the conventional, the accepted picture. How far this conventional picture is confirmed by the *Verse Edda* and other literary sources we may examine later.

Snorri's first mention of Valhalla (*Valhöll* "the hall of the slain") is in *Gylfaginning* II where he describes the arrival of king Gylfi in Asgard. Gylfi "saw a hall towering so high he could scarcely see above it. It was slated with shields of gold like a shingled roof, a fact alluded to by Þjóðólfr of Hvin who also implies that Valhalla was thatched with shields:

> Their backs were ablaze
> (though battered with stones)
>   with Odin's hall shingles,
>   those stout-hearted men.

Gylfi caught sight of someone standing in the hall entrance juggling with daggers keeping seven in the air at once. This person hinted that he might like to give his name and he said 'Wayweary' who had foot-slogged all the side roads, who was looking for a shakedown for the night and who wanted to know 'who owns this hall'? The other answered it was their king 'and I'll take you to see him. You'd better ask him his name yourself'. He turned into the hall in front of Gylfi, who followed and at once the great door ground to on his heels.

"He saw there a wide, open floor and many people, some playing games, some drinking steadily, others armed and fighting. Then he blinked swiftly about and thought many things he saw there quite unbelievable. . . ."

Then in *Gylfaginning* XX we learn that "Odin is called All-father because he is father of all the gods; he's called, too, Val-father or Father of the Slain because all those are his sons by adoption who fall in battle; he billets them in Valhalla and Vingólf, and they are called Einherjar (*or Champions*). . . ."

Chapter XXIV of *Gylfaginning* contributes this further information: "Freya is the most beautiful of the goddesses. Her home in heaven is called Fólkvangr (*or the People's Plain*). When she rides to battle she takes one half of the corpses and Odin the other half, as it says here:†

> It is called Fólkvangr
> where Freya rules
>   who shall have seats in the hall;
> half of the dead
> she chooses each day
>   and Odin rakes up the rest."

Snorri regards the Valkyries as being similar in status to the lesser goddesses, for after speaking of the Ásynjur he comments:‡ "There are others too whose lot it is to wait on in Valhalla, to carry round the drinks, to keep the table going and the ale-cups brimming; there's a list of them given in *Grímnismál*:§

Hrist and Mist	*Shaker, Mist*
bring the horn when I list.	
Skeggjöld and Skögul	*Axe-time, Raging*
Hildr and Þrúðr,	*Warrior, Strength*
Hlökk and Herfjötur,	*Shrieking, Host-fetter*
Göll and Geirönul,	*Screaming, Spear-bearer*
Randgríðr and Ráðgríðr	*Shield-bearer, Plan-destroyer*
and Reginleif	*Gods' kin*
carry ale to the Einherjar.	

These folk are called Valkyries. Odin despatches them to every battle where they make a choice of men destined to die and

† *Grím.* 14.   ‡ *Gylf.* XXXVI.   § *Grím.* 37.

decide who shall have victory. Guðr and Róta and the youngest of the norns (called Skuld) always ride to choose the slain and order the fighting."

In Chapter XXXVIII Gylfi remarks to Hárr (i.e. Odin) " 'You tell me every man jack who has fallen in battle from the beginning of the world is now come to Odin in Valhalla. How does he manage to victual them all? I think there must be hosts of them.'

"Hárr said, 'You are right—as usual: there *are* hosts of them, and there'll be millions more yet, in spite of which their numbers won't stretch far enough at the time when the Wolf comes. Still, there will never be so mighty a multitude in Valhalla that the pork of the boar Sæhrímnir won't go round. Cooked every day, he comes alive and well again each night. But as to this question you have just asked me: it seems to me beyond all likelihood that few men are wise enough to tell truthfully all the ins and outs of it. Well, the cook's name is Andhrímnir Sootyface and the pot is called Eldhrímnir the Smoky, just as this says:†

> Andhrímnir cooks
> in Eldhrímnir
> > Sæhrímnir's seething flesh
> juiciest of pork;
> but few people know
> > what fare the Einherjar feast on.'

"Next Gylfi asked,‡ 'What do the Champions have to drink which keeps them equally satisfied as their meat—or is water the only tipple there?'

"Hárr said, 'Now isn't this a pretty wonderful sort of question he asks? He wants to know if the Father of All will ceremoniously invite kings and jarls and other proud nobles into his home and give them—water! By the hokey! I'll wager many who come to Valhalla would feel they had paid dearly for their drink of water if they didn't receive better entertainment there—

† *Grím.* 18. ‡ *Gylf.* XXXIX.

those who had worked their passage to death through blood and fire! Water! What I have to say to you about this gives a quite different account. The nanny-goat called Heiðrún stands on her hind legs in Valhalla and nibbles the needles of the branches of that very famous pine named Læraðr; and mead squirts so copiously from her two teats that every day she fills an enormous vat: big enough anyway to get all the Champions roaring drunk on.'

"Gylfi observed,† 'There's a goat and a half for them if you like: must be a pretty good tree she browses too. . . . In fact, these are astonishing things which you now relate. What a vast—what an eye-staggering edifice this Valhalla must be. And yet I suppose there are queues and double-queues quite often before its doors?'

"Hárr replied, 'Look, why don't you ask plainly how many doors there are in Valhalla, and how big they are? When you've heard that told, you may see it will be a very strange thing indeed if whoever wishes to, may not go in—or out! It can be said without a word of a lie that there is a seat and a free entry for all who earn it. You can hear this in *Grímnismál*:‡

> Five hundred doors
> and forty more
>   I vow are set in Valhalla:
> eight hundred warriors
> abreast walk through each
>   when they march to meet the Wolf.'

"Then said Gylfi,§ 'Certainly, there's a multitudinous concourse of men in Valhalla, therefore I need no persuasion to believe Odin to be an almighty chieftain when he commands so big a battalion. How do the Champions fill in their time when they are not tossing the pots?'

"Hárr answered, 'Every day as soon as they are dressed they don their armour, file orderly on to the parade ground, fight and flatten each other: that is their sport; then when second

† *Gylf.* XL.   ‡ *Grím.* 24.   § *Gylf.* XLI.

breakfast-time comes they scamper home to Valhalla and sit themselves down to their drinking, as it says here:†

> All the Einherjar
> in Odin's barracks
>   crack each other's crowns every day;
> they bundle up the dead,
> ride back from the fight,
>   and sit to their drink all healed and sound.' "

So much for the *Prose Edda*. If we summarize Snorri's information about the Choosing of the Slain, we get the following results: he believes that Odin's hall of the slain is in Asgard; it is a viking warrior's paradise—a man's paradise—of eating, drinking, gaming and fighting; during daylight hours the warriors fight and maim or kill each other only to come whole again by evening ready to fight next day, and this will continue until the Ragnarök when the Einherjar fulfil the purpose for which they are gathered together, namely to assist the gods against their enemies; food for the warriors is provided by the everlasting boar Sæhrímnir and drink by the goat Heiðrún; the ale is carried round in Valhalla by Valkyries (i.e. Choosers of the Slain) of whom Snorri gives no physical description but who from their names (Axe-time, Raging, Warrior, Shield-bearer, etc.) appear to be Amazon-like; from a direct statement of Snorri's and again from such names as Host-fetter and Plan-destroyer it seems that the Valkyries are able to "order the fighting", to decide victory and defeat; Snorri is vague about the actual choosing of the slain and their disposition in Asgard, for he implies that there is really no "choosing" about it since "every man jack who has fallen in battle from the beginning of the world is now come to Odin in Valhalla", but at the same time he paraphrases and quotes *Grímnismál* 14 in which Freya is said to share the slain with Odin.

When we consult the *Verse Edda* we are forced to the conclusion that Snorri has based his account mainly if not entirely

† *Vaf.* 41.

on the eddaic poems and in particular on *Grímnismál*: there is
nothing to suggest that Snorri's version owes anything to
sources no longer available to us or (what is more important)
that he has done violence to the sources he used. In fact, here
we find Snorri including information from sources which
appear to be mutually contradictory when, for instance, in the
one case he names Odin as the receiver of the slain and in the
other he states that Odin and Freya share the chosen fallen
equally.

2

THE VERSE EDDA

To begin with *Grímnismál*: stanzas 8, 9 and 10 contain the
following information, that Valhalla, shining bright with gold
stretches far and wide in Glaðsheimr: anyone who comes to
Odin can easily recognize the hall, for its rafters are spears, it is
tiled with shields and the benches are strewn with war-coats,
while over the western door hangs a wolf with an eagle hover-
ing above it; here every day does Odin "choose men killed
with weapons". Stanza 23 tells of the "five hundred and forty
doors" in Valhalla's walls, each wide enough to allow through
"eight hundred"[63] men, shoulder to shoulder, at one time.
These doors are mentioned as being for use particularly when
the warriors double forth "to fight with the Wolf", i.e. at
Ragnarök. But the outermost gate, called Valgrind "the holy
barred-gate of the slain" of which "few people can tell how
tightly it is locked",† is the one entrance to Valhalla available
to those killed in battle. Even before they reach Valgrind, the
"host of the slain" must wade through the loudly roaring river
Þund. Stanza 21 is a difficult and important one; it says:

> Loud roars Þund;
> Þjóðvitnir's fish
>   swims and sports in the flood,

† *Grím.* 22.

but the host of the slain
are hard put to it
to trudge through that wild torrent.

The difficulty lies in the interpretation of the kenning "Þjóð-vitnir's fish"; such kennings are characteristic of skaldic poetry but rare in the *Verse Edda*. The name Þjóðvitnir means "Mighty Wolf", presumably a synonym for Sköll the wolf who is to swallow the sun. In the kenning "Þjóðvitnir's fish", the sun is called a fish because she is regarded as swimming in the river Þund which flows round Valhalla. But the actual sun moves across the sky, through the river of air, and so the "loudly roaring Þund" is the turbulent air-stream which the sun moves through with ease (as anybody can see) but which the slain have difficulty in wading. This is the one piece of circumstantial evidence in the *Verse Edda* for the slain rising to Valhalla through the sky, on foot, and not on the horses of the Valkyries.[64]

Once safely past the obstacles of the river Þund and the gate Valgrind the "men killed with weapons" enter Valhalla where Andhrímnir the cook prepares succulent stews of the boar Sæhrímnir's flesh in the mighty cauldron Eldhrímnir. For drink the warriors quaff the sparkling mead provided by the nanny goat Heiðrún who browses on the branches of the tree standing outside Valhalla called Læraðr.

Grímnismál 14 says that Freya shares the slain with Odin, and Vigfusson and Powell[65] saw in this the meaning that she had a "Walhall of her own for women". Whether this be the case or no, it seems certain that Freya had a dark side to her character (cf. p. 161); but there is nowhere any mention of *women* being received from earth into Valhalla, which would indicate that Vigfusson and Powell were wrong in their assumption.

The last information in *Grímnismál* on the subject of choosing the slain is the list of thirteen Valkyries in stanza 37 quoted by Snorri in his own account.

If we compare the *Prose Edda* and *Grímnismál* in this matter of the choosing of the slain it is obvious that Snorri's errors are those of omission and not commission. Snorri has missed at least two important points: first, the obstacles to entering Valhalla in the shape of the air stream Þund and the barred gateway Valgrind; and second, the "wading" of Þund by the slain. On the other hand, Snorri presents additional information to be found in other sources. One such piece of information comes from *Vafþrúðnismál* 41 (which Snorri paraphrases and then quotes): this is an isolated stanza but nevertheless of prime importance, for it contributes the idea of the everlasting battle, of the warriors who daily wound and kill each other only to be healed and revived at night ready for the next day's fighting. It is perhaps significant that *Grímnismál*, which gives such a full account of Valhalla and the Einherjar, should make no mention of the everlasting battle: whether the everlasting battle was originally connected with the warriors who are mustering in Valhalla to help Odin and the Æsir at the Ragnarök, we are not yet in a position to determine. It is surely significant too that *Grímnismál* (although including the list of Valkyries in both manuscripts, *Codex Regius* and the *Arnamagnæan Codex*) does nowhere say that the Valkyries choose the slain: the Valkyries in *Grímnismál* wait on in Valhalla and the slain "wade" to Valhalla through Þund, the stream of air. In fact, the phrase *kjósa val* "to choose the slain", is used in *Vafþrúðnismál* of the Einherjar themselves when at the end of the day's fighting in Valhalla they pick up their fallen comrades.

But the name *Valkyrja* means a "female chooser of the slain", a notion which must have been inherent from the first coming of the word; so that when *Grímnismál* includes a list of Valkyries but gives an account of how the slain get to Valhalla independent of the Valkyries, we must concede that at the time of the composition of the *Verse Edda* poems there was difference and confusion in men's minds about how the slain got to Valhalla.

There is little else to be added from the *Verse Edda*: *Hárbarðs-ljóð* 24 contains a suggestion that "the noble who fall among the slain go to Odin while Thor takes the thralls"; but it is doubtful whether this is reliable information because *Hárbarðs-ljóð* in the form we have it is relatively late, it is corrupt, and in any case one of those "flyting" poems where the contestants are prone to exaggerate and not to respect the truth. In *Völuspá* 30 we have a list of Valkyries who are "ready to ride over the earth" (but who have different names from the roll in *Grím-nismál*):

> She viewed far and wide
> Valkyries assemble,
>   ready to ride
>   to the ranks of the gods;
> Skuld held a shield
> and Skögul another,
>   with Gunnr, Hildr, Göndul
> and also Geirskögul
> now you have heard
> of Herjan's maids the list
>   of Valkyries ready
>   to ride o'er the earth.†

There are two other lists of Valkyries' names given in the Rhymed Glossaries or *Þulor*,[66] in the first there are nine and they are (it seems) connected with the fates or norns; in the second list there are twenty-nine names. In both the *Þulor* lists the Valkyries are said to be Odin's Valkyries or Odin's Maids: their strong connection with Odin and with "riding over the earth" are significant. Whatever the Valkyries were to begin with, by viking times many sources and their very names suggest Amazon-like women riding over the earth. Finally, *Völuspá* 42 mentions the cock-crow which at the Ragnarök awakens the Einherjar.

> Then to the gods
> crowed Gullinkambi‡

† Skuld = *Shall be* (the youngest norn).   Skögul = *Raging.*
　Gunnr, Hildr, Göndul = *War, warrior, ?.*   Herjan = *Lord of Hosts.*
‡ Golden-comb.

who wakes the heroes
in Herfather's hall.

There are two skaldic poems which go back to the tenth century, *Eiríksmál* and *Hákonarmál*, which treat the theme of a king's entry into Valhalla. I shall touch on these two poems in the next section.

3

VALKYRIES

As I have said, the name Valkyrja means "a female chooser of the slain". It is not peculiar to the Norse tongues but occurs also in Old English as *wælcyrge* (*walcyrge*, *walcrigge*). There is too a phrase in Old Norse, *kjósa val* "to choose the slain" of which (simple as it seems) we are uncertain of the real meaning. The phrase may mean either to pick up the dead from the battlefield, or to decide on those who are to die on the battlefield.

To begin at the end, Snorri's and the *Verse Edda*'s picture of the Valkyries is of a domesticated type of warrior woman who is equally at home serving drink in the hall or riding splendidly horsed and armed above the battlefield. Such is the picture in *Völsungakviða* 16:†

High under helmets
across the field of heaven,
     their breastplates all
     were blotched with blood,
and from their spear points
sparks flashed forth.

The two skaldic (as distinct from eddaic) poems which go back to the tenth century also support this picture of the Valkyries in whole or in part: I am referring, of course, to *Eiríksmál* and *Hákonarmál*.

† Also called *Helgakviða Hundingsbana* I.

Eiríksmál or *The Song of Eric* has for its subject the entry of king Eric into Valhalla. This poem has a direct interest for the English: Eric Blood-axe, the brave but luckless son of Haraldr Fairhair, having been pushed out of Norway landed in North-umbria and made himself king at York. Eric was in turn driven from York in A.D. 954 and shortly afterwards killed in battle by an under-king of "Edmund (Eadred?) Edwardsson" king of the English.[67] After Eric's death, his wife Gunnhildr had the poem *Eiríksmál* made on the subject of his entry into Valhalla; it begins with Odin's waking up one morning in Valhalla with a dream still fresh in his mind. He cries out:

> What dream was that? I thought I rose by daybreak to freshen up Valhalla for the fallen men;
> I wakened the Einherjar, warned them to jump to it to strew the benches and broach the beer-casks, the Val-kyries meanwhile to bear a king's wine.
> Therefore I expect the arrival of chiefs, nobles from the Earth, and so my heart is glad.

The god Bragi then awoke and hearing the approach of Eric and his men cried:

> What's that sound of thunder, a thousand men marching, an army approaching us?
> Every bench is trembling—is Balder coming back home to Odin's hall?

In this account, Odin plays the same part as an earthly king or jarl expecting a noble visitor; the Einherjar are reduced to the status of retainers and servingmen; and the Valkyries act the ladies of high birth who carry round wine at the banquet just as we find described in our own *Beowulf*. The slain march with a thunderous tramping up to Valhalla and there is no sug-gestion of their being *chosen* or led there by Valkyries.

On the other hand, the *Hákonarmál* though composed some thirty years later than *Eiríksmál* (i.e. about A.D. 980) seems truer to the older conception of Valkyrie as a chooser of the slain.

This poem *Hákonarmál* too is of interest to Englishmen, for its subject king Hákon the Good was a foster son of the famous English king Athelstan the victor of Brunanburgh. Hákon was killed by the sons of Gunnhildr, and in the poem Göndul and Skögul reappear as the Valkyries who conduct him to Valhalla. They are depicted as noble, dignified personages in byrnie and helmet, sitting high on horseback and directing the fight according to Odin's orders. *Hákonarmál* begins:

> The Father of Gods sent Göndul and Skögul
> to choose a kingly champion,
> one of Yngvi's lineage to enter Odin's service
> valiant in Valhalla. . . .

The battle takes place and Hákon is mortally wounded:

> The king was sitting with his sword drawn,
> his shield was scored and his byrnie shot-holed.
> Sadly low in spirit were
> the ones bound for Valhalla.
> Göndul then speaking, said leaning on her spear-shaft
> "The Æsir's army's swelling
> now Hákon is bidden with a great host
> home to the heavenly Powers."
> Vanquished, the king heard the Valkyries chatting
> seated in their saddles,
> bravely they bore themselves under their helmets
> with shields upon their shoulders.

Hákon said:

> Why did you sway the struggle so Skögul, yesterday?
> Didn't we deserve more gain from the gods?

Skögul answered:

> We so worked it, that you won the field
> and that your foes should flee.
> But now we two must gallop to the gods' green home—
> cried the powerful Skögul—

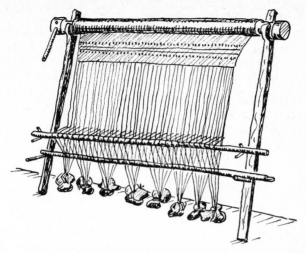

FIG. 15 LOOM

From Lyngen, north Norway. A loom of the kind the poet had in mind in
Darraðarljóð, with human heads replacing the stone weights.

> Odin must be told a mighty king is coming
> to meet him face to face.

There is another remembrance of Valkyries in one of the
hero lays from the *Verse Edda*, in *Helgakviða Hjörvarðssonar* 17.
But here the maidens have nothing to do with the choosing of
the slain; instead they fulfil the role of guardian angels at sea by
bringing Helgi's ships safely to harbour:

> There were three nines in ranks;
> one maid rode ahead
>   with a helmet and all in white;
> when their horses reared
> there rippled from their manes
>   dews into the deep dales,
>   hail into the high woods,
>   whence men their harvests have.

Here we are reaching the realms of faery; but there is a memory
of something wilder, fiercer, much more primitive and uncon-

ventional in such eddaic Valkyrie names as *Hlökk* Shrieking, *Göll* Screaming, *Skögul* Raging. This memory of cruder figures is even stronger in the skaldic poem *Darraðarljóð* the "Lay of Darts"; here the Valkyries weave the web of war much as Gray depicted them in his poem *The Fatal Sisters. Darraðarljóð* is comparatively late and must have been composed after A.D. 1014, the date of the Battle of Clontarf to which it refers. The poem is spoken by Valkyries who call themselves Odin's friends and who tell of a great warp raised on spears into which they are running a red weft. This web of victory is dripping with blood—"it is raining blood"; the warp itself is made of men's guts weighted with human heads; the shuttles are arrows. The Valkyries, who are weaving the web before the battle takes place, call themselves Hildr, Hjörþrimul, Sangríð, Svipul, Gunnr and Göndul; and they say plainly

> *Eigo Valkyrjor vigs um kosti*
> We Valkyries are able to order the battle,

after which they cry "Let us ride off far away on our bare-backed steeds with our drawn swords in our fists!"

Such creatures, exulting in blood and slaughter, are unlike the dignified Amazons of Snorri; but they are akin to those others depicted in the sagas, creatures for instance such as were dreamed of by king Haraldr Harðráði's men before their ill-fated expedition left Norway to fight Harold of England at Stamford Bridge. On this occasion one man, Gyrðr, "had a dream. He thought he was on the king's ship, and saw a great witch-wife standing on the island, with a fork in one hand and a trough in the other . . ."[68] Evidently the fork was intended to rake up the dead and the trough to catch the blood. Another man, Tord, dreamt that "before the army of the people of the country was riding a huge witch-wife upon a wolf; and the wolf had a man's carcass in his mouth, and the blood was dropping from his jaws; and when he had eaten up one body she threw another into his mouth, and so one after another, and he swallowed them all."[69] It is perhaps significant that Laing should have used the word "witch-wife" in translating the word of these two passages; it may be suggestive that *Grímnismál*, listing thirteen Valkyries by name should make up the same number as the witches coven.

It is quite certain that in tenth-century England the *wælcyrge* has a place alongside witches and malefactors as an enemy of the Christian god;[70] and a tradition which was tough enough to be recorded as late as the fourteenth century in the North West Midland dialect poem *Cleanness*[71] puts witches and Valkyries alongside each other.

It is difficult to decide whether our Anglo-Saxon ancestors had the same suspicion of witchcraft in mind when they glossed *wælcyrge, walcyrge, walcrigge* with Tisifone, Eurynes, Herines (Erinys), Allecto and Bellona.[72] A recent writer has said of these Greek "Furies" that "the Erinyes . . . are old: older than the gods who came to power with Zeus. They say this themselves when they appear on the stage—for example, in the play by Æschylus whose title is their other name, the *Eumenides*. They have serpents in place of hair. Their skins are black, their raiment is grey. . . . Whenever their number is mentioned there are three of them. . . . But . . . they can all be invoked together as a single being, an Erinys. The proper meaning of the word is a 'spirit of anger and revenge'. . . . The Erinyes were not always winged. . . . The smell of their breaths and bodies was intolerable. From their eyes poured a poisonous slaver. Their voice was often like the lowing of cattle; but usually their approach was heralded by a sound of barking, for they were bitches, like Hekate. The whips they bore were brass-studded thongs. They carried torches and serpents. Their home was below the earth in the Underworld. One of them was called Allekto, 'the Never-Ending'; the name of the second, Tisiphone, contains the word *tisis*, retaliation; the name of the third, Megavia, means envious anger. All three were virgins, but above all they represented the Scolding Mother. Whenever a mother was insulted, or perhaps even murdered, the Erinyes appeared. Like swift bitches they pursued all who had flouted

blood-kinship and the deference due to it. They defended the
rights of the father, and also of the elder brother; but especially
they supported the claims of the mother, even when these were
unjust."[73]

In another Old English passage[74] the word for Valkyries
appears as a gloss for Gorgons:

> Lat.   *hae bestie oculos habent Gorgoneos*
> O.E.   *þa deor habbað wælcyrian eagan*
>   these beasts have Valkyries' eyes.

And in one MS. of Aldhelm's *De Laudibus Virginitatis*[75] the
word *wælcyrie* is given as a gloss for *veneris*.

In reviewing the traditions concerning Valkyries I ought to
mention Swan Maidens—women who can assume the shape
of a swan and are able to fly. Swan Maidens appear in *Völundarkviða* where Völundr (*Wayland the Smith*) and his two
brothers come upon three "maids from the south" by the shore
of a lake. The prose introduction (written in Christian times)
says of the three maidens "near them were their swan-guises,
for they were Valkyries". In passing, we may note that the
goddess Freya is known to possess a "feather-coat", a bird-guise
which gives the wearer the power of flight. Völundr and his
two brothers live in love with the three swan maidens for seven
years, but in the eighth year "a longing came again" to the
maidens and they disappeared—not only from Völundr and
his brothers but from the poem too.

Again in *Hrómundar saga* VII a woman appears in the guise
of a swan and flies above the head of a warrior in battle and
chants spells to prevent his defeat.

In neither of these cases is the word *valkyrja* mentioned in the
actual source. The Swan Maiden story (without the Völundr
appendage) became one of the most popular German folk-
tales: and there are definite indications that the story came to the
north from Saxon regions.

What sort of order are we to get from these conflicting ideas?
The name *valkyrja* means "a female chooser of the slain"; it is

FIG. 16   FRANKS CASKET

This beautiful piece of seventh century Northumbrian craftsmanship is carved out of walrus ivory. The front panel (here depicted) is particularly interesting for placing side by side a scene from pagan myth (the story of Wayland Smith, Norse Völundr, *left*) and one from the Bible (the Magi presenting their gifts, *right*). The runes read clockwise, beginning at the bottom of the left-hand "box", as follows:

Hronæs ban, fisc flodu	The whale's bone from the fishes' flood
a-hof on fergenberig;	I lifted on Fergenbury;
warþ gasric grorn	he was gashed to death in his gambols
þær he on greut giswom.	as he swam aground in the shallows.

(British Museum)

found in O. English as *wælcyrge* and so the idea of choosing the slain must date from before *c.* A.D. 450 after which date the Angles, Saxons and Jutes left the Continent for England. Next we are to note that the Valkyries are strongly connected with Odin: *Völuspá* 30 calls them Herjan's (i.e. Odin's) Maids, the *þulor* lists call them Odin's Maids and Odin's Valkyries, *Darraðarljóð* refers to them as Odin's Friends and *Hákonarmál* describes them as doing their work for Odin, and of course Snorri takes the same point of view.

Are these two ideas of closeness of association to Odin and of choosing the slain necessarily as old as each other? My contention is that they are not. Odin was originally the god of the furious wind rushing across the sky and as such he is remembered to this day in folklore as the leader of the Wild Hunt and in the folk tale of Gabriel's Hounds. The creatures associ-

ated with this early Odin are noted for their noise and com-
motion and we have a memory of them in the Valkyrie names
meaning Shrieking, Screaming, Raging and Shaker: these are
the associates of Odin the leader of souls—they may even have
been at first the souls themselves—or more likely, if we are to
accept the Greek analogy of the Furies, they were the tormentors
or spirits of retribution upon the souls. The point is that
valkyrja is a later name for a being already in existence in men's
minds, and at the time of the application of the name *valkyrja*
the conception of the being had changed or was changing. We
may guess that the name *valkyrja* was adopted when Odin began
to assume the attributes of a war god, when he began to ascend
in the hierarchy, i.e. about the first century A.D. Then these
beings associated with Odin really became "choosers of the
slain" and their occupation was limited to choosing slain from
the battlefield. It is surely from these times that the warlike
Valkyrie names date; names such as Gunnr (*war*), Hildr
(*Warrior*), Geirönul (*Spear bearer*) and Randgríðr (*Shield
bearer*); other names such as Ráðgríðr (*Plan destroyer*) and
Herfjötur (*Host fetter*) suggest extension to the Valkyries of
Odin's power over the fortunes of war. The idea of control
of the battle and the death of many fighters probably led
to the inclusion of the norn Skuld in the number of the
Valkyries.

A later development still would seem to reflect the hall-
society of Migration Times, I mean the regarding of Valkyries
as dignified and elevated serving maids carrying round the
drink in Odin's own hall, Valhalla. Other conceptions like
those of the Swan Maiden, the Guardian Spirit and the Maiden
Difficult of Attainment (e.g. Brynhild) were not originally
connected with the Valkyries at all.

4

THE EVERLASTING BATTLE

I have already referred to two sources of the story of the everlasting battle. In answer to the question "How do the *Einherjar*
(*Champions*) fill in their time when they are not tossing the
pots?" Snorri says in *Gylfaginning* XLI "Every day as soon as
they are dressed they don their armour, file orderly on to the
parade ground, fight and flatten each other: that is their sport;
then when second breakfast time comes they scamper home to
Valhalla and sit themselves down to their drinking, as it says
here . . ." after which Snorri quotes *Vafþrúðnismál* 41.

Snorri is here basing his account of fighters who do battle
one day, kill or wound each other, and are revived and restored
to continue fighting next day, on *Vafþrúðnismál* 40, 41. This is
the only source in the *Verse Edda* telling of the resurrection of
warriors; it is the only source in the *Verse Edda* telling of the
everlasting battle. In both manuscripts[76] in which *Vafþrúðnismál* is extant an older copyist appears to have run stanzas 40
and 41 together, but fortunately Snorri quotes what must have
been the original stanza 41 in full:

Allir einherjar	All the Einherjar
Oðins túnum í	in Odin's barracks
höggvask hverjan dag,	crack each others' crowns every day,
val þeir kjósa	they bundle up the dead,
ok ríða vígi frá,	ride back from the fight
sitja meir of sáttir saman	and sit together healed and sound.

The sentence *val þeir kjósa* (which means literally "the slain they
choose" and which I have translated "they bundle up the
dead") is combined with the preceding line in Snorri's para-
phrase. In other words, he does not accept the idea of the Einherjar *choosing* the slain, but he combines the idea of *höggvask*
"hew at each other" and *valr* "the slain" into "fight and flatten

each other"; the word I have translated "flatten" being *drepa*, an accepted euphemism for "to kill". Other than this line *val þeir kjósa* there is nothing in the two *Eddas* to suggest that the Einherjar choose the slain in the way that the Valkyries do.

The notion of the everlasting battle did not originate in Norse myth, and except for Snorri's account and *Vafþrúðnismál* 41 I know of no other extant source connecting the everlasting battle with the Chosen Warriors who are to assist the gods at the Ragnarök.

There are plenty of Norse accounts of dead warriors being resuscitated on the battlefield and fighting on. In *Hrólfs saga Kraka* LI Skuld, daughter of king Helgi and an elf woman, raises an army against her half-brother Hrólfr, and though Skuld's men are chopped and sliced in pieces they immediately rise up and fight again. Böðvarr Bjarki, Hrólfr's champion, calls these animated dead by the name *draugar*, a word which appears to mean the same as Haitian "zombie". Skuld is said to raise these dead by evil magic as soon as they fall. Another raiser of dead warriors by magic is Hildr. Snorri himself tells the story in *Skáldskaparmál* XLIX of how Hildr prolonged a fierce battle between her lover's and her father's armies by raising the dead fighters by night: "Now Hildr went to the slain by night, and with magic quickened all the dead. The next day the kings went to the battlefield and fought, and so did all those that had fallen on the day before. So the fight went on one day after the other: all who fell, and all those weapons which lay on the field, and the shields also, were turned to stone; but when day dawned, up rose all the dead men and fought, and all the weapons were renewed. It is said in songs that in this fashion the Hjaðnings will continue until the Ragnarök." According to this version of the story the scene of the battle is laid in the Orkneys. Saxo Grammaticus has a dim memory of Hildr's handiwork:† "They say that Hilda longed so ardently for her husband, that she is believed to have conjured up the spirits of the combatants by her spells in the

† Ch. V.

night in order to renew the war." Another account is given in
Sörlaþáttr from *Flateyjarbók*: here a mysterious woman called
Göndul forces the lover to carry off Hildr, but Göndul is only
working for the goddess Freya who creates the everlasting battle
as a labour imposed on her by Odin in order that she may re-
trieve her necklace. Saxo gives another description of the battle
seen by the hero Hadding on a journey to the Underworld
whither he is led by a mysterious woman: "Going further, they
came on a swift and tumbling river of leaden waters, whirling
down on its rapid current divers sorts of missiles, and likewise
made passable by a bridge. When they had crossed this, they
beheld two armies encountering one another with might and
main. And when Hadding enquired of the woman about their
estate: 'These', she said, 'are they who, having been slain by
the sword, declare the manner of their death by a continual re-
hearsal, and enact the deeds of their past life in a living spec-
tacle.' "

From these stories one may draw the conclusion that the everlasting battle myth was not invented by Snorri nor by the poet
of *Vafþrúðnismál*. The battle did not, of course, take place in
Orkney (as *Hrólfs saga Kraka* says); then where is it supposed to
be fought? Snorri and *Vafþrúðnismál* say in Valhalla; Saxo (in
one account) says beyond a "river of leaden waters, whirling
down on its rapid current divers sorts of missiles". This is the
river Slíðr which in *Völuspá* 34 is said to "flow from the east
out of poisonous dales" and to be a river of "daggers and
swords". Slíðr is also listed in *Grímnismál* 29 as among those
rivers which, having their source in Hvergelmir, run near the
lands of men and thence drop down to hel. The supposition is
then that the battle is connected with the other world—whether
originally Valhalla in Asgard or in hel we are left to decide.

There are stories in the sagas telling of battles in burial
mounds or other situations beneath the earth, as for instance the
tale of Þorsteinn Uxafótr in *Flateyjarbók*. Here beneath a mound
with a hall-like interior twelve black and evil men do battle
with twelve fair men dressed in red. Even after what would

appear to be deadly wounds, the men get up and fight again. Another story of dead and mutilated warriors in a howe rising to fight again is met with in *Bárðar saga Snaefellsáss* XX. These are only two examples of many similar tales.

It seems that the connection between the everlasting battle and the burial mound, howe or underworld is more likely to be the earlier notion. The battle is hardly of Norse origin: Panzer[77] has suggested a Celtic source. An Irish story with most striking resemblances to *Grímnismál's* account occurs in *The Death of Muircertach Mac Erca.*[78] A woman called Sin, who is closely connected with a fairy mound, shows her magic powers by calling upon two bodies of warriors who maim and kill each other but who rise up and eat food created magically by the woman Sin. This food consists of wine made out of water and pork made of fern leaves which (Sin promises) "she will give them forever and forever the same amount". In the Welsh *Mabinogion* there are variations of the everlasting battle in the stories of *Kulhwch and Olwen* and *Branwen the daughter of Llyr.* I have little doubt but that the Middle English alliterative poem *Sir Gawayne and the Greene Knighte* (with a narrative mainly derived from Celtic sources) has a variant of the battle story in the beheaded knight who rises to return the blow which should have killed him—his head being severed. Significantly, the knight is attached to a "Green Chapel" which from a description in the poem is evidently an ancient grave mound.

The development I would suggest of the everlasting battle story, as far as Nordic myth goes, is as follows: there is first a fight between dead men in a grave mound; usually there is a woman in the background—presumably a corpse-raiser; secondly the story is connected with the gods through the woman who becomes identified with what is to become the *Prose Edda's* conception of the Valkyrie through such women as Skuld (in *Hrólfs saga Kraka*), Hildr and Göndul (in the Hjaðning's story) women who are not yet Valkyries but all with names which are borne by Valkyries. The third and final development removes the battle from the mound or Underworld to Valhalla and Asgard and completes the development of the witch-like corpse-raiser into the dignified chooser of the slain. The warriors are linked with the final battle at the Ragnarök, possibly because in the stories the battle is an everlasting one, and certainly because the warriors became identified with the Einherjar, i.e. the Chosen Slain.

CHAPTER VII

A Dynamic Mythology

A BIRD'S EYE VIEW

A BIRD'S eye view of Northern Mythology may help us to a better understanding of it. There are dangers in such a view, for in taking it we may suppose that the body of myth has a beginning, middle and end, that it came into being complete at some point in time, that all its parts are logically connected with each other and that it is worked out according to a time scale which we imagine can be depicted as a straight line.

This is, of course, not the case.

We have seen, for instance, that Odin as Allfather is not the same as the Ancient Skyfather; that some ancient and important gods (such as Hœnir) have almost disappeared off the stage by viking times; and that new gods (such as Balder, Njörðr, Frey and Freya) have made a comparatively late entrance. In fact, in Northern Myth we have not a homogeneous oil painting by one master, but a jig-saw puzzle of pieces from different sets forced by different hands at different times willy-nilly into place and more often than not on top of one another.

Nevertheless, Snorri does present the tales as though they did have certainly a beginning and end, and a rather amorphous middle: he begins with his tales of creation and finishes with the doom of the divine powers and the suggestion of a new creation. That such was the commonly held view, at least during viking times, is borne out by the evidence of the eddaic poems: *Völuspá* presents such a picture beginning with Ginnungagap and ending with Ragnarök and the new creation; *Vafþrúðnismál* does the same. It is this picture that I hope to present now in outline.

The one who was there from the beginning of time was called Allfather. In the beginning too, there was Ginnungagap, a yawning chasm. Within Ginnungagap to the north part lay a region of freezing and fog called Niflheim, to the south a region of fire and flame named Múspellheim ruled over by a fire giant, Surtr, who grasped a flaming sword. Surtr is on the scene at the beginning of things; he is also there at the Ragnarök when he flings fire over all. Boiling and bubbling up from the centre of Niflheim surged the great source of all rivers the Roaring Cauldron Hvergelmir. The north quarter of Niflheim was frozen solid with glaciers and mountains of ice formed from Élivágar or Icy Waves, a river which had welled up from its source from time immemorial. Some evil influence was at work in Élivágar, for poison drops yeasted to the top and formed a hard scum of ice. Where the hazy heat of Múspellheim met the poisonous frost of Niflheim a thawing occurred and there was formed a giant in the likeness of a man. He was called Ymir or Aurgelmir (*Mud Seether*). Ymir began to sweat and under his left hand there grew a male and female, while his one foot begot a son upon the other: from these sprang the race of Frost Giants.

Ymir was sustained by milk from the teats of the primeval cow Auðumla (*Nourisher*) also sprung from the ice. The cow licked the icy rocks which were salty to her taste: by the evening of the first day there appeared from the ice, at the spot where she was licking, the hair of a man; on the second day, a man's head; on the third day, a man complete. This was Búri, beautiful, great and strong. His son was Bor who married Bestla a giantess, daughter of Bölþorn (*Evil Thorn*). The sons of Bor and Bestla were Odin, Vili and Vé.

The sons of Bor and the old giant Ymir fell out and the three sons killed the giant. So great a torrent of blood flowed from Ymir's wound that the rest of the Frost Giants (all except Bergelmir and his wife) were drowned. Odin, Vili and Vé removed Ymir's corpse to the middle of Ginnungagap and made the earth out of it. Lakes and seas they made from his blood;

his flesh formed the very earth, his bones and teeth became rocks, screes and mountain crags.

From the earthy-flesh of Ymir there now came as maggots, but shaped like humans, the dwarfs.

The sons of Bor took Ymir's skull to form the heavens with four of the dwarfs stationed at the corners to support it aloft. According to some authorities, the sons of Bor made the heavenly lights from sparks blown up out of Múspellheim. From this work came the tally of nights and days. The earth was round, and about it in a ring lay the sea. Along the outer shores of the sea the sons of Bor gave a grant of land to the giants to live in; but towards the centre of the earth they built a fortress from the brows of Ymir and they called it Midgard. They flung Ymir's brains to the winds and so created the clouds.

We may pause here for a moment to take up the story of Bergelmir which we left unfinished on page 62. The giant Vafþrúðnir says in *Vafþrúðnismál* that he has a memory which goes back to the time when the giant Bergelmir "was laid on a mill". The connection here is undoubtedly with the story of a great cosmic mill which ground out the earth and rocks from a giant's body. The mill known to our forefathers was the quern or handmill consisting of two circular stones one above the other. The lower mill-stone remained stationary, the upper was turned round and round by means of a handle set upright in the stone near its periphery. This handle had the name *möndull*, a word which appears cognate with Mundil—in the name Mundilfari. And so we take Mundilfari to be the one who turned the cosmic mill grinding out from the carcase of Bergelmir the rocks, skerries, islands and mainland of the world. But who *is* Mundilfari? He is the father of Sól and Máni, Sun and Moon, and for this reason probably to be identified with the old Sky Father. We seem then to have here a more ancient version of the creation of the world myth than that which makes the main protagonists Odin, Vili and Vé.

Yet a third version of the creation story is left us not in any broken narrative even, but merely in the continued existence of three names Hœnir, Langifótr and Aurkonungr, which as I have already suggested, relate to the creation of the world from the cosmic egg laid by the great bird.

A fourth version of the creation of the earth is that in which appear the descendants of Nörfi, a giant. Nörfi seems to be a name for the Dark Moon, and he had a daughter called Night whose *second* husband is known to us only by the name Annarr which means "the second". Their child was Earth, and so it becomes evident that Annarr is the Sky Father and we can regard as confirmation of this that Annarr was later used as a bye-name of Odin. Night also had children by Naglfari and Dellingr. Dellingr is Dayspring or Dawn and Naglfari is Twilight; in other words Dellingr and Naglfari are simply manifestations of particular aspects of the Sky Father. The Sky Father as Dawn begat Day upon Night, and as Twilight he begat Space. The Allfather (i.e. the Sky Father) then despatched Night and Day each with a chariot and pair of horses to drive round the heavens once in every twenty-four hours. Sól and Máni I have just mentioned and have suggested that originally their father Mundilfari may have been identified with the Sky Father in his role of the Great Turner of the heavens.

The three sons of Bor (now called Odin, Hœnir and Lóðurr as well as Odin, Vili and Vé) created men to people the world. They are said to have brought into being Askr and Embla, man and woman, from trees or from logs of driftwood.

These, then, are the remains of the primitive myths and they are mainly concerned with the creation of the world and man, the heavenly bodies, night and day: and at the centre of them all we may suspect the presence of Allfather, the Sky Father. These are the remnants of the ancient myths, the tales which were current among the Indo-European tribes before they split up and wandered afar from each other. Many tales are lost; others live on in a modified form connected as they are with gods whose roots reach back to Indo-European times: such stories are those which tell how Odin lost his eye, how Týr lost his hand (both gods in these cases are hypostases of the Sky Father), how Heimdallr should be the son of nine mothers, and so on. Mímir the giant of the deep with his well of wisdom seems to belong to these early tales as does Urðr and her two sister fates, and Ægir god of the sea.

The body of myth now begins to take on a form which we have come to recognize as peculiarly Northern, and by "now" I mean a date round about the birth of Christ. Odin, originally Lord of the Wind and a leader of souls rushing through the air, is assuming the attributes of *Djevs the Sky Father, and *Djevs himself is developing into the Northern Týr, a pale god of war. Odin sits "now" on the skiey throne Hliðskjálf; he has usurped the seat of *Djevs—although he is still often depicted as a wanderer through the world under such guises as Gangleri "Wayweary". Odin looks out over all the worlds, "now" conceived of as being supported by "Odin's Steed" Yggdrasill the World Ash: he looks over Asgard, Midgard, Jötunheim and hel. As a patriarch Odin is the father of the Æsir, the progenitor of the race of gods by his wife Jörð (Earth) or Frigg. But, as in even the best regulated families, things are not what they seem: Odin is the father of Thor, Heimdallr, Hermóðr, Höðr, Týr and Víðarr in the same make-believe way as Peter Pan is father of the Lost Boys. Certain of the gods and goddesses are said plainly to be of another race, the Vanir; and their presence in the Northern pantheon is explained by the tale of the war in heaven. After the war between Æsir and Vanir, hostages were exchanged and Njörðr (a fertility god who became god of the sea) was brought among the Æsir together with his two children Frey and Freya.

There is among the Æsir a creature of evil, namely Loki. Loki is no relation to the inhabitants of Asgard except that he is a blood-brother of Odin. By a witch-like giantess Angrboða, Loki fathers three monstrous and evil beings, Fenriswulf (who is destined to destroy Odin), Jörmungandr the World Serpent (who will kill Thor), and Hel. For the time being the gods stave off disaster by binding Fenriswulf (at the sacrifice of Týr's hand), by casting the World Serpent into the sea and Hel into Niflheim where she becomes queen of the dead.

It is evident that the gods are in the hands of fate and steadily moving towards their doom, the Ragnarök. On this day, the forces of evil, Frost Giants, Mountain Giants, Fire Giants, Hel and her children all led by Loki and Surtr will march against the gods. It seems that Balder is in some way connected with the Doom: his death will presage the onset of Ragnarök and for this reason the gods deem it meet to take extraordinary methods to protect his life, but Balder is slain by the machinations of Loki whom the gods bind in the underworld.

Such a fateful mythology was evidently to the taste of the men of the viking age. Odin for them takes on the character- istics of a warrior and a general in war. Ably assisted by Thor, he directs the continual struggle against the forces of evil, the giants, and he continues his part as a leader of souls by be- coming the patron of all fighters killed in battle. These are to congregate with him in his hall of the slain, Valhalla, there to wait for the ominous cock-crow on the morning of Ragnarök.

At the Ragnarök the demons destroy the gods and the world; but a new heaven and a new earth arise after the fires of Surtr have done their worst. Two human beings, Líf and Lífþrasir hide in Hoddmímir's Holt and survive the cataclysm: they repeople the earth. And Balder, Hœnir and other gods re- turn in peace to heaven.

We can see that there are two beginnings to this system of mythology, one belonging to Indo-European times with the Sky Father in a supreme place and with its early stories of creation; the other, with Odin as chief deity, belonging to Gothonic times and more specifically in the early centuries of the Christian era to Scandinavia and Iceland. I have dealt with the old creation stories in some detail in Chapter II; before I go on to the myths connected with particular gods I want to sum- marize the early narrative of the Odinic system of tales: this is concerned largely with the Golden Age which was brought to an end by the stealing of Iðunn's apples and the war in heaven.

2

THE GOLDEN AGE

The Golden Age of the Æsir is described by Snorri in *Gylfaginning* XIV: "In the beginning Odin appointed his chief helpers and bade them assist him in arranging the fates of men and the running of the fortress; this took place at Iðavöllr or Idavale which lies in the middle of their stronghold. Their first task was to build that edifice in which stand their twelve thrones and one higher than the rest for the Father of All. That building is the best in the world and the vastiest: within and without it is like burning gold. Men call it Glaðsheimr ('Place of Joy'). A second hall which they built was a fane for the goddesses; it too was very fair: men call it Vingólf ('Friendly Floor'). Their next job was a workshop in which they set a forge and made besides a hammer, tongs and an anvil, and by means of these all other kinds of tools. Next they made metal, stone and wood—particularly that metal called gold, enough to have all their delf and dishes of gold. That's why this time is called the Golden Age, before it was destroyed by the coming of the Women, they who came from Giantland."

For his account, Snorri was drawing on the *Verse Edda*: occasionally he omits a detail, occasionally he merely repeats or transcribes a bit of obscure information of whose meaning he himself is patently unsure. One such obscure passage is the recital of the termination of the Golden Age by "the women who came from Giantland". But before I discuss this, I may note other details of the Æsir's life in the morning of their time. According to *Völuspá* 8, their recreation, as they peacefully passed their days, was a game of tables resembling chess or draughts. It was ever summer,† with green grass, blue seas,

† *Völ.* 58, 61.

cataracts drifting down like veils from the high crags above which the eagle soared and below which fish flickered in the clear rivers. Fields were ripe with self-sown grain. Time had no meaning, no existence, and all the world was young. The Æsir maintained their eternal youth by eating the apples of the goddess Iðunn. Snorri says,† "Iðunn guards within her ashwood casket the apples which the gods have to nibble at as they age and fail—then all at once they are young again: this goes on right up to the Ragnarök."

This idyllic existence was terminated by the "coming of the Women, they who came from Giantland". We are nowhere told directly who the "Women" are. *Völuspá* 8 is the source and it does give a little more information than Snorri passes on. It says there were *three* of these women; that they were giant maidens *þursa meyjar* from Jötunheim (*Giantland*); and they were possessed of immense power. These attributes may be applied most fittingly in Northern Myth to the three Nornir. The chief Nornir are three in number and they are said in *Vafþrúðnismál* 49 to be of giant race. There is no doubt of their possessing immense power: they are the Fates. They determine the period of men's lives and in *Gylfaginning* XVI they are depicted as the preservers of the fabric of all creation as they sprinkle the water from Urðr's well over the trunk of the World Ash. The Anglo-Saxon race maintained their belief in the tremendous power of the oldest of the three sisters, Urðr, long after they had been converted to Christianity. Urðr in Old English has the form *Wyrd* which means "fate" the compelling power and final destiny which no man and no thing may escape: the word occurs with this meaning nine times in the O.E. poem *Beowulf,* and lived in the English language at least down to Shakespearean days with much of its original sense,‡ and to the present in the Scots' idiom "to dree one's weird". As far as the Northmen were concerned not even Odin could

† *Gylf.* XXVI.

‡ Cf. *Macbeth:* the Weird Sisters—*three* witches with power to foretell the future and apparently to affect the course of events.

escape his "weird" in spite of his communing with it in any great crisis. Thus the Nornir could be said to be all-powerful. That the Nornir are pre-Odinic is suggested by the fact that Odin is in their power; this suggestion is bolstered up by the further fact of the Nornir's going back to Indo-European times. The ancestresses of the Nornir were those beings who also gave rise to the Greek Moirai, the goddesses of Fate. According to Greek Myth the Moirai were amongst the children of Night: and Night, as we know, was one of the more ancient beings of Northern myth—older at any rate than the viking god Odin. The Orphists said that the Moirai lived in heaven, in a cave by a pool whose white water gushed from the cave. This, says Kerényi[79] is a clear image of moonlight. The name *moira* means "part" and "their number, so the Orphists claim, correspond to the 'parts' of the moon; and that is why Orpheus sings of 'the Moirai in white raiment'."[80] The Nornir are of course connected strongly with a well, Urðr's well, which is also said to be situated in heaven, and whose water is evidently *white* if we are to judge by its effect on Yggdrasill which turns white as the film inside an egg wherever the water from Urðr's well drops on its roots and trunk. We may suspect with good reason then, that originally the Nornir and the phases of the moon had much in common, especially the phases of the moon as an ancient measure of time. We have found that Odin's supremacy in the Norse pantheon dates from later times, from about the beginning of the Christian era: it is reasonable therefore that the three ancient Fates should have power over him. But if the Fates date from Indo-European times, as *fates* they must have had dominion over the Sky Father as well. How can we reconcile the idea of two omnipotent powers co-existing? The clue to the position is surely contained in the association, identification rather, of the Fates with the moon. Our ancestors were witnesses of the Shining One's, the Sky Father's daily omnipotence and nightly displacement by the moon. Certainly he did come to full life and power each morning, but still each night the moon replaced him in one of her *three* different aspects, Crescent (*Urðr*), Full (*Verðandi*) and Waning (*Skuld*).

The names of the three Nornir are Urðr, Verðandi and Skuld, words which may be translated Past, Present and Future: so that when "the three giant maids came from Giant-land" they brought with them *time*; then the timeless existence of the youthful gods in the Ancient Asgard ceased, and they put off their immortality. From the "coming of the women" the predestined events must take place one after the other until the Doom of the Gods.

3

THE STEALING OF IÐUNN'S APPLES

Another story which tells of the letting in of time is that relating how Iðunn was kidnapped from Asgard. The Æsir, deprived of the youth-giving apples, began to grow old. Although this tale is told only by Snorri there is no doubt of its currency during heathen times. There is a reference to it in *Hárbarðsljóð* 19 where Thor says he killed the giant Þjazzi and cast his eyes into the heavens to serve as stars. Snorri's version of the myth goes like this:

"The three gods Odin, Loki and Hœnir set out from home and tramped through the mountains and desert places until they were hard put to it to know where to look for food. At last, they dropped down into a valley where they saw a herd of cattle grazing and cornering an ox, they set about roasting it. When they thought it ought to be cooked they kicked away the embers only to find that it wasn't done. They let an hour pass and once more scattered the fire, but still the meat was not done. 'Now what's going on here?' they said to one another. They heard words coming from an oak tree over their heads, saying that he who sat there had held up the cooking. Glancing that way they saw perching on a bough an eagle—and no pigeon. The eagle enquired, 'Will you give me my fill of the ox if I allow it to cook through?' They all said yes. So he let himself glide down out of the tree, went to the fire and began at once to gobble the two hams and both shoulders. Loki was incensed at this and grabbed up a long stave which he swung as hard as he could right at the eagle's body. The eagle hopped away sharply from the blow and took off. In an instant the stave stuck to the eagle's back and Loki's two hands to the other end of the stave. The eagle then flew at such a height that Loki's legs bashed against rocks and screes and bushes, while he felt as though his arms would be torn out of his shoulders. He yelled at the top of his voice asking the eagle to come to terms, and the eagle said he should never get loose unless he swore him an oath to entice Iðunn out of Asgard along with her apples; which Loki did, and was at once set free to hobble back to his comrades. Nor is there anything else worth telling about this journey before they came back home.

"At the time arranged, Loki drew Iðunn out of Asgard into a certain wood by saying that he had discovered some apples which she of all people must think to be without price. He told her to bring her own apples so that he and she could compare them.

"Then the giant Þjazzi came in his eagle's guise and seized Iðunn and flew off with her to his dwelling in Þrymheimr. But the Æsir took Iðunn's disappearance much to heart and quickly they began to grow aged and grey. The Æsir then met together to discuss with one another what was the latest that had been heard of Iðunn and came to the conclusion that she had last been seen walking out of Asgard with Loki. At once Loki was caught and frog-marched to their meeting where they threatened him with torture and death. When he was sufficiently scared he promised to search for Iðunn into Jötunheim provided Freya would lend him the hawk skin she owned. He took the hawk skin, flew north into Jötunheim and came one day to the giant Þjazzi's. Þjazzi was rowing out at sea, but Iðunn was at home. Loki turned her into the likeness of a nut which he clutched in his talons and flew off like the wind.

FIG. 17 EAGLE IN FLIGHT

A motif from the Sutton Hoo shield. The eagle figured prominently in Northern Mythology, as for instance in the story of Hræsvelg, the giant in eagle's guise whose flapping wings caused the wind, Odin stealing the mead of poesy, or Þjazzi stealing Iðunn's apples.

"But when Þjazzi returned home and missed Iðunn he took his eagle skin off the hook and zoomed after Loki with a great rushing noise in his flight.

"The Æsir saw where a hawk clutching a nut was flying, and overhauling him an eagle, so they hurried out under Asgard walls carrying with them a bin full of wood shavings. When the hawk flew into the fortress he let himself glide down by the ramparts and at that moment the Æsir struck fire to the plane shavings; but then the eagle lost the hawk and could not stop his flight; the rising flames ran through his feathers and he dropped to the ground. The Æsir were waiting and they killed the giant Þjazzi right in the entrance to Asgard gates—and that struggle is a very famous one.

"But Skaði, daughter of the giant Þjazzi took helmet and byrnie and all the weapons of war and went to Asgard to avenge her father. The Æsir offered her reconciliation and compensation, and first of all that she should choose herself a husband from among the Æsir provided she made her choice only by seeing his ankles and no more of him. She saw one man's feet which were surpassingly fair and said, 'I choose this one: there can be little about Balder that's ugly.' It was, however, Njörðr

of Nóatún. The other condition attached to the reconciliation
was that the Æsir should do a thing which she believed to be
quite impossible, to make her laugh. So Loki fastened a cord
to a billy-goat's beard and knotted the other end round his own
balls: each one gave way in turn and both of them screeched
loudly. At last Loki allowed himself to fall on to Skaði's lap
at which she burst out laughing: and so a reconciliation was
effected between her and the Æsir.

"They do say that Odin also compensated Skaði by taking
Þjazzi's eyes, flinging them up into the vault of heaven and
making a pair of stars out of them."

One may see from the myth just recounted that it is unreasonable to expect detailed consistency in the stories: they are
not history. If the myth of the stealing of Iðunn's apples were
to be consistent, then either the *áss* Hœnir would not have been
journeying with Odin and Loki or else the *vanr* Njörðr would
not be among the Æsir to marry Skaði nor would Freya be
there to lend her feather coat: for, after the war between Æsir
and Vanir, Hœnir was exchanged as a hostage for Njörðr and
went to live in Vanaheim. The best one can say is that the
stealing of Iðunn's apples was regarded as taking place early in
the gods' occupation of Asgard. The same may be said of the
war between Æsir and Vanir, for the *Vanr* hostage Njörðr
(together with his children Frey and Freya) takes part in most
of the myths relating to the Æsir.

4

THE WAR IN HEAVEN

The details of the myth about the war in heaven are confusing;
but the fundamental ideas are easy to grasp. The war between
Æsir and Vanir represents a struggle in men's minds between
the older religion of the north as seen in the beliefs about Odin,
Thor, Hœnir and other gods with Indo-European affiliations
set against the cults of Njörðr, Frey and Freya who were in-

truders from the south, from Asia Minor. In such a case of warring gods it is usual for one side to be vanquished and to be driven (literally) underground: the old gods become the demons, goblins, elves and fairies of the new regime. But in the fight between Æsir and Vanir the result was a draw, with a reorganized pantheon made up of gods and goddesses from both races, certain of the Æsir being displaced to make way for the so-called "hostages" from Vanaheim.

It is certain that the Æsir lost Hœnir (not really because he was banished to Vanaheim, but because he had become a nonentity—the myths about him had been forgotten); it is less certain that the other hostage, Mímir, was ever a true *áss*. Balder and Frigg are certainly intruders from the south east as well as the Vanir, but appear to have got established in the Æsir pantheon before Njörðr, Frey and Freya, and so are regarded as members of the Æsir.

What then of the confusing details of the war in heaven? It appears that Freya the incomparable goddess of beauty, love and fruitfulness was stolen from Asgard by the Frost Giants. Nothing in nature prospered and the air was filled with rottenness.† It looks as if that other emblem and mainspring of life and fertility, the Sun (as well as the Moon), had been stolen away too. The rape of Freya was in some way connected with an evil woman, a witch from Giantland who had insinuated herself into Freya's good graces in Asgard. When the Æsir discovered their loss, they took the witch and meted out to her the age-old Indo-European punishment for sorcery: they burnt her alive, and they did it ceremonially, spitting her at the apex of an arch of spears which they held over the long-fire running down the middle of Valhalla. Though carbonized, the witch was not destroyed but came alive again: three times they burnt her and three times she lived. On the last occasion, Loki found her living heart among the ashes of her body and swallowed it.

† There appears to be a remembrance of this myth in *A Midsummer Night's Dream* where Titania describes the reversal of the seasons following on her quarrel with Oberon over the 'Indian Boy'.

This evil heart, working within the evil Loki, fertilised him and he gave birth to the wolf Fenrir from whom sprang all the race of wolves, including those who were to swallow the sun and moon.

When the Vanir heard how the Æsir had murdered the witch they demanded restitution at a Thing; for it seems that the evil witch was a relative by marriage of one of their number being, ironically enough, the mother-in-law of Frey whose sister Freya the murdered witch had been instrumental in abducting. Such a situation, a struggle between love and duty, was of course dear to the Nordic mind and there was to the Northman nothing ridiculous in the Vanir's demand for wergild for a person who had done them an injury but who was nevertheless a relative. Not to attempt every means of obtaining restitution or revenge would have been craven and therefore unthinkable. But, for their part, neither would the Æsir give way. Odin brought the Thing to an end by flinging his spear. War between the two sets of deities followed and the walls of Asgard were broken down and the "war-wise Vanir were able to tread the field". The phrase "to tread the field" *völlu sporna* appears to be a parallel to the O.E. *wigstead healdan* "to possess the (battle) field" met with so often in the *Old English Chronicle* during the years of the viking invasions. Such a phrase seems to indicate a victory but a rather incomplete one; at any rate, the opponent lives to fight again.

The Æsir and Vanir patched up a truce according to the terms of which two Æsir (Hœnir and Mímir) were exchanged for Njörðr, father of Frey and Freya who also came to live in Asgard. Another deity, Kvasir (by some accounts a *Vanr*, by others a product of the mixture of Æsir's and Vanir's spittle) is also mentioned as a hostage in Asgard.

The sources on which I have based the above account of the War are poems from the *Verse Edda*, Skaldic poems, Snorri's *Edda*, *Ynglinga Saga* and Saxo's *History of the Danes*: no one can be certain that the account is as I have given it. The trouble is that the sources relating to the War are fragmentary, allusive

5 BRONZE AGE SUN IMAGE

Found in Trundholm Mose (North Zealand). The sun-disk stands on a six-wheeled carriage of bronze which also supports a bronze horse; originally traces had passed from a loop on the front edge of the disk to the horse. The belief that the sun was drawn across the heavens by his steed was commonly held by the Scandinavian peoples.

6 THE SYMBOLISM OF THE TREE

The theory of the phallic symbolism behind Yggdrasill, the World Ash, is given
support by various medieval pictures of the tree of Jesse. But whereas these are all
to some extent stylised, the above drawing is blunt and unmistakable: it represents
Adam as *prima materia*, pierced by the arrow of Mercurius. From the 14th century
MS. 'Miscellanea d'alchimia', Biblioteca Medicea-Laurenziana.

and show events in a confused order. There are half-a-dozen or so stanzas on the subject in *Völuspá*; but confusion is worse confounded because the order of the stanzas in the two manuscripts of *Völuspá* (*Codex Regius* and *Hauksbók*) is quite different. For instance, the two stanzas which tell of the air filled with decay, of the abduction of Óðr's bride (Freya) and the anger of Thor, come together in both manuscripts. But while in *Hauksbók* these events start the train and give a reason for the Æsir's murdering the evil witch, in *Codex Regius* the two stanzas come *after* the account of the murder of the witch and *after* the war between Æsir and Vanir. Yet another variant is given by Snorri (in *Gylfaginning* XLII) who quotes the two stanzas to support a different myth altogether—the tale of the first building of Asgard walls. In Snorri's account, Freya, together with the sun and moon, is merely promised to the giants who in the end are baulked of their reward by a trick: in other words Freya is not delivered to the giants. But other accounts show that Freya does spend a time in captivity with the Frost Giants and we can safely say that Snorri is backing up one myth with a quotation from another. Freya's captivity and Thor's anger at it are part of the same fertility myth. It seems probable that this anger is remembered to this day in the folklore assertion that summer lightning ripens the corn, i.e. brings back fertility to the fields (whether Freya or Sif is the goddess concerned in this anger of Thor's is really immaterial).

In the *Verse Edda* there is no myth of the first building of Asgard walls such as Snorri gives to account for the birth of Sleipnir, Odin's eight-legged horse. But Snorri's bringing together of the idea of Freya, sun and moon being promised to the giants, and the two stanza quotation from *Völuspá* about Óðr's maid being given to the giants, etc., and the tale of the building of a wall round Asgard, all suggests that this building was originally a re-building of the walls after they had been breached by the Vanir.

5

THE BUILDING OF ASGARD WALLS

Snorri says,† "It happened early on in the dawn of the gods' settling here: they had finished Midgard and just built Valhalla when up came a certain Master Mason who promised to build them (within the space of three seasons) a fortress so stuggy and steep it would be proof against both Hill Trolls and Frost Giants—even though they managed to burst into Midgard. His wages? He asked them for the hand of Freya—oh yes, and he wanted the sun and moon thrown in.

"The gods called a meeting-extraordinary and set to arguing the matter out one against the other. They made this bargain with the Mason: he should get what he asked for provided he could build the bastions in one winter alone. If, by the first day of summer, the last of the stones was unfaced even, then the payment as agreed on should be off. Nor was he to get help with his task from anybody. When they told him these conditions he asked if he might just have the assistance of his horse called Svaðilfari, and Loki's advice weighted the beam and they agreed to it.

"He marked out the foundations of the walls on the first day of winter, and that same night hauled up boulders by means of his horse. It set the gods back quite a bit to see what mountainous rocks that animal could drag, for it seemed the horse was doing half as much again of that superhuman task as the Mason was. Moreover there had been strong witnesses to the solemn agreement, and many binding oaths, for it didn't seem right to the giant to be among the gods without a safe-conduct, especially if Thor should chance to come home. But at that time he was knocking about the east hunting trolls.

"Now as winter melted away, the stronghold was nearly done and was so lofty and stout it could not possibly be taken

† *Gylf.* XLII.

by storm. And when it needed only three days to summer the job was finished right up to the fort gate. Then the gods sat down in their judgment seats and scratched their polls and bickered one with another as to who it was had advised the delivering up of Freya into Giantland or the destruction of the sky and the heavens by taking away the sun and the moon and giving them to the ettins. Everyone agreed these things must have been advised by the person notorious for his evil counsels, Loki Laufeyjarson, and they said he deserved an ill death if he didn't hit on a plan to diddle the Mason out of his pay: moreover they gave him a good drubbing. Then, when he was at his wit's end with fear he swore oaths he would so work it out that the Mason should lose his reward, let the cost be what it may.

"That very evening when the Mason drove off for stones with his stallion Svaðilfari, there trotted from the forest a mare who whinnied to the stallion as she did so. When he recognized the new horse for a mare his loins tingled, he snapped his traces and lept for her and she away under the trees, and the Mason after, intending to capture his beast of burden. But those horses vanished away all that night and the work could not proceed for the time being. Dawn came and no building went on as it had been wont to do. When the Mason realized that he would not finish his task in time he flung into a gigantic fury; and when the gods saw for certain that a giant of the mountains had indeed come amongst them they thought 'Oh blow!' to their oaths and hollered out for Thor. He rushed up quicksticks and next minute his hammer Mullicrusher soared into the sky. It was he who paid the Mason his wages, and not with the sun or moon. In fact, he even denied him the right to live in Giantland. He let fly but the one blow so that his skull exploded into dust, and sent him down under into Niflheim.

"But Loki had such carryings on with Svaðilfari that some time after he gave birth to a foal: it was a grey and had eight legs. And this horse is the best among gods and men. As it says in the Spaewife's Song:

Then strode the heavenly Powers
to their judgment seats,
   and the holy gods
   put their heads together
to seek the would-be causer
of the blacked out skies
   and the loosing to the Giants
   of Óðr's lady.

Solemn oaths were broken
word and bond
   and binding pledges
   which had passed between them.
Thor alone hammered,
knotted with anger:
   could he sit quiet by
   hearing such shocking schemes?"

These then are the stories of the early days of the Æsir. Now
we come to tales of the individual gods.

CHAPTER VIII

Tales of Odin and Thor

I HAVE told the stories (in Chapter IV) of how Odin won wisdom at the price of his eye and at the price of privation by being wounded and hanged on the "Windy Tree". Many tales concerning the gods have been lost, and as far as Odin is concerned we are reminded of our loss by some of his nicknames (recounted in *Grímnismál* and elsewhere) connected with his behaviour in half-forgotten myths. There is a certain amount of evidence that one such half-forgotten myth comes into the wisdom-winning category: I am referring to the wresting of wisdom from Mímir. There are two recognizable versions remembered in *Völuspá* 28 (where Mímir drinks mead from Odin's eye every morning) and in *Völuspá* 45 (where wisdom comes from Mímir's severed head). The explanation of the cutting off of Mímir's head usually given is that already told, namely that the Vanir decapitated him: but there are relics of a quite different account:

I

ODIN AND MÍMIR'S HEAD

What were the details of the original myth which the following scraps are hiding, is anybody's guess: Odin in *Grímnismál* 50 says "I was called Sviðurr and Sviðrir at Sökk-Mímir's when I fooled the old giant and single-handed became the death of that famous son of Miðvitnir". From this we gather that Odin journeyed to the underworld to *Sunk-Mímir* (*Mímir of the deep*) as usual in disguise. His identity was covered by the name Sviðurr or Sviðrir, who appears to be the same as Svigðir or Svegðir (a name connected with "swig") mentioned in *Ynglingatál* 2 and a noted drinker. In other words, the purpose of Odin's visit to Sökk-Mímir the son of Miðvitnir (? Mjöð-vitnir of *Völuspá* 11 "Meadwolf"—the stealer of the mead of inspiration, poetry or wisdom) was to gain a "swig" of the mead. In the course of gaining his drink of mead Odin slew Sökk-Mímir. This slaying appears to be referred to in *Sigrdrí-fumál* 12 and 13: stanza 13 runs "He stood on the cliff with Brimir's sword and wearing a helmet on his head: then Mímir's head spoke the first word and uttered verses of truth". Stanza 12 says "Hroptr [the Sage, a nickname of Odin] read them [the runes of wisdom], cut them and thought them out from the lees which had leaked out of Heiðdraupnir's skull and out of Hoddrofnir's horn". One great difficulty of interpretation arises from the proper names. There is a giant Brimir who has a mead hall in a part of the underworld which marches with Niðavellir, in a region called Ókólnir "the Never Cold". *Völuspá* 35 says "there stood in Ókólnir the mead hall of the giant called Brimir". As for Heiðdraupnir ("Clear-dripper") and Hoddrofnir ("Treasure-opener") they are nicknames and seem to mean Mímir. The culmination of the story may be found in *Haleygjatál* 2

> . . . *hinn es Surtz or Sökkdaolum*
> (*far-maognoðr*), *fliugandi bar* . . .†

"He, the mighty traveller who flying bore (the mead) from Surtr's deep dales. . . ." One manuscript of *Grímnismál* has an extra half line among a list of "best things" which names "Brimir best of swords" (*C.P.B.* I, p. 77).

It is tempting to see these scraps of a jig-saw puzzle falling into place something as follows: Odin visited the underworld in disguise to obtain a draught of the mead of wisdom, inspira-tion or poetry; the mead had been stolen by the giants (actually by Miðvitnir "the Mead Wolf") and was kept in Ókólnir, a name which suggests a region of fire and flame such as that where Surtr lived. Indeed, we are told that the mead was car-ried by Odin from "Surtr's deep dales". But before he could

† (*C.P.B.* I, p. 252.)

come at the mead Odin had to cut off Sökk-Mímir's head with the best of swords which belonged to Surtr. Odin achieved his quest. With the materials remaining we can hardly say more.

2

ODIN AND THE WINNING OF POESY

This is the story according to Snorri in *Skáldskaparmál* I: When the Æsir and Vanir had appointed a peace-meeting to terminate their war, each side went up to a vat and spat their spittle into it. After the meeting, the Æsir were loath to see the peace-token perish and so from the mixture of salivas they created Kvasir, a person so wise that no question ever found him lacking an answer. He went up and down the earth instructing men and came at their invitation to the home of two dwarfs, Fjalarr and Galarr. This pair treacherously killed him and drained his blood into two vats and a cauldron. The name of the cauldron is Óðrerir and of the vats, Són and Boðn. The dwarfs mixed honey with Kvasir's blood to produce that mead by virtue of which any man who drinks becomes a poet or scholar. The dwarfs reported to the Æsir that Kvasir had choked on his own shrewdness, there being none wise enough to question *his* wisdom.

Fjalarr and Galarr next invited to their home a giant called Gillingr and his wife. The dwarfs entreated the giant to go rowing with them and when they were far from land and in choppy water they overturned the boat and drowned the giant who could not swim. They then righted the boat and rowed back to land.

Gillingr's wife was noisily upset at the drowning of her husband. The blubbering got on Fjalarr's nerves and he decided to do away with the mourning giantess. He asked her if it would ease her heart to gaze on the sea where Gillingr had perished and she said it would. Fjalarr then spoke quietly to his brother Galarr, instructing him to climb up over the doorway and to drop a millstone on the giantess' head as she walked out. This was done.

When the news came to the ears of Gillingr's son Suttungr, he went off to the dwarfs, collared them and rowed them out to a reef which was covered at high tide. Fjalarr and Galarr, despairing of their lives, begged Suttungr to take the precious mead as a wergild for his father's death. Suttungr accepted the mead, transporting it to his home and concealing it in the place called Hnitbjörg (*Lock Rock*) and setting his daughter Gunnlöð to watch over it.

The mead eventually came into the possession of the Æsir and in this manner. Odin left home and reached a certain place where nine thralls were mowing hay. He asked if they would like their scythes sharpened and when they said yes he took a hone from his belt and whetted the scythes. They were so pleased at the result that they asked to buy the hone. He said the price on the hone was an exceedingly dear one but they agreed to pay it. At this, Odin flung the hone into the air, the nine thralls ran at once with their scythes over the shoulders to get it and in their eagerness fatally chopped each other's necks.

Odin then sought a night's lodging with the giant Baugi the brother of Suttungr. Baugi complained that his farming would fail since his nine thralls had killed one another for he could get no other workmen. Odin (who gave his name as Bölverkr— *Balework*) declared that he would do nine men's work for Baugi in return for one drink of Suttungr's Mead. Baugi said he had no control at all over the mead but that he would go with Odin to his brother and try to get him a sup. Odin did nine men's work all summer for Baugi and when the winter came he asked for his wages. They set out for Suttungr's together and Baugi told his brother of the bargain. Suttungr refused flatly to give up a drop of the mead. Odin suggested a stratagem: he pulled out the auger called Rati and invited Baugi to bore through the rock to get at the mead. Baugi did so and finally declared the rock bored through, but the wily Odin blew into the hole and found the chips flying back into his face.

Baugi would have deceived him. Odin ordered Baugi to bore once more until the hole went right through the rock. Odin tested this by blowing, when the chips went inwards. Then Odin changed himself into a snake, crawled into the auger hole and had he not been quick, Baugi would have destroyed him for he thrust after him into the hole.

Odin crawled to where Gunnlöð was and lay with her for three nights; after which she gave him leave to take three drinks of the mead. In the first draught he drank every drop out of Óðrerir; in the second he emptied Boðn; and in the third, Són. After which he turned himself into the shape of an eagle and flew off as furiously as he could. But when Suttungr saw what had happened, he too turned himself into an eagle and pursued Odin.

When the Æsir saw Odin flying, they set out their vats in the courtyard and when Odin came into Asgard he spat the mead into those vats. Still, he came so near to being caught by Suttungr that he squittered some of the mead backwards and no heed was taken of it. Whosoever wants it may have it: it is called the poetaster's port. But Odin gave Suttungr's mead to the Æsir and to those men who have the ability to compose.

This story is alluded to in *Hávamál*. The allusions are tantalizing for they seem to hold details of a version of the myth different from that just related. Odin declares in *Hávamál* 13–14: "The heron of forgetfulness hovers over banquets and steals away men's wits: I myself was fettered with that bird's feathers when I lay in Gunnlöð's house. I was drunk—I was dead drunk at the wise Fjalarr's: and the only comfort is that a drunkard's wits do come home when he's sober." Again in stanzas 104–110 Odin says "I sought out the old giant,—now I have come back. I should not have got far there by keeping mum: many a word I spoke to my profit in Suttungr's hall. Gunnlöð gave me a drink of the precious mead as I sat in a golden chair; I let her have an ill repayment for her loyal heart and faithful love. I let the point of Rati gnaw through the rock, so that the paths of the giant lay above and below me

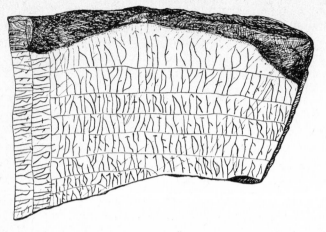

FIG. 18   THE RÖK STONE

This stone from Rök, East-Gotland, Sweden, is 13 ft. high and has the longest
extant single inscription in runes. The top line reads *Aft Uamuþ stonta runar þar*,
"These runes stand after Uamuth."

both: that's how I risked my neck. The fraud-got mead has
profited me well and the wise man lacks nothing now that
Óðrerir is come up into the midst of men on earth. I doubt
whether I should ever have escaped from the giants' garth if
Gunnlöð had not helped me—that best of women within
whose arms I had lain. Next day, the frost giants came...
asking after Bölverkr, whether he was back with the gods or
had Suttungr managed to kill him?" The poet then permits
himself this comment, "Odin, I am sure, had taken the oath
on the ring: who shall ever believe his word again? He
swindled Suttungr out of his mead and left Gunnlöð to
weep."

There is one other reference to the winning of inspiration in
Hávamál 140. Óðin says, "I learnt nine mighty charms from
the son of Bölþorn the father of Bestla; and I got a drink of the
precious mead poured out from Óðrerir." Bestla was, of course,
the mother of Odin, and the son of Bölþorn must then have
been Odin's uncle. It has been suggested that this uncle was

Mímir who gave Odin nine charms which enabled him to win the mead. Who knows?

3

ODIN AND BILLING'S DAUGHTER

Another cryptic tale is contained in *Hávamál* 96–102: Odin says, ". . . I crouched in the rushes, waiting for my love: the gentle maiden was to me as my own flesh and blood, and yet I never had her. I found Billing's daughter, white as the sun, sleeping upon her bed: an earldom seemed empty to me living without her fair body. 'Odin,' she said, 'you must return in the evening if you wish to talk with me. It would be my ruin if any but us two knew of our unlawful love.' I turned away, I was blind with love, I was certain I would win her body and soul. And so I came again in the gloaming only to find the armed retainers all awake with burning torches and flaming lights: I had had my walk for nothing. Then, when I came once more, near morning time, all the hall-retainers were snoring and I saw only the fair lady's hound chained upon her bed."

One may suspect that a good deal of this story is missing; that originally it told of a succession of attempts by Odin upon the love of Billing's daughter. If this is so, then the events it resembles most are those recounted by Saxo (Bk. iii, 78 ff.) when Odin attempted to win the love of Rinda in order to beget a son to avenge Balder. The three references to Rindr (*Rinda, Wrindr*) in the verses are a curious refrain by Cormac Ogmundsson, *Baldrs Draumar* 11 and *Grógaldr ok Fjölsvinns-mál* (*Svipdagsmál*) 6. Cormac in his *Sigvodardrapa* merely says† *Seið Yggr til Vrindar* "Yggr (*Odin*) put a charm on Rindr", which recalls Saxo's account (iii, 79) of how Odin attempted to kiss Rindr at which "she repulsed him so that he tottered and smote his chin upon the ground. Straightway he touched her with a piece of bark whereon spells were written, and made her

† *C.P.B.* II, 33.

like unto one in frenzy". In the guise of a woman skilled in leechcraft Odin pretended to cure Rindr of her condition and took his opportunity of getting his son Váli upon her body. *Baldrs Draumar* 11 says "In the Western Halls Rindr shall bear a son, Váli, who when but one night old shall avenge Odin's son. He shall neither wash his hands nor comb his hair before he bears to the funeral fire the killer of Balder." And *Svipdagsmál* speaks of a charm which Gróa sings over her son, "The first charm I chant thee is one such as Rindr chanted over Rani: it will stand thee in good stead in casting off from thy shoulder whatever evil thou encounterest: trust in thine own powers."

On the one hand, in the myth of Billing's daughter we see solar allusions in the adjective *sól-hvíta* "white as the sun" applied to the maiden, together with the fact that during the day she is absent from her couch; and on the other hand, the solar allusions are there too in the story of Rindr who bears her son in the "Halls of the West" where the sun sinks and is renewed, and in Váli who achieves his purpose in the course of one day.

In spite of the hundred and sixteen names and nicknames for Odin given in *Þulor* (C.P.B. II, p. 426) there is little else left to be told specially of him. What remains will be better kept for the account of the Doom of the Divine Powers.

4

THOR AND GEIRRÖDR

Thor's traditional occupation was going on journeys to the east where he killed giants and trolls: Snorri quite often refers to this and Thor himself mentions it several times in the eddaic poem *Hárbarðsljóð*. In *Hárbarðsljóð* 23 Thor is made to say "I was off in the east knobbling the evil-doing giant women ...."; in stanza 29 he observes "I was off in the east guarding the river where the sons of Svarangr sought me, hurling rocks at me. Little joy did they have of winning when they came before me to ask for peace"; and in stanzas 37 and 38 he mentions encounters at "Hlésey" with the "wives of Berserkers" who appeared in the guise of wolves.

Apart from such allusions there are at least four accounts of Thor's adventures in Giantland: the first of these to be related concerns Thor and the giant Geirröðr which is told by Snorri in *Skáldskaparmál* XVIII:

"There's quite a tale to be told on the score of Thor's visit to Geirröðr's Garth: on that occasion he didn't have with him his hammer Mjölnir nor his Strength-Increasing-Belt nor his iron gloves. But Loki was travelling with him; because it befell Loki once when he was enjoying himself in Frigg's hawk's guise that he flew out of curiosity into Geirröðr's Garth, and saw there a great hall and fluttered up to and looked in through a window; but Geirröðr glanced that way and ordered someone to catch the bird and bring it to him. It was with some difficulty the man sent on the errand was able to clamber up the hall wall, Loki was so high. In fact Loki was amused at the climber's toil and trouble and had no intention of flying any higher for a while until he had really put the man through the hoop. Just as the fellow reached out for him, he stretched his wings and struck out hard with his feet—only to find them stuck fast. Loki was seized and carried off to the giant Geirröðr, who, when he looked into his eyes, recognized him for a man and ordered him to speak, but Loki would not. So Geirröðr locked him in a chest and starved him there for three months.

Then when Geirröðr let him out and ordered him to speak, Loki said who he was and in return for his freedom he swore an oath to Geirröðr that he would inveigle Thor to Geirröðr's Garth without either his hammer or his Girdle of Strength.

Thor came up to the giantess called Gríðr who was the mother of Víðarr the Silent and took lodgings for the night. She told Thor all the truth about Geirröðr, how he was a crafty old giant and hard to deal with. She lent him her own belt of strength and iron gloves and her staff called Gríðarvölr† as well. So Thor went on until he came to the river Vimur which is of all rivers the greatest. Then he buckled about him the strength-increasing-belt and supporting himself with Gríðarvölr struck downstream while Loki clung to his belt. But when Thor reached the middle, the waters of the river rose without warning right up to his oxters. Thor cried out:

> Wax not Vimur
> Just when I want to wade you
>   and get into the giants' garth;
> You see (do you not?)
>   that my own strength swells to heaven?

Just then Thor looked up a ravine and saw Gjalp, Geirröðr's daughter with her legs wide open astraddle the river; it was she who was causing the flood.

Thor plucked a huge rock up out of the river bed and hurled it at her, saying at the same time 'You should always dam a stream at its source'. Nor did he miss the target at which he had aimed. Just at that very moment, he reached the other side and grabbed a rowan tree standing out from the edge of the water: after which the proverb arose about the rowan being 'Thor's deliverance'.

When Thor and his companion arrived at Geirröðr's, they were shown first of all for their lodgings into the goat house with a single stool for a seat, and Thor sat on that. He suddenly realised that the stool was moving under him up to the roof, so he shoved Gríðarvölr into the rafters and thrust himself sharply down on to the stool. There was a great crash followed by a screech. Geirröðr's two daughters Gjalp and Greip had been hiding under the stool and Thor had broken both their backs.

Geirröðr next had Thor called into the hall in order to play him up. There were great hearth fires right down the middle of the hall. When Thor came opposite Geirröðr, the giant with a pair of tongs picked out of the flames a white hot iron bar and

† *Gríðr's wand.*

flung it full at Thor. Thor caught it with the iron gloves and
pitched it into the air while Geirröðr scrambled behind an iron
pillar in order to save his skin. Thor then hurled the white hot
bar which pierced the pillar, and Geirröðr, and the wall behind him, and so on out into the ground."

That, naturally was the end of Geirröðr.

5

THOR AND ÚTGARÐALOKI

Thor's most famous journey to Giantland was that in which
he strove with Útgarðaloki or Loki of Outgard. Snorri tells
the story at length and delightfully in *Gylfaginning*;† it is
alluded to also in *Hárbarðsljóð* 26, *Hymiskviða* 37 and *Lokasenna*
60 and 62. "The start of this tale is that Driver-Thor set off on
his travels with his goats and chariot, and accompanied by the
god known as Loki. As the sun was setting they drove up to a
farmer's so they took lodgings with him for the night. During
the evening Thor led away his goats and slaughtered both of
them. After that they were flayed and duly brought in to the
stewpot; when they were cooked Thor and his companions sat
down to supper. Thor had invited the farmer, his wife and
their two children to share the meal: the son was called Þjálfi
the Swift and the daughter Röskva Holdfast. Then Thor
spread out the goatskins in front of the fire and told the farmer
and his family to pitch the bones on to the hides.

Þjálfi, the farmer's son, caught hold of one of the goat's
thighbones and split it open with his knife point to get at the
marrow.

Thor rested there that night and in the blackness before
sparrow-peep he stood up and put his clothes on. Next he
caught hold of his hammer Mullicrusher (*Mjölnir*), made one
or two passes over the goat skins and blessed them: at once the
goats scrambled to their feet, though one was now lame of its

† *Gylf.* XLIV.

hind leg. Thor spotted it and said either the farmer or some bumpkin in his family hadn't dealt wisely with the bones of the goats: he knew the thigh-bone had been split. There's no need to make a long story of it all; any fool can understand how muckstruck the farmer must have been when he saw Thor let his eyebrows sink down over his eyes, but when he looked at the orbs themselves!—why, he felt himself swooning away before their lightnings. Thor clawed his fists round the hammer shaft until the knuckles showed white. The farmer and all his household did only as was to be expected: he hallooed to some purpose and yammered for pardon, offering every penny he had in compensation. When Thor saw their terror, his rage left him and he allowed himself to be pacified, at the same time accepting in settlement the two children, Þjálfi and Röskva: they became his servants and have followed him ever since.

After that he left his two billies† and went on foot eastward in the direction of Giantland as far as the shore where he put out over the deep sea. When he made landfall he disembarked —he and Loki and Þjálfi and Röskva. Having trudged a little way they found a great forest rise before them, and they tramped through it all that day until nightfall. Þjálfi was the fleetest runner on earth; he was carrying Thor's knapsack, though they weren't very well off for provender. By dark they were looking about for a spot to spend the night and saw a monstrously large hall in front of them. It had a great door co-extensive with the gable end.

They found themselves a corner to sleep in.

Now in the middle of the night they had a simply terrifying landslide; the earth quaked underneath them and the hall trembled. Thor got up and yelled to his companions and together they fumbled about until they found a room leading off to the right and about halfway down the hall. Thor squatted in the doorway, the others being further in beyond him, pretty shaken, and Thor gripped his hammer-shaft and thought

† *Gylf.* XLV.

7 FRANKS CASKET

This celebrated casket of walrus ivory, worked by a 7th century Northumbrian craftsman, is notable for depicting biblical and pagan themes side by side. The top (pictured above) shows Egil, whose name is given in runes as Ægili, the archer who is equated with Örvandill in Norse mythology and Orion in Greek mythology.

8 MOUNT HEKLA IN ERUPTION

Both the Verse and the Prose Edda suggest that their writers must, in certain
passages, have been influenced by the recollection of Mount Hekla in eruption.
The above photograph vividly recalls Völuspá's description of the end of the world
when 'fire and reek burl upwards and break with hazy heat against heaven itself'.

about saving his skin: especially when they heard a loud murmuration and a snorting.

When dawn broke Thor stepped outside and saw a man stretched before him a little way off in the forest—a man, but by no means a dwarf: he was asleep and snoring like a pig. Then Thor began to understand what the noise was during the night, so he buckled his belt of strength around him and his muscles swelled with divine power. But just at that moment the person awoke and stood up smartly. It's said that for once Thor was too startled to smite with his hammer, instead he asked the other his name and got the answer 'Vasty (*Skrýmir*)! And there's no need for me to ask what you're called: Thor of the Gods, isn't it? Now what did you have to pinch my glove for?' Vasty stretched out his hand and picked up his 'glove'. Thor saw it was what they had taken for a hall during the night, and the 'side chamber' was the thumbstall of the glove!

Vasty enquired if Thor was prepared to accept his company on the way and Thor had to say 'yes'. So Vasty set about un-lacing his own provision bag and started into his breakfast while Thor and his party did the same a little distance off. Vasty said it ought to be nice to make a common store of their food and again Thor had to agree. Without a pause Vasty stuffed all their rations into one bag and threw it over his shoulder.

All that day he stalked in front taking pretty long strides and when evening came on he looked about for a place to rest and decided on the foot of a gigantic oak tree. Vasty then said he thought he would lie down and sleep and 'here, catch hold of the provision bag and help yourselves to supper'.

In a twink Vasty was asleep and snoring while Thor picked up the bag to undo it. Now what I'm going to say must appear to be a lie: he couldn't untie a single knot and no lace-end was any looser than another. When he saw his labour went all for nothing he flew into a violent rage, he gripped his hammer Mullicrusher with both fists, took one step towards the spot where Vasty lay and cracked him over the skull.

Vasty woke up mumbling something about a leaf having dropped on to his head and asked if the others had eaten and were quite ready for bed? Thor muttered that they were just about to go to sleep, and they trooped off to the shelter of another oak. Now this is perfectly true—they were not entirely free from anxiety as they settled down to their slumbers.

About midnight Thor heard Vasty snoring so that the rumbling of it shook the forest. He got up and, quickly and fiercely clasping his hammer, tiptoed towards him and flung a dunt full in the centre of his crown: he even felt the hammer face sink deeply into his head.

Vasty woke at once: 'What's up now?' he grumbled. 'An acorn maybe? Fell off the tree on to my nut? Oh. Ah. Thor—and what's biting you?' But Thor was already falling over himself backwards mumbling at the same time he had just been wakened himself and it was still dark and it wasn't time to get up yet.

Then Thor cogitated privately to himself thinking if he got the chance of a third wallop Vasty would be the last to know anything about it. He lay down with his ear cocked to listen if Vasty were fast asleep. A little before the grey of dawn he heard Vasty snoring and he got up and lept at him swinging the hammer with all his power and drove it down on his up-turned temple: the hammer head sank in as far as the helve.

But Vasty only sat up and rubbed his cheek, murmuring 'Dang those dirty birds roosting up the tree! You know, I just realized—half asleep half awake—the nasty little beggars have messed on me through the twigs! Oh! so you too are awake, Thor? Ah well, I suppose it's time to get up and get dressed. As a matter of fact you aren't far now from the stronghold known as Outgard (*Útgarðr*). I've heard you gossiping among yourselves about my not being exactly a shaveling—well, let me tell you this: you'll see men a trifle bigger in Outgard. Now just let me give you some sound advice: don't go putting on airs. Loki of Outgard's retainers won't stomach any showing off from such toddling tinies as you are. Or better still—why don't you turn back? I do really believe that would be your best plan. If you do aim to go on, this is where you turn off to the east yonder. My way lies north to the mountains you can see there.' Vasty slung the provision bag across his back and made off into the wood: they do say that the gods didn't even wish him 'safe home'.

Thor and his friends set their best foot forward and travelled on until noon when they saw soaring high above them the stronghold set in the middle of an open plain.† Even though they pressed back the crowns of their heads on to the napes of their necks they still couldn't see its battlements. They walked round to the main gate and found it blocked by a great grille. Thor went up to the grille but couldn't budge it. They were determined to get in and did so by sidling between the bars.

Next their eyes were caught by a vast edifice towards which they went. The door was open so they entered and saw there crowds of men sitting up to two trestle-tables. Men? They were giants!

Almost at once, they found themselves in front of King Loki of Outgard saying 'How do you do?' to him. But he was slow to notice them and when he did, his upper lip drew back from his teeth and he sneered, 'Of course, news travels slowly to us here at the Back of Beyond and I may be quite wrong in what I think; but is it—can this young bully-boy be Two-goat Thor? Oh no, no: there must be far more about you than appears at the moment. Look, here's your chance—tell us just what talents you reckon you and your cullies possess. No one stays long here with us unless he's clever in some art or science more than the general run.'

The one who was bringing up the rear, Loki, blurted out 'I know an art which I'm very willing to put to the test. It's that nobody in this hall can eat a good square meal quicker than I can.'

Loki of Outgard observed, 'Yes. That *is* something of a feat if you can bring it off: we'll test you.' He bellowed out across

† *Gylf.* XLVI.

the tables that the one called Blazeaway (*Villi-eldr*) should step on to the floor and pit himself against Loki. Next, a long wooden trough was dragged into the hall and piled high with meat. Loki took up his station at one end and Blazeaway at the other. Both began to gobble as fast as they could with the result that they met dead in the middle of the trough. Loki had eaten every morsel of meat off the bones, but Blazeaway—*he* had eaten the meat *and* the bones *and* his half of the trough as well!

Of course, it was obvious to everybody that Loki had lost that little game.

Loki of Outgard then asked if the young fellow could do anything and Þjálfi said he was prepared to race anyone Loki of Outgard would put forward. Loki of Outgard said that was a notable sport indeed but he would certainly need to be very fleet of foot if he was to win this particular race. He gave the order for it to be quickly put to the trial. Loki of Outgard stood up and strode outside to where there lay an excellent running-track along a level plain: he called up to him his page-boy named Wit (*Hugi*) and told him to run a match against Þjálfi.

They ran the first heat in which Wit gained enough on his rival to be able to turn back and meet him at the end of the race. Loki of Outgard said, 'Þjálfi, you'll have to try and put a bit more guts into it to win. Mind you, it's perfectly true I don't believe I've seen any man come here who was fleeter footed than the way you've just run.'

They began the second heat in which Wit ran there and back and when he turned to look for Þjálfi, the poor lad still had a bowshot to go. Loki of Outgard said, 'I'm quite certain in my own mind that Þjálfi is a good runner, but I don't see how he can win now: let's find out—they can run one final heat.'

They raced again, Wit running to the end of the track and turning to meet Þjálfi when he was only halfway on the first lap. Everybody said that contest had been well and truly decided.

Loki of Outgard turned to Thor and asked what particular

bit of prowess he was going to put on display for them—they had heard so much talk about his exploits. Thor said he would rather than anything else have a drinking match with any man. Replying that that might well be, Loki of Outgard went into the hall and shouted for his cupbearer to bring in the drinking horn which his retainers were accustomed to bib from. At once, the cupbearer came forward lugging the horn which he dropped into Thor's hands. Loki of Outgard made the observation 'It's looked upon as good drinking when you toss off this horn in the one draught, though some men take two. Nobody is so unparched as not to be able to down it in three swigs.'

Thor examined the horn which, though it did not appear to be over wide, was pretty long; still, he had a fine drouth on him. He began to ingurgitate with such huge swallows he believed he wouldn't need to bow his head over the horn more than once. At last his breath gave out and to see what progress he had made in the drinking he peeped inside the horn: there seemed to be scarcely any difference between the level now and before he started. Then said Loki of Outgard, 'Oh! well drunk! Though—I wonder? No, I see you haven't swilled in excess. Do you know, if anyone had told me Thor of the Gods couldn't quaff larger than that I should never have believed him. I know what you're up to—you intend to make quite certain of polishing it off in two goes!'

Thor didn't say a word. He jammed the horn rim into his mouth intending to drink the drink to end all drinks—and did so, up to the final squeak of wind in him. There was one drawback; he couldn't raise the point of the horn as high as he would have liked.

When he took the vessel from his lips and looked, it seemed to him there was even less difference in the levels than with the first draught. Loki of Outgard chimed in, 'What's up now, Thor? Aren't you holding yourself back just a bit too much for your last drink? It seems to me if you're going to drain the horn with the third drink it'll need to be the biggest yet.

Naturally, we can now hardly allow you here among ourselves the sort of inflated (shall I say?) reputation you have back home among the gods; unless, of course, you give a better account of yourself in other feats than you seem to me to be giving in this one.'

Thor was furious. He rammed the horn into his teeth and sucked like a whirlpool just as long as he was able, and, when he looked inside, certainly this drink had dropped the level more than either time before: but Thor thrust the horn from him and would not drink again. Loki of Outgard said, 'It's obvious now that your capacity isn't as large as we thought. Would you like to try something else? You don't seem to have got much change so far.'

Thor growled, 'I'm game for anything—anything at all! As a matter of fact, it would have surprised me back home among the gods if such draughts as I've just drunk here had been called so little. However: what other tricks have you got up your sleeve for me?'

Loki of Outgard said, 'There's a game the little boys play here, and for that reason we can scarcely call it a miracle—it's picking up my cat. Now, I'd hardly know how to mention such a thing to Thor of the Gods (save us!) if I hadn't already seen you are of much less account then I used to think.' Almost at once, a cat (a grey tabby, rather a large one) gambolled across the end of the hall floor. Thor went straight to it and placing his hand under its belly he shoved up, but the cat arched its back every time Thor pushed. Even when he pushed upwards as far as he could stretch, the cat only lifted one paw off the ground; and that was the most Thor could achieve in this particular ploy. Loki of Outgard said, 'I thought so. The cat is rather a large cat while Thor is short—stunted even, compared with the giants we are accustomed to.'

Thor snapped, 'Stunted as you say I am—let somebody step up quick and wrestle with me! Now, I really am angry!'

Loki of Outgard glanced along the tables and replied, 'Do you know, I don't see a single man present who wouldn't consider it beneath his dignity to wrestle with you.' And then he added, 'Let me see first: I've got it!—give a shout for the old lady, my foster mother Annodomini (*Elli*), and Thor shall try a fall with her if he will. She's often put down people who seemed to me a lot stronger than Thor is.' The very next instant an old, old woman hobbled into the hall. Loki of Outgard said she should try a hold with Thor of the Gods. Well, not to make a long story of it, the bout proceeded in such a way that the more strenuously Thor exerted himself the more rock-like she stood. Then she herself began to buckle to and finding Thor a little unsteady on his feet she wrestled all the fiercer: it wasn't long before she had Thor down on one knee!

Loki of Outgard stepped up to the strugglers and ordered them to break saying at the same time that Thor had no need to offer to wrestle with any other of his men. By this time it was well into the evening: Loki of Outgard showed Thor and his companions to their seats and they ate and drank with the best for that night.

When day dawned† Thor and his friends got up and put their clothes on ready to leave. Loki of Outgard came along and had a trestle-table laid for their breakfast; again there was no shortage of meat and drink. After wiping the last crumbs away, they set off on their return journey, Loki of Outgard following them out and going with them beyond the gates of the stronghold. As they were about to part he addressed Thor, enquiring whether he was pleased with his trip or if he felt he had come across people of more consequence than himself. Thor grunted he couldn't say he hadn't been taken down a peg or two 'so I know you must think me something of a man of straw; and that goes against the grain.'

Then Loki of Outgard replied, 'Now that we're out of the stronghold at last, I'm prepared to let you into a secret—and I might say in passing that given my health and strength you'll never get inside again: I'll tell you flat, you never would have got inside at all if I'd known then what I know now about

† *Gylf.* XLVII.

your pith and brawn, which brought us all to within an ace of destruction. I bewitched you into seeing certain hallucinations. The first was when I purposely met you in the forest (you remember Vasty?). When you tried to undo the provision bag I had clamped it closed with adamantine wire which you weren't able to unloose. After that, when you struck at me three times with your hammer, although the first blow was the least, it would have put paid to me if it had got home. Well, you remember seeing a saddle-back crag by the hall in the forest? And you saw three box shaped valleys, one much deeper than the other two? Those were the imprints of your hammer: I slipped the saddle-back crag in front of each stroke, but you couldn't see it! Likewise with the various contests your party had with my retainers. Take the first one which your man Loki tried: he was certainly famished and gobbled quick enough in all conscience, but his opponent Blazeaway—well, *he* was wildfire and burnt up the trough just as fast as the meat. When Þjálfi tried racing the boy called Wit he was pitting himself against a *thought* out of my head and you could hardly expect Þjálfi to win over such opposition. Now, you yourself, you swigged from the horn and thought you were making slow progress; but strike me dumb! It was a prodigy—something I wouldn't have believed possible—for the end of the horn unknown to you was plunged in the Ocean! And when you come to the sea you can find out what difference you've made between the old and the new levels.' (Nowadays, we call it the foreshore.)

And then he added: 'You know, I thought it was some going when you pushed up the cat's belly; as a matter of fact, there wasn't a fellow there not shivering in his shoes when they saw you raise one of its paws off the ground. Of course, the cat wasn't what it seemed to you: it was the World Serpent which lies completely encircling the land; by gripping the tip of its tail in its jaws it is just long enough to do the job for the earth. But you thrust up so far it wasn't a great way off heaven! An equal wonder was during the wrestling when you stood firm so long and only went down on one knee in your struggle against Annodomini. For there's never been a man, nor ever will be a man, who can live to old age and not take a fall from this same Annodomini. Now I'll tell you the truth: we must part company here and it will be better for all concerned if we never meet again. In future, I shall always protect my stronghold with such like spells or other new ones so that you'll never be able to get at me!'

When Thor had heard out this stupendous tale he seized his hammer and swung it into the air, but before he could strike one blow, Loki of Outgard had vanished. So he whipped round to face the stronghold intending to smash it to bits. But he saw there a smiling valley, open and empty: and no stronghold. Then he turned once more and set his foot on the path for home, nor did he stop before he got back to the Paddocks of Power (*Þrúðvangar*)."

6

THOR AND THE GIANT HYMIR

Snorri goes on to say† that Thor "determined to leave no stone unturned in bringing about a meeting between himself and the Midgard Serpent. . . . It's common knowledge that he didn't sit quiet at home very long before he was off on another jaunt, this time without goats or chariot or any company. He left the shores of Midgard disguised as a young blade and on a certain evening arrived at a giant's called Hymir. Thor stayed the night with him as a lodger. At daybreak, Hymir got out of bed, dressed and prepared his row boat to put to sea fishing. Thor too sprung up and quickly got ready, asking Hymir to let him row the boat on the sea with him. Hymir said he couldn't see his being much help, so small and youthful as he was, 'and you'll freeze if I stay so long and so far out as I am in the habit of doing.' Thor replied if that was so he should be

† *Gylf.* XLVII.

sure to row a good distance from the shore for he didn't think he would be the first to ask to row back. In fact Thor was so enraged with the giant he was ready at any time to let his hammer crash down on him: but he held himself in since he firmly intended to try his strength in another quarter.

He asked Hymir what they were to use for bait and Hymir grunted he must see to himself for bait. Thor turned at once to where he saw a herd of oxen belonging to Hymir. He grabbed the hugest ox, called Himinhrjóðr *Heavenspringer*, cut off its head and went with it to the shore; by which time Hymir was launching the boat. Thor lept aboard, made himself comfortable in the bottom, picked up a couple of oars and started to row. In spite of his efforts at pulling, they seemed to Hymir to be crawling along. Hymir rowed forrard in the prow and did his best to speed up the strokes. At last he said they were come to the fishing-banks where he usually angled for flat-fish, but Thor protested he wanted to row much farther out: so they pulled on smartly for a bit. Again Hymir spoke: they had come so far out it was dangerous to hang about there on account of the World Serpent; and again Thor answered they ought to row for a spell. He got his way and Hymir took it good humouredly. Thor at last dropped his oars and busied himself with a fishing rod, rather a huge one, nor was the hook either small or weak. Thor fastened the ox's head on to his hook and cast it over the side, when the hook sank to the bottom of the sea.

Now, I'll tell you something; the World Serpent's belly hadn't really befooled Thor when he tried to lift it up, but Loki of Outgard had indeed made him into a laughing-stock. Well, now it was the World Serpent's turn to swallow the ox-head, but the fish-hook stuck in his gullet, and when the Serpent realized it he threshed about so monstrously that Thor's wrists were skinned along the gunn'l. This made him fizz with rage and he called up all his divine power and dug in with his heels, bracing both feet so hard against the boat bottom that he hauled the Serpent up to the side!

I can tell you this for a fact: nobody ever saw a more blood-freezing sight than Thor did, as his eyes goggled down at the Serpent, and the Great Worm from below glared up and blew a cloud of poison. At that, they say the giant Hymir blenched, then turned yellow in his terror, what with the Serpent and the sea swashing into the boat and out of the boat! But Thor grabbed his hammer and flung it above his head just as Hymir fumbled for the knife he used for cutting bait and hacked Thor's fishing rod overboard!

The Serpent sank down into the depths of the sea.

But Thor cast his hammer after it, and some people think he would have liked its head and horns. I myself think it is true to say that the World Serpent still lives and lies weltering at the bottom of the Ocean. Still, Thor raised his fist in mad mortification and made a dead set at Hymir so that he plunged into the sea and the last Thor saw of him was the soles of his feet. Then Thor waded ashore."

There is another version of this tale to be found in the *Verse Edda* piece called *Hymiskviða* or *The Lay of Hymir*. The *Hymiskviða* is deemed to be comparatively late, say round about A.D. 1000–1050. As a poem it is an inferior piece of work and seems to have been cobbled from two or three different tales. Nevertheless, in spite of its defects, *Hymiskviða* has a foundation in myth.

Ægir, a giant and god of the sea agreed to brew ale for the gods if they would procure a famous kettle of fabulous size. Nobody knew where this kettle or cauldron was until the god Týr said that it was in the possession of his "father" the giant Hymir who lived at the "end of Heaven to the east of Élivágar".

Týr and Thor set out in the goat-drawn chariot to get the cauldron. They left the goats with one, Egil, and proceeded on foot until Týr found his grandam, a nine-hundred headed giantess, and his mother "the bright-browed one" who was married to Hymir. From the context it seems evident that the grandmother was a giantess and Hymir's own mother, while "the bright-browed one", Týr's mother, belonged to the race of the gods. Týr's mother hid her son and Thor under the very cauldron they had come to take away, for her husband Hymir was of uncertain temper. When Hymir did get back from hunting, his beard rattled with icicles for he was a frost giant, and when he knew of Týr's and Thor's presence he glanced in their direction. His gaze was so fierce that a beam supporting eight other cauldrons above the two gods' heads broke asunder and all the kettles except the one hiding Týr and Thor were cracked apart. Still, Hymir remembered his duties as a host and had three oxen prepared for food—of which Thor gobbled two.

It appears that next morning Hymir decided to go fishing and Thor asked to come too. He also asked the giant for bait at which he was directed to the cattle yard, for said Hymir, he should find it easy to get bait from the oxen meaning, of course, an insult to Thor in that he should use dung. Thor professed to misunderstand the giant and cut off the head of an ox much to Hymir's chagrin. The two rowed out to fish as in Snorri's version of the story. Thor hooked the Midgard Serpent but it got away. Hymir asked if Thor would row back or would he carry the whales they had caught from the shore to the house? Thor jumped out of the boat, heaved it and the catch on to his shoulders and waded ashore and up to the giant's house. Bested again, Hymir said he would call nobody strong, no matter how well they rowed, unless they could smash his glass goblet. Thor threw the goblet at the stone pillars of the house, but it was the pillars which were shattered and not the goblet. Týr's mother let the gods into the secret that Hymir's head was the only object against which the glass would break: and there Thor broke it.

Hymir next set the two gods the feat of lifting his mighty cauldron. Týr could not budge it, but Thor seized the rim, upturned the vessel over his head and ran off with the handles clattering about his heels. The two gods had not gone far before they found themselves pursued by Hymir and a throng of giants. Thor cast the cauldron off, and turning with his hammer, killed them all.

7

ODIN, THOR AND HRUNGNIR

Thor's famous encounter with the giant Hrungnir gave rise to his nickname Smiter or Killer of Hrungnir. The story is told by the skald Þjóðólfr of Hvin in his poem *Haustlöng* and by Snorri in *Skáldskaparmál* XVII where *Haustlöng* is quoted in full:

"Once when Thor was knocking about the east killing trolls, Odin rode Sleipnir into Jötunheim and came to the giant's called Hrungnir. Then Hrungnir enquired who that could be in the golden helmet, riding over sea and sky, for he remarked, he owned a nice bit of horse flesh. Odin answered he would wager his head that there wasn't another horse to equal him in Jötunheim. Hrungnir agreed it was a good mount but declared he himself owned a far fleeter one called Gullfaxi Goldmane. Hrungnir was nettled and lept up on to his horse and galloped after Odin intending to pay him out for his bragging. But Odin went at such a lick he was always breasting the next hill ahead, which put Hrungnir into such a gigantic fury that before he knew it he had lept in over Asgard gate. When he pulled up at the hall doors, the Æsir invited him inside to drink. He walked into the hall and called for something to quaff and those puncheons were brought out from which only Thor was accustomed to drink: Hrungnir drained them every one. As he got drunk he found no difficulty in laying his tongue to vaunting words, for he said he intended picking up Valhalla and carting it off to Jötunheim; he said he would sink Asgard and knock off all the Æsir except Freya and Sif whom he would take home to live with him. Freya was the only one not afraid to carry drink to him for it seemed he intended to bib all the ale of the gods. And when the Æsir were afraid of his big talk they called on Thor.

In a twink Thor stepped inside the hall with his hammer held high and fuming with rage: he asked who could possibly have advised allowing cunning giants to drink there or who had given Hrungnir a safe conduct to be in Valhalla or why Freya should carry ale to him at a feast of the gods? Hrungnir himself answered, for he saw no look of friendship in Thor's eyes: he said Odin had invited him to drink and Odin was responsible for his safety. Thor said Hrungnir would be sorry for this little party before he got away. Hrungnir said Thor of the Gods had just about enough courage to kill him when he was unarmed; it would be a better test of his valour if he had the guts to fight him on the frontier of Grjótúnagarðr 'and I've been and gone and done a daft bit of work in leaving at home my shield and my whetstone', he said, 'but if I only had my weapons here, we two should now try our strength in a duel— otherwise, I say you're yellow, if you kill me when I'm unarmed!'

Thor would by no means fail to meet him in single combat since he was challenged, especially as he had never failed yet. Hrungnir then took his departure and galloped prodigiously until he came to Jötunheim and his journey became very famous among the giants as did the appointment for his meeting with Thor: the giants thought there was a good deal at stake, whoever should gain the victory; they could expect little good from Thor if Hrungnir lost for he was the strongest giant among them. And so the giants made a clay man in Grjótúnagarðr and he was nine leagues high and three leagues broad under the armpits; they couldn't find a heart big enough to fit him until they took one out of a mare, and even that didn't beat very steady when Thor came up. They say that Hrungnir had a heart made of hard rock shaped like a triangle (just like the rune which afterwards came to be called 'Hrungnir's heart'); his head was made of stone, and his shield also was a stone one, wide and thick. He held his shield in front of him when he stood awaiting Thor in Gjótúnagarðr, while he had a whetstone for his weapon which he carried over his shoulder: it wasn't a pleasant sight.

On the other side of him stood the clay giant who was

called Mökkurkálfi *Cloudcalf* and pretty nigh frightened to death: they say he wet himself when he saw Thor.

Thor went to this combat along with his servant Þjálfi. Then Þjálfi ran forward to where Hrungnir was standing and said to him, 'Hey giant! You're being careless, standing there with your shield in front of you! Thor has seen you and he's coming below ground; he's bound to attack you from underneath.' Thereupon Hrungnir shot his shield under his feet and stood on it holding his whetstone two-handed. Immediately, he saw fire and heard great claps of thunder, and caught sight of Thor in his divine wrath: he was rushing like a thunderbolt, whirling his hammer, which he cast at Hrungnir when he was still afar off. Hrungnir thrust up the whetstone with both hands and then flung it against the hammer; it met the hammer in mid flight and the whetstone was shattered to bits. One part of it fell on the earth and gave rise to all the outcrops of rock fit for making hones; the remainder of it sank into Thor's head so that he fell flat on the earth; but the hammer Mjölnir hit Hrungnir on the head and crushed his skull to powder so that he fell forward over Thor and one of his legs lay across Thor's neck.

Þjálfi attacked Mökkurkálfi, who simply sluthered to the ground in a heap. Then Þjálfi ran up to Thor and set about lifting Hrungnir's leg off him only to find he couldn't do it. So all the gods came up when they heard Thor had fallen and they in turn tried to lift up the leg and they all failed. Then came Magni, the son of Thor by Járnsaxa: he was at that time three nights old; he tossed Hrungnir's leg off Thor and said, 'Now, dad, just look at the pickle you're in because I've turned up late! You know, I reckon one blow of my fist would have put paid to this giant if only I had got at him.'

Then Thor stood up and thanked his son heartily and said he was a promising lad 'and I've made up my mind', said he, 'to give you the stallion Gullfaxi who used to be Hrungnir's.' Odin spoke up and said Thor did wrong to give away that good steed to the son of a giantess rather than to his father.

"Thor went home to the Paddocks of Power with the chunk

of whetstone fixed in his skull. He was visited by the wise-woman called Gróa, wife to Örvandill the Brave: she sang her spells over Thor until the whetstone became loose. When Thor felt it, and it looked as though he would get the stone away, he was agog to reward Gróa for her healing art, and to make her happy he told her how he had waded north over Icywaves and how he had carried away out of Jötunheim back from the north in a basket slung over his shoulder, none other than Örvandill her husband; as a proof of what he was saying, one of Örvandill's toes had stuck through the basket and got frost-bitten and Thor had had to break it off and had thrown it up into the sky and made a star out of it, the one called Örvandill's Toe. Thor went on to say it wouldn't be long before Örvandill came home which made Gróa so glad she forgot to chant her spells before the whetstone was finally freed, so there it sticks still in Thor's cranium: and it stands for a warning never to throw a hone across a room because when that happens the hone in Thor's head moves."

8

THE STEALING OF THOR'S HAMMER

It is extraordinary that Snorri nowhere refers to the eddaic poem *Þrymskviða* or the subject with which it deals, the stealing of Thor's hammer by the giants. Extraordinary, because *Þryms-kviða* dating from *c.* 900 is one of the oldest poems in the *Verse Edda* and artistically one of the best; it has been preserved too (in *Codex Regius*) in first rate condition with no serious gaps or inserts.

The story runs as follows: the god Thor woke up one morning in Asgard to find his hammer missing. Wrathfully he fumbled about him, his red beard and hair tossing in violent anger. He shouted for Loki and broke to him the astounding (and alarming) news. He dragged Loki off to the palace of the goddess of love and beauty, Freya. Thor asked Freya if she

would lend her feather-coat so that someone might wear it and
fly into Giantland to seek the stolen hammer—for it was
obvious that only the giants would have taken it. Freya willingly lent the coat which Loki put on. He flew off at once to
Giantland. From a distance he saw Þrymr, the giant king,
sitting on a mound plaiting leashes of gold for his dogs and
trimming the manes of his horses: without stopping, Þrymr
asked Loki how the gods and the elves were doing—knowing
full well the stew they were in over the loss of the one weapon
which could protect them from the giants. Loki answered
frankly that the gods and the elves were ill at ease, and asked
straight out if Þrymr had hidden Thor's hammer. Þrymr was
equally frank, saying he had hidden Thor's hammer eight
rösts beneath the earth and nobody would get it back until
Freya was brought to him to wife.

Loki flew back to Asgard as quick as he could go, and before
he was able to alight, Thor was there asking for news. He was
told where the hammer was and the terms by which it could be
redeemed.

Thor dragged Loki once again before Freya and bluntly
ordered her to put on a bridal veil to drive with him to Giantland. Now it was Freya's turn to be angry. Her breast swelled
with such fury that she broke the famous necklace Brísingamen
asunder: she flatly refused to marry any giant.

The gods called a council and debated what should be done.
Heimdallr, the whitest of the gods, suggested a plan, namely
that Thor himself should be got up as a bride, draped with the
veil, and with petticoats hiding his legs, with a housewife's
keys dangling from a chain at his waist, brooches on his bust—
and above all, to show that it really was "Freya", he must wear
the mighty necklace of the Brísings.

Thor was extremely reluctant to dress up as a woman, he felt
the other gods would call him a sissy; but Loki added his per-
suasions and offered to go along with him disguised as a maid
servant. It was either that or the giants would crowd in over
Asgard walls. Thor at last assented and the gods and god-

desses got ready the "bride". The goats were led in, harnessed to the chariot and with rumbles of thunder and flashes of lightning, Thor and Loki drove into Giantland.

Þrymr heard the approach of the chariot re-echoing around the hills of Jötunheim. He called to his giants to strew the benches, to broach the ale, set up the tables and prepare the wedding feast for his new bride Freya. He thought of the gold horned oxen with jet black hides abiding in his paddocks; of the gold and jewels he kept in his coffers; he seemed to need only Freya to complete his happiness.

By this time it was early evening and the feast was set. The "bride" ate a whole ox, eight salmon, all the dainties intended for the ladies and washed the lot down with three tuns of mead. Even Þrymr was astonished enough to observe that he had never seen a maiden with such an appetite or thirst. Cunning "maid servant" Loki put it down to "Freya's" having been too excited to eat or drink for a week before coming to be married. Þrymr wanted to steal a kiss and he lifted a corner of the bride's veil, but the flashing eyes he saw there made him leap back in surprise. Handmaid Loki said "Freya's" eyes were fiery because she hadn't slept for a week before driving to Giantland. Þrymr's sister next asked "Freya" for the bridal fee—for a present of all the red gold rings "she" was wearing on "her" fingers.

At last, Þrymr called for the marriage to be celebrated in the traditional way by Thor's hammer being laid on the bride's knee while both bride and groom swore their vows to the goddess Vár. As soon as Thor felt Mjölnir within his grasp, his heart chuckled in his breast and with the first swipe he felled the giant king; with the next the greedy sister who got death from the hammer instead of many rings.

And that was how Thor got his hammer again.

CHAPTER IX

Tales of other Gods and Goddesses

THERE is evidence that originally each god or goddess was a comparatively simple being: for instance the stories represent Odin basically as having *two* sides to his make-up—the All-father and the Leader of Souls and that only because he is a combination of *two* gods; Thor is the fighter of giants, the protector of Asgard and Midgard. Similarly, we shall see other gods as basically representing one mythic idea; and some gods and goddesses show their essential similarity by representing the same idea in a different dress. For example, Frey is remembered in the mythology really by the story of his lovesickness, his failing and restoration to health by his winning (at a loss) Gerðr for his bride; Balder is the dying god who is lost to Hel but who returns after the Ragnarök; Freya is the goddess who is stolen away while nature languishes, but who is eventually restored to her friends; Heimdallr is the protector and educator of men; Loki is the mischievous destroyer of all. I have told the stories of Odin and Thor (such as remain to us) now it is the turn of the others.

I

FREY'S LOVESICKNESS

There are two versions of the myth of Frey's falling in love, one in *Gylfaginning* XXXVII and the other in the *Verse Edda* piece known as *Skírnismal*. We may take the later one first and try to work back to the original story:

"There was a man called Gymir† whose wife Aurboða was kin to the hill giants. Their daughter was Gerðr, of all women

† *Gylf.* XXXVII.

the most ravishingly fair. Now one day the god Frey had sneaked up to Hliðskjálf and looked out over the world; glancing across the vistas of the north, his eye caught sight of a town, where stood a magnificent dwelling-place and a maiden was walking towards it. As she raised her hands to unlatch the door in front of her, a beautiful light shone from them both so that earth and sky and sea were the brighter for it. But Frey was so paid out for his pride in sitting in that Holy Seat that he staggered away sick at heart, and arriving home he would not speak. He would not sleep, he would not drink, and nobody dared offer a word to him.

At last, his father Njörðr had Frey's servant Skírnir called to him and ordered him to go to Frey and speak to him and ask him why he was so put out that he hadn't a word to throw at a dog. Skírnir said he'd go if he must, but he wasn't eager; what's more, he knew (he said) that he'd get plenty of kicks and few ha'pence in return. When he did stand before Frey he enquired what could have made the god so put out as not to speak to anybody. Frey answered and said he had cast eyes on a beautiful woman and for her sake his heart was heavy with love-longing; he wouldn't be able to live much longer if he didn't win her, 'and now—you're just the man to go and ask her hand in marriage for me. Bring her back here whether her father will or no. I'll reward you well.'

Skírnir said he would run that errand when Frey gave him his sword (this was so good it fought of its own accord); Frey wouldn't even let him go short of that, but gave him the sword. Skírnir went off and asked for the maiden's hand for him. She pledged herself to come a week later to the spot called Barrey, thence to proceed to her wedding with Frey. When Skírnir told Frey the results of his mission he cried out:

> One night is long!
> Another is worse!
> How can I thole for three?
> Often a month seemed

shorter to me
than half this night to my nuptials!

This is the reason why Frey was caught without a normal
weapon when he did battle with Beli and struck him down
with a hart's horn."

There are puzzling things in this account which Snorri puts
into the mouth of Hárr (i.e. High = Odin). King Gylfi no
doubt expressed the puzzlement of Snorri when he said to
Hárr, "You know, it makes me scratch my head a bit that such
a captain as Frey would willingly part with his sword seeing
he hadn't another equally as good. It must have been no end of
a bother to him when he fought the one you call Beli. I'll bet
my boots he ate his heart out over that particular gift." Hárr
then replied, "His scuffle with Beli was nothing: he could have
killed Beli with his little finger. But a time will come when
Frey's blood will freeze for want of his sword; and that's when
the Sons of Múspell gallop out a-harrying."

The puzzle, to my mind, is not that Frey should have
parted with the sword, but that Snorri makes him give it to
Skírnir. Surely the sword was the price the giants asked for
Gerðr's hand, and Skírnir was merely the bearer of it to them?
We may be able to prove this contention later, but before that
we should refer to *Skírnismál*.

Skírnismál in its present form probably dates from 900–950.
The prose introduction sets the scene as Snorri has it, with Frey
seeing Gerðr from Hliðskjálf and falling into "a mighty love-
sickness". Njörðr bids Skírnir to ask Frey why he is languish-
ing. Frey replies to Skírnir asking how he can tell so heavy a
grief to the "young hero", and Skírnir says he must tell it for
"old times" sake, reminding Frey how "since days of old when
we were young together we always shared each other's secrets".
Frey unburdens his heart and observes that none of "the gods
or the elves" will allow him and Gerðr to come together. It
would appear (from Snorri's version) that in a missing stanza
Frey asks Skírnir to fetch him Gerðr. Skírnir agrees to do so

provided Frey gives him "the steed which goes through the dark and through the magic flickering flames, and the sword which fights of itself". Frey gives the horse and the sword. Skírnir sets out for Giantland.

The journey is a difficult and dangerous one through darkness and wild mountains, but at last Skírnir comes upon a herdsman sitting on a mound outside the stockade surrounding Gymir's abode. There are fierce hounds tethered in front of the gateway and Skírnir asks the herdsman how to get past the hounds and speak with Gerðr.

The herdsman suggests that Skírnir will die before he can speak to Gerðr. Apparently, Gerðr inside the house hears the altercation outside and asks her handmaiden what it can be, for there is much noise, the ground shakes and Gymir's house trembles. The maid answers that there is "a man outside who has lept from his horse and lets it loose to graze". Gerðr orders "the man" to be bidden inside to drink good mead though (she says) she fears that the one outside must be her brother's slayer.

When Skírnir enters, Gerðr asks if he is of the race of the gods, the Vanir or the elves, and how he managed to come alone through the leaping flames? He replies he is not of the gods, Vanir or elves, and that he comes to offer her eleven golden apples if she will betroth herself to Frey. Gerðr refuses. Skírnir next offers the famous gold ring belonging to Odin called Draupnir and which has the power of producing eight similar rings every ninth night. Gerðr still refuses to be bought. Skírnir then utters a series of threats: first he will strike off Gerðr's head with the keen, bright sword he holds in his hand; Gerðr says Gymir her father will prevent that; Skírnir says Gymir is doomed to die before the blade. Next, Skírnir says he will strike Gerðr with his magic wand (*tamsvöndr*, lit. *taming wand*) and "tame her to work his will"; she will then be forced to go to the "eagle's hill" at the end of heaven overlooking Hel, where her meat shall become loathsome to her. Hrímnir, a fearsome frost-giant will be there. She will suffer rage, longing, fetters, wrath, tears and torment. She will suffer every terror "in the giants' home". She will dwell for ever with three-headed giants or never know any other husband; she will be gripped with longing, she will waste away and be like a dried up thistle cast and crushed in the barn.

Next (stanza 32 of *Skírnismál*) Skírnir utters three lines which seem to be out of place: "I went to a holt and to a wet forest (or sappy tree) to get a magic wand (*gambanteinn*). I got a magic wand."

Skírnir says Odin grows angry, Frey is angry, the magic wrath of all the gods is directed at Gerðr. He cries out to the frost-giants, the sons of Suttungr and the gods too, to hear his banning of Gerðr's meeting with men. She shall be given to the frost-giant Hrímgrímnir in the depths by the Corpse Gate (*Nágrindr*); to the frost-giants' halls she shall daily crawl and crave in vain and without hope. Under the root of Yggdrasill which stretches towards the frost-giants, every day shall vile thralls give her to drink horns of goats' piss. Skírnir cries that he is risting the rune þ (*Þurs*) and three other names as a spell inducing upon her longing, madness and lust. But, should Gerðr repent her refusal he may still unwrite his charm.

At this mighty curse, Gerðr is won over, offers Skírnir the welcoming cup of mead and intimates her willingness to marry Frey. Skírnir wishes to know how soon will she meet Frey, and Gerðr fixes a rendezvous at "Barri, a fair forest known to us both, where after nine nights I will grant his wish to the son of Njörðr".

Skírnir then rode back and gave his news to Frey, and the poem finishes with the stanza already quoted by Snorri:

> One night is long!
> Another is worse!
>   How can I thole for three?
> Often a month seemed
> shorter to me
>   than half this night to my nuptials!

Even with this account—some three hundred years earlier than Snorri's—we are still not arrived at the original myth. But there is additional information: for instance we now see Frey's sword presented not as a reward to Skírnir for undertaking the dangerous mission, but as one of the tools (along with the horse which goes through the dark and the magic flickering flames) to help Skírnir do the job. It is doubtful whether *this* is the real reason for the sword's being taken: for though the horse was necessary for the journey, the sword is merely used to threaten Gerðr and she takes no notice of that particular threat. Other important additional information is (1) Frey and Skírnir have been close friends from childhood, (2) it appears that the "gods and the elves" oppose Frey's marriage to Gerðr. Why? Is it because she must be paid for by the sword which can then be used by the giants against the gods and their close friends the elves at the Ragnarök? (3) Skírnir's journey is an extremely dangerous and difficult one involving distance, darkness, wild country, a giant herdsman, fierce dogs and magic flames. (4) Skírnir is supplied with a number of priceless gifts to win over Gerðr such as eleven golden apples (obviously Iðunn's apples of eternal youth) and Odin's remarkable ring Draupnir. Such gifts often go in groups of three, the first two being rejected and the third accepted. Was Frey's sword originally the third gift, the one which was to be accepted? (5) Gerðr refuses all Skírnir's approaches until he utters a curse of sterility upon her; but according to Snorri, as soon as Skírnir asked for Gerðr's hand for Frey, she "pledged herself to come a week later". (6) There is a cryptic reference to Skírnir's going to "a wet wood" or "a sappy tree" to get *gambanteinn*: Snorri has nothing of this.

Before we attempt any conclusions there is one other *Verse Edda* poem on the subject of a maiden difficult of attainment at which we ought to look: I mean *Svipdagsmál*.

2

SVIPDAGR AND MENGLÖÐ

Two eddaic poems, *Grógaldr* (*Gróa's spell*) and *Fjölsvinnsmál* (*The Lay of Fjölsviðr*) are so obviously connected that most editors unite them under the title of *Svipdagsmál*. Both poems survived only in late paper manuscripts none of which antedate the seventeenth century: to this lateness Brodeur[81] attributes "the frequent errors in mythology", while Vigfusson and Powell believed part of the poem to be such a jumble that they did not bother to translate it in *Corpus Poeticum Boreale*. But Viktor Rydberg in his *Teutonic Mythology* decided there was a good deal of sense in the nonsense. The story of Svipdagr and Menglöð is not mentioned either by Snorri or anywhere else in the *Verse Edda* under those names. Both are nicknames rather than proper ones: Svipdagr means "Swift Day" and Menglöð "Necklace Glad". Svipdagr's mother Gróa is mentioned by Snorri as a wise-woman (wife of the archer Örvandill) who almost charms the broken hone of Hrungnir out of Thor's head. Svipdagr gives his father's name as Sólbjartr "Sun bright".

The story of Svipdagr and Menglöð runs like this: A false woman whom Svipdagr's father has married after Gróa's death lays a task upon her stepson: Svipdagr must go where none may fare to seek Menglöð. Young Svipdagr remembers what his mother Gróa told him namely that in any sore trouble he was to seek her help at her grave mound. He does so, crying into the mound that he is only young, that he fears death on his journey, and praying Gróa to give him charms to help him. Gróa chants protective charms over her son, first such as Rindr chanted over Rani to enable him to throw off from his shoulder anything harmful and to be self-reliant; second a charm for him wandering bereft of will, when the "bolts of Urðr" shall guard him on his road; third, of use when streams threaten his death, both the rivers Horn and Ruðr shall turn and dwindle back to hel; fourth, a charm for use against men who would wish to hang him; fifth, a spell to loosen fetters; sixth, to calm magical storms at sea and prevent shipwreck; seventh, a protection against killing frost on the high fells; eighth, a charm for use when, wandering by night on the Niflveg (*Mist Way*) Svipdagr may be cursed by a "dead Christian woman"; and lastly, a charm for use when he is caught up in a deadly argument with a warlike giant. Thus armed Svipdagr sets out on his quest and *Grógaldr* ends.

Fjölsvinnsmál begins with a broken stanza: seemingly Svipdagr has arrived before the gates of Menglöð's abode and he is accosted by Fjölsviðr who wishes to know "who is that standing in the forecourt and around him the fires are flaming?" In turn, Svipdagr asks who is barring his way, to be told "Fjölsviðr I am called. But you shall never find entrance here". Svipdagr answers that few men will leave the sight of their loves if they can help it: he sees the gates glowing with gold and he knows that here he will find bliss. Fjölsviðr asks him his lineage. Svipdagr says he is Windcold (*Vindkaldr*), son of Springcold (*Várkaldr*), son of Muchcold (*Fjölkaldr*), and asks who rules that hall. The answer is Menglöð whose mother was married to the son of Svafrþorinn. Young Svipdagr then enquires the name of the gateway and is told "Þrymgöll (*Loud Clanging*) which was made by the three sons of Sólblindi (*Sun-Blinded*). It holds as fast as though in fetters any wayfarer who lifts its latch". "What do they call the house itself?" asks Svipdagr: "Gastrópnir (*Guest-crusher*)," says Fjölsviðr, "and I made it myself of old from the limbs of Leirbrimir (*Clay-giant*) to stand as long as the world." Svipdagr's next question is "What do they call the tree that casts its branches over every land"? "It is Mímameiðr (*Mímir's Tree*): few men know what root runs beneath it, nor what shall fell it for neither fire nor iron will." "What fruit," asks Svipdagr, "grows from the tree?" and Fjölsviðr replies, "Women in labour shall bear its fruit to the fire when that which was within shall come out and so it will be mighty with men." The insatiably curious Svipdagr next wants to know the name of the cock which glitters with gold on the tree's highest bough. "Víðópnir," says Fjöl-

sviðr, "and greatly does he grieve both Surtr and Sinmöra."
This questioning and answering proceeds as follows:

Svipdagr: What are the two fierce hounds called there in front
of the house?

Fjölsviðr: Gífr one, Geri the other.

Svipdagr: May no one hope to enter the house while the dogs
sleep?

Fjölsviðr: They never sleep together. When they were put on
guard it was arranged that one should sleep by night, the other
by day.

Svipdagr: Is there no meat one could tempt them with and
leap within while they eat?

Fjölsviðr: Yes, there is—the two wing joints belonging to the
cock Víðópnir.

Svipdagr: And what weapon would one need to kill
Víðópnir?

Fjölsviðr: It is called Lævateinn (*Wounding wand*) which
was forged by Loptr down below by the Corpse Gate. It's kept
beside Sinmöra under nine locks in the coffer of Lægjarn
(*Lover of ill*).

Svipdagr: How can a man get the weapon?

Fjölsviðr: By taking the bright sickle feather from Víðópnir's
tail and giving it to Sinmöra the giantess. . . .

Thus is the circle of impossibilities (it seems) closed: for to
get past the dogs, Svipdagr would have to kill the cock; to kill
the cock he would need to get the sword from Sinmöra; she
will only give up the sword in exchange for the cock's sickle-
feather, and no one can pass the dogs to get it without offering
them the bird's wing joints.

Svipdagr's next questions elicit the information that the hall
before which he stands and which is ringed with flickering
magic flames, is called Hýrr (the "Joyous") and that it shall
long tremble on the sword's point. In answer to the question
which of the gods built the hall, Svipdagr is told, "Uni, Íri,
Óri, Bári, Varr, Vegdrasill, Dóri, Úri, Dellingr, Atvarðr,
Líðskjalfr and Loki." The questioning then proceeds:

Svipdagr: What is the name of the mountain on which I can see the lovely maiden lying?

Fjölsviðr: Lyfjaberg; a hill which has long been a solace to the sick and sore; for any woman, no matter how sick she has been, is cured when she climbs that mountain.

Svipdagr: Who are the maidens sitting so happily at Menglöð's knees?

Fjölsviðr: Hlíf (*Helper*), Hlífþrasa (*Help-breather*), Þjóðvara (*Folk-guardian*), Björt (*Shining*), Bleik (*White*), Blíð (*Blithe*), Fríðr (*Peaceful*), Eir (*Kindly?*) and Aurboða (*Gold-giver*). These maidens help and serve to protect the sons of men who give offerings on the holy altars.

Svipdagr: And is there any man alive who may dare to sleep within Menglöð's lovely arms?

Fjölsviðr: Only Svipdagr! The sun-bright maiden was destined to be his bride.

Svipdagr: Then fling wide the gates for Svipdagr is here! Go see if Menglöð is ready to give me joy.

Fjölsviðr: Do you hear, Menglöð? Here stands a man before whom the hounds are fawning and the gate opens wide. I believe it to be Svipdagr himself.

Menglöð: You shall be hanged high from a gallows, ravens shall peck out your eyes if indeed you are lying about the hero coming to my hall! Tell me, where do you come from? How did you get here? I must know what your kinsmen call you and what your lineage is before I can be certain that I am destined to be your bride.

Svipdagr: My name is Svipdagr, my father is called Sólbjartr (*Sun bright*) and I came hither by the wind-cold ways. No man may quarrel with Urðr's decrees be her rewards merited or not.

Menglöð: You are more than welcome for I have waited long. Come, take the welcoming kiss! The yearned-for meeting of lovers is the greatest joy of all! Day after day, day after day, I have waited for you here on Lyfjaberg! And you too have hungered after me! But now henceforward we shall live our lives together to the end!

In his *Teutonic Mythology* Viktor Rydberg erected a glittering
structure upon his interpretation of the *Lay of Svipdagr*. It may
be true (and most likely is) that Menglöð the "Necklace Glad"
is a hypostasis of Freya, the beautiful owner of the necklace of
the Brísings; it seems certain that Menglöð is depicted as awaiting Svipdagr in Asgard and that the main scene of *Svipdagsmál* takes place at Asgard gate: Fjölsviðr may even be Odin.
But Odin (as consort of Frigg-Freya) ought to be identified as
Svipdagr too. When Rydberg comes to employ such proofs as
that the sword mentioned in the poem was made by Völundr
(*Wayland the Smith*) because it was made by Loptr ("Airy")
and because Völundr in *Völundarkviða* 14 is supposed to refer
to himself as "Wind" (*Byr*), then one must suppose that such
"proofs" are similar to those employed to "prove" that Bacon
was Shakespeare. Surely a more fruitful line of enquiry is to
compare these stories of Skírnir and Svipdagr and find what,
if anything, they have in common: to do this, I will analyse the
three versions side by side.

SNORRI (*Gylf* XXXVII)	SKÍRNISMÁL	SVIPDAGSMÁL
1. There is a beautiful maiden difficult of attainment—Gerðr.	There is a beautiful maiden difficult of attainment—Gerðr.	There is a beautiful maiden difficult of attainment—Menglöð.
2. Love of her causes Frey to fall sick.	Love of her causes Frey to experience "a heavy grief".	
3. A young man Skírnir (*Shining*) undertakes a mission to the maiden apparently at the instigation of a father (*Njörðr*).	A young man Skírnir (*Shining*) undertakes a mission to the maiden apparently at the instigation of a father (*Njörðr*).	A young man Svipdagr (*Bright Day*) undertakes a mission to the maiden on the orders of his step-mother (unnamed).
4. Skírnir agrees to make the journey if Frey will give him his sword "which fights of its own accord".		

SNORRI (*Gylf* XXXVII)	SKÍRNISMÁL	SVIPDAGSMÁL
5.	The journey is extremely dangerous and Skírnir asks for Frey's sword and Odin's horse to help him. As we find out later, Skírnir is also in possession of [Iðunn's] golden apples and Odin's ring Draupnir.	The journey is extremely dangerous and Svipdagr has protective charms chanted over him by his dead mother.
6.	A herdsman outside Gerðr's dwelling suggests that Skírnir will die before he can get inside. There are fierce dogs and magic flickering flames before the door. Gerðr, however, orders the man to be bidden in.	Fjölsviðr outside Menglöð's dwelling acts as a warder. There are two fierce hounds before the gate and a hall is ringed with magic flickering flames. No one can enter the hall unless he first gets a magic sword to kill the cock on Mímameiðr and offer its meat to the hounds.
7. Skírnir asks for the maiden's hand for Frey and she agrees to meet him at "Barrey" a week later.	Skírnir offers the apples and Draupnir to Gerðr. She refuses them. He threatens to kill her with the sword; he utters other threats, but she is unmoved until he threatens her with "longing, madness and lust". She agrees to come to Frey a week later at "Barri".	Svipdagr mentions his name and is at once invited in to receive Menglöð's love.

From an analysis such as this it becomes obvious at once that Snorri's story of Skírnir, the stories contained in *Skírnismál* and in *Svipdagsmál* must have come from the same source. It seems likely from a comparison of the three tales that the original ingredients were as follows: a young man falls in love with a beautiful maiden difficult of attainment. He makes a dangerous journey to find her. A magic sword plays an important part in the journey: since we are not told of its being used against anybody, and since in one version it seems to form one of a group of three treasures to be offered as bribes for the maiden, it would seem likely that the magic sword was originally the price of the maiden's love. With the handing over of the sword the maiden is won.

Having reduced the myth to such terms one might say that the sword is an obvious phallic symbol and the whole a representation of the sexual act—and particularly a representation of the first experience by both parties to the act. But such assertions must wait for their discussion in the *Conclusion*.

It may be useful here to mention another myth connected with Freya, the stealing of her necklace Brísingamen. The priapic characteristics of both Frey and Freya link the two together, if indeed they do not identify them. For just as Frey loses his sword, his greatest treasure, so Freya loses her greatest treasure, her necklace. Frey's sword is the equivalent of Brísingamen. And the loss of both represents the loss of virginity, or the loss of erection and the broken hymen.

Little has been left of the myth of Brísingamen, but the story was known to others of the Gothonic peoples besides the Northmen. *Beowulf* 1197–1200 runs:

Nænigne ic under swegle	I have heard tell of no
selran hyrde	better treasure fit for
hordmaðm hæleþa,	princes since Hama car-
syþðan Hama ætwæg	ried off Brísingamen (that
to þære byrhtan byrig	ornament and gem) to
Brosingamene,	the shining citadel. . . .
sigle and sincfæt. . . .	

And a reference in Úlfr Uggason's *Húsdrápa* goes:

> The famed rain-bow's defender,
> Ready in wisdom, striveth

At Singasteinn with Loki,
Fárbauti's sin-sly offspring;
The son of mothers eight and one,
Mighty in wrath, possesses
The stone ere Loki cometh. . . .[82]

To which Snorri refers in *Skáldskaparmál* VIII when he says of Heimdallr that "he is the Frequenter of Vágasker and Singasteinn, where he contended with Loki for the Necklace of the Brísings . . . they were in the form of seals". Again Snorri says of Loki (*Sk.* XVI) that he may be nicknamed "Thief of Brísingamen".

If we piece these allusions together we may suppose that Loki stole Brísingamen from Freya, as he stole Sif's hair and Iðunn's apples, and that in each case the mythic meaning was the same; that Brísingamen was left on a skerry or rock in the sea (*singasteinn*, cf. O.E. *sincastān*, *treasure stone*); that the god Heimdallr (O.E. *Hama*) found out its whereabouts, swam out to it in the form of a seal, contended with Loki at the rock in the same form, beat Loki and eventually carried the treasure back to Asgard (*Beow.: "to þære byrhtan byrig"*).

3

HEIMDALLR—RÍGR

There is another story told of Heimdallr under the name of Rígr. The prose introduction to the *Verse Edda* poem *Rígspula* says, "Men tell in old stories that he of the gods who is called Heimdallr set out along a certain sea strand, and arriving at a house, called himself Rígr. This poem (*Rígspula*) follows these old tales. . . ." In the first stanza of *Rígspula* the god is described as being "old, strong, wise, mighty and brisk" and as "striding out". He called at the hovel of Ái (*Grandfather*) and Edda (*Grandmother*) a hoary old couple dressed in old-fashioned clothes. They refreshed him with heavy bread coarse with husks and a bowl of broth. Rígr shared the bed of Ái and Edda, lying for three nights in the middle; then he went on his way.

Nine months later, Edda gave birth to a son with black hair who was named Þræl (*Slave*). He grew into a big hulk of a man, with wrinkled rough skin, knotted knuckles, thick fingers, twisted back, protruding heels and an ugly face. He was strong and worked hard all day long. Soon Þræl married a woman similar to himself, her name was Þír (*Serving-woman*); she was bow-legged, with stained feet, sunburnt arms and a flat nose. The sons of Þræl and Þír were called Hreimr *the Shouter*, Fjósnir *the Herd*, Klúrr *the Coarse*, Kleggi *Horse-fly*, Kefsir *Whore-master*, Fúlnir *Stinker*, Drumbr *the Log*, Digraldi *the Fat*, Dröttr *Lazybones*, Hösvir *the Grey*, Lútr *the Bowed*, Leggjaldi *Big-legs*; and the daughters were Drumba *the Log*, Kumba *Stumpy*, Økkvinkalfa *Fat-legs*, Arinnefja *Hearth-nose*, Ysja *Harridan*, Ambátt *the Servant*, Eikintjasna *Oak Peg*, Tötrughypja *Raggyskirts* and Trönubeina *Cranelegs*. All these children worked every day about the house or muck-spreading, digging turf, herding swine and goats according to the ways of serving folk; for from them did the thralls arise.

But after Rígr had passed away from the hovel of Ái and Edda he came to a hall where lived Afi (*Grandfather*) and Amma (*Grandmother*). Afi was shaping wood for a loom: his beard was trimmed, his hair curled on his forehead, his clothes fitted close, while his wife sat spinning with a distaff. Amma wore a band round her head, on her body a smock and a kerchief with clasps round her shoulders. Rígr was refreshed with stewed calves' flesh and after supper lay in bed between the man and wife. After three nights he again passed on his way.

Nine months later Amma bore a son, Karl the Yeoman, with a rosy face and sparkling eyes. He grew up to own oxen and ploughs, to make carts and houses and barns. Karl's wife (with keys rattling at her waist) was called Snør (*Daughter-in-law*), and they had many children. Their sons were Halr *the*

Man, Drengr *the Strong*, Höldr *the Farmer*, Þegn *Freeman*, Smiðr *Craftsman*, Breiðr *the Broad*, Bóandi *Yeoman*, Bundin-skeggi *Trimbeard*, Búi *Householder*, Boddi *Farmholder*, Brattskeggr *High Beard* and Seggr *Goodfellow*; and their daughters Snót *Good Wife*, Brúðr *the Bride*, Svanni *the Slender*, Svarri *the Proud*, Sprakki *the Fair*, Fljóð *Good Woman*, Sprund *the Vain*, Víf *the Wife*, Feima *Bashful* and Ristill *the Graceful*. From all these are descended the race of yeomen farmers.

But once more did the god Rígr pay a call, this time upon Faðir and Móðir (*Father* and *Mother*) in their castle-hall. Father was winding strings for his hunting bow and making spears, Mother was wearing a gay cap, a blue gown with brooches on her breast and a broad train. A feast was set for Rígr on a table covered with a cloth of bright embroidered linen; there were thin loaves of white bread, well cooked meat and game in silver dishes all washed down with goblets of wine. Rígr did as formerly and went to bed between Father and Mother for three nights: then he went away.

Nine months later Mother gave birth to a blond-haired bright-cheeked baby with fierce proud eyes. They called him Jarl the Earl and as he grew he spent his time with lances and shields, bows and arrows; he learnt to ride horses, to handle a sword, to hunt with hounds and to swim. Then Rígr came striding back out of the grove and taught runes to Jarl, called him after his own name Rígr, and claimed him for a son and urged him to hold on to his heritage.

Afterwards, Jarl rode through a dark forest over frosty fells until he came to a hall. He fought and conquered. He ruled over men. Then Jarl sent his messengers to Hersir (*Lord*) who had a fair, slender-fingered daughter named Erna (*Capable*), and the outcome was that Jarl married Erna. Their children were Burr *the Son*, Barn *the Child*, Jóð *Youth*, Aðal *Off-spring*, Arfi *Heir*, Mögr *Sonny*, Niðr *Descendant*, Niðjungr *Chip-of-the-old-block*, Sonr *Son*, Sveinn *Boy*, Kundr *Kins-man*, and King the Young.

King the Young apparently assumes the mantle of Hiem-
dallr—as far as a mortal may be able. He learnt the use of magic
runes and eventually won the right to be called Rígr. But of his
particular exploits we know little or nothing, for the manuscript (*Codex Wormanius*), is incomplete.

There is little more to be told of Heimdallr-Rígr at this time;
but it is convenient to turn to his enemy, his opposite and complement, Loki.

4

LOKI STEALS SIF'S HAIR

Loki was well known as a mischief-maker and a thief. The
story of how he was instrumental in the stealing of Iðunn and
how he himself stole her apples has already been told; so has
what remains of the tale of Loki's stealing of Freya's necklace
Brísingamen. Now we come to the robbery of the long golden
tresses of Sif the wife of Thor. This story has probably led to the
slanderous rumours coupling Loki's name with Sif: for instance Hárbarðr taunts Thor with these words† "Sif has a lover
at home: go and have a crack at him—you'd be using your
beef to good purpose then!" And Loki himself says meaningly
to Sif‡ "Well, *I* know one at least who went where Thor should
have been."

This then is the story of the stealing of Sif's hair and the way
in which the gods turned it to good. It is told by Snorri in
Skáldskaparmál XXXV to explain why gold is sometimes
called "Sif's hair":

"Out of a spirit of mischief, Loki Laufeyjarson had shorn
Sif until she was bald as a coot. When Thor got to know, he
seized Loki and went the right way to break every bone in his
body until he promised he would so work it with the Dark
Elves as to get them to make for Sif a head of hair out of gold
which would proceed to grow like natural hair. So Loki

† *Hárb.* 47.   ‡ *Lok.* 53.

journeyed to those dwarfs called the Sons of Ívaldi and they made the hair and in addition the ship Skíðblaðnir and the spear Gungnir which came into the possession of Odin.

Then Loki wagered his head with the dwarf named Brokkr that his brother dwarf Sindri could not make three treasures equal in worth to these others. When they went into the smithy, Sindri laid a pigskin on the coals and ordered his brother Brokkr to blow the bellows and not to leave off blowing until he had taken that out of the fire which before he had put on. Thereupon Sindri left the smithy but as Brokkr pumped, a fly settled on the back of his hand and bit him: but he continued to blow as before until the smith came and withdrew from the glowing coals a boar with bristles of gold.

Next, Sindri placed some gold in the fire and told Brokkr to blow the bellows and not leave off blowing until he came back. He went away: and a fly came and settled on Brokkr's neck and bit him half as hard again as before. But still he continued pumping until the smith pulled out of the fire that golden ring which is called Draupnir.

Lastly, he laid iron on the hot coals ordering Brokkr to blow and remarking that everything would be spoilt if he stopped. At once a cleg alighted between his eyes and stung his eyelid until the blood dripped down into his eye and he couldn't see. He made a grab at the fly as fast as he could when the bellows sank down and swiped the beast off him just as the smith returned to observe that it would be a near go but that what was in the fire would be ruined. Sindri took out of the coals a hammer.

He placed all the treasures into his brother Brokkr's hands and told him to go to Asgard to get the wager settled. When Brokkr and Loki displayed their treasures, the Æsir sat on their judgement stools and the decision was to rest with Odin, Thor and Frey.

Loki gave the spear Gungnir to Odin; he gave the hair which Sif was to have to Thor; and to Frey he presented the ship Skíðblaðnir. He explained the properties of all the treasures which were these: the spear would never stop in its lunge, the hair would grow to the flesh once it reached Sif's head, and as for Skíðblaðnir, she should have a favourable wind as soon as the sail was hoisted to go wherever it was desired, but she could be folded up like a handkerchief and carried in the pocket if one wished.

Then Brokkr brought forward his treasures. He gave the ring to Odin, saying that every ninth night eight other rings equally precious would drop from it. To Frey he gave the boar saying it would run over air and sea, night or day, better than any horse, nor would it ever be so dark either at the dead of night or in the worlds of darkness that the boar wouldn't have enough light to see by wherever he went, his bristles sparkled so. Then he gave Thor the hammer and said he could smite with it as hard as he wanted at whatever was before him and the hammer would never fail, moreover once he had thrown it the hammer would never miss, nor would its flight be so long but it would return to his hand if he wished: lastly it was so small he could carry it inside his shirt. There was one blemish, the handle was a bit on the short side.

The gods pronounced judgement that the hammer was best of all those treasures and the finest defence against the frost giants; and they gave their verdict that the dwarf had won the wager. At that, Loki offered to redeem his head but the dwarf said, no, that was not what he expected. 'Catch me then!' cries Loki; and when the dwarf wanted to capture him he was well out of the way. Loki owned those shoes which enabled him to run on sky and sea. Then the dwarf prayed Thor to corner him, and he did so, when the dwarf would have chopped off his head; but Loki yammered that he should have the head but not the neck.

So the dwarf took a thong and a pointed knife intending to pierce holes in Loki's lips and stitch up his mouth: but the knife just wouldn't go through. He said it would have been better had his brother's awl been there, and no sooner said than done—there was the awl, and it pierced the lips. He sewed up the mouth, though Loki tore the thong from the lace holes. This thong by which Loki's lips were fastened together is called Vartari."

But the one story connected with Loki which will ever be remembered by gods and men, is that which caused the death of Balder the Beautiful and brought about the Doom of the Gods. Because the story is really part of the events leading up to the Ragnarök it will be best told in the next chapter.

CHAPTER X

Ragnarök

As I have argued before in Chapter IV, the god Balder is strongly linked to the cult of the "Lord" which flourished in Asia Minor and the Eastern Mediterranean. His bloody death and descent to hel to remain in the keeping of Hel the ruler of the underworld is paralleled in the Greek myth of Adonis. And the Northern myth-makers embodied the story of Balder in the myth of the Doom of the Gods, and his return from the underworld is not a yearly one like that of Adonis, but must wait until the old order has been destroyed and a new one arises: *then* does Balder come back.

Balder is the first of the gods to experience death and his baleful dreams were held to be a forewarning of his death and indeed of the beginning of the chain of events which were to lead to the Ragnarök.

I

BALDER'S DREAMS

The *Verse Edda* poem *Baldrs Draumar* (*Balder's Dreams*) says that the gods and goddesses held a council to discover why Balder had had baleful dreams. The poem does not say what the dreams were, though we might have guessed had we not been given the information in another source: Saxo (III, 77) says that in the night "Proserpine was seen to stand by him in a vision, and to promise that on the morrow he should have her embrace. The boding of the dream was not idle; for when three days had passed, Balder perished from the excessive torture of his wound . . . ". The fact that the Queen of the Underworld (whether called Proserpine or Hel) was to "embrace" Balder is an additional proof of the god's connection with the Adonis myth.

According to *Baldrs Draumar*, the outcome of the Æsir's deliberations is that Odin is despatched to the eastern gate of hel to exorcise a *völva* or *seeress*. He saddles Sleipnir and rides ever down "to Niflhel deep" past the growling hound until he comes to the *völva's* grave. Odin utters charms and raises the dead. The *völva* asks what person it is who has dragged her from the grave? Odin gives a false name, saying he is Vegtamr Valtamssonr (*Wanderer son of Battler*), and enquires for whom are the tables laid and the benches spread in hel? The *völva* says that the mead is brewed and the drink sparkles for Balder: she entreats her questioner to allow her to sink back to death.

Odin wants still more information: "Who will be Balder's murderer?" he asks, and the *völva* replies, "Höðr will carry the far-famed branch. He will kill Balder. Unwillingly, I have spoken; now I would be quiet."

"Not yet!" cries Odin, "Tell me who shall avenge Balder?"

"Rindr bears Váli to Odin in Vestrsalir (*the Western Halls*). He shall neither wash his hands nor comb his hair until he brings Balder's slayer to the funeral fire. Now let me go!"

"No!" cries Odin, "tell me who are the maidens who then shall weep and toss the sails up to heaven?"

At this question the *völva* realises that her questioner sees into the future as well as she and can be none other than Odin. "You are not Vegtamr!" she cries. "Nor are you a *völva*," says Odin, "but rather the mother of three giants!" The three giants most likely to be in Odin's thoughts are Fenriswulf, Jörmungandr and Hel, and if this is the case then the *völva* is none other than their mother Angrboða. Whoever she is, she finishes by saying "Ride home Odin in your pride. No man shall seek me again till Loki is set free from his bonds and the Destroyers ride to the Ragnarök".

Much the same story is contained in stanzas 31–33 of *Völuspá* where the *völva* says she saw the destiny of Odin's son Balder, the bleeding god. She saw the mistletoe full grown in strength.

A shaft from the tree was shot by Höðr. Balder lay dead but Odin's son (Váli) avenged his brother before ever he washed his hands or combed his hair; in fact, before he was one night old. Only Frigg (who could see into the future) wept sorely in Fensalir for Valhalla's need. Further, the *völva* saw Loki lying bound, with his wife Sigyn staying at his side.

Snorri gives a connected and most moving account of the events of Balder's death.

2

THE DEATH OF BALDER

"Now I must tell you† of events which to the gods seemed most ominous. It all began like this: Balder the Good dreamed premonitory dreams touching the safety of his life. When he told the gods his dreams they pooled their suggestions and it was decided to seek protection for Balder from every conceivable kind of hurt; and to this end Frigg exacted oaths from fire and water, iron and every sort of metal, stones, earth, trees, diseases, beasts, birds, poisons and serpents that they would never harm Balder. And when all this had been seen to, it became a sport and a pastime at their meetings for him to stand up as an Aunt Sally while all the others either shot at him or cut and thrust or merely threw stones. No matter what they did, he never took the slightest harm, which seemed to everybody the best of good sport.

Loki Laufeyjarson saw all this and liked it the worse when Balder was never injured. Disguised as an old crone, he went to see Frigg at Fensalir. Frigg asked the old woman if she knew what the gods were doing at their meeting today? She said they were all shooting at Balder without hurting him a bit. Frigg explained, 'Neither weapon nor wand will ever wound Balder, I have their given word—all of them.' The old crone croaked, 'Do you mean to say every single thing has given its oath to

† *Gylf.* XLIX.

protect Balder from harm?' 'As a matter of fact,' Frigg said, 'there is one young sprout growing in a wood over to the West of Valhalla (they call it Mistletoe) far too immature for me to ask it to swear oaths.'

The 'old crone' turned on 'her' heel at once, but Loki cut the mistletoe down and took it with him to the meeting. Höðr stood away on the edge of the ring of gods because he was blind. Loki whispered to him, 'Why aren't you shooting at Balder?' and he replied, 'Because I can't see where he is; and another thing—I have nothing to throw.' Then said Loki, 'Do as the others are doing and show honour to Balder as they do. I'll guide you to where he is standing: here, pitch this shaft at him.'

Höðr took the mistletoe and threw it at Balder just as Loki told him. The shaft flew full at him and he fell down dead to the ground—the cruelest tragedy that ever happened to gods and men.

As soon as Balder dropped, the gods were dumb-struck and their limbs went weak as water and they looked the one at the other with but a single thought in their heads 'who did this shameful thing'? which no one could ever avenge. They thought they had taken every precaution. And when at last the gods did find their voices the first sounds they made were wails of affliction, nor could one address the other for the distress within his throat. Even so, Odin had the bitterest grief to bear since his knowledge was the keener of how portentous to the gods was the slaying and loss of Balder.

When the gods had composed themselves a little, Frigg spoke up, 'Who is there', she asked, 'on our side who will earn the love and dying gratitude of all the gods by riding down the road to hel and trying to find the ghost of Balder, who will ask the ransom Hel desires—provided she is willing to allow Balder to come back home to Asgard?'

He who is called Hermóðr the Swift, a son of Odin, said he was ready to go.

Then Odin's horse Sleipnir was led from the stables; Hermóðr strode into the saddle and galloped away.

The gods lifted up Balder's corpse and carried it down to the sea shore. Balder's ship was called Hringhorni. This was the greatest of all vessels which the gods were about to launch, and amidships they built Balder's funeral pyre, only to find they were unable to budge the boat. So they sent into Giantland for a giantess called Hyrrokkin who came astride a wolf with a viper for a bridle. As she lept off her steed, Odin shouted up four berserkers to manage the brute, which they were quite unable to control until they stunned it. Hyrrokkin stepped up to the ship's prow and heaved it ahead at the first short, sharp shove, so that the sparks feathered up from the rollers and the ground trembled. Thor was suddenly enraged and flew to his hammer intending to smash open her skull; but the gods pacified him for her sake. Then Balder's body was carried out on to the ship, and when his wife, Nanna the daughter of Nep, saw it she cried out in her grief and anguish; she was born in the fire and she perished in the fire. Thor then stepped in front and blessed the pyre with Mullicrusher, and at the same time a dwarf named Litr ran in under his feet; Thor lunged at him savagely with his toe, flinging him into the midst of the blaze and he burned to death.

All manner of people gathered for the burning: first, let me mention Odin, and with him Frigg and his Valkyries and his ravens; Frey, and drawing his chariot the two boars called Goldenbristles and Tearingtusks; Heimdallr riding his horse Goldtopping; Freya with her cats; then thronged a great host of frost giants and hill trolls. Odin flung into the fire his gold ring called Draupnir the Dropper: it had a supernatural power in that every ninth night there dropped from it eight other such rings of equal weight. Balder's horse in full harness had already been laid on the pyre.

But to speak now of Hermóðr: he rode nine days and nights down ravines ever darker and deeper, meeting no one, until he came to the banks of the river Gjöll which he followed as far as the Gjöll Bridge: this bridge is roofed with burning gold. Móðguðr is the maiden's name who guards the bridge. She asked him his name or lineage, saying only the day before five droves of dead men had passed over the bridge 'but the bridge echoed less under them than thee. Anyway, you haven't the pallor of a dead man: why are you riding down the Hel Way?'

He replied, 'I ride to hel to seek out Balder. You don't happen to have set eyes on Balder on the road to hel?'

She said Balder had already ridden over Gjöll Bridge 'and the road to hel lies down still and to the north'.

Hermóðr galloped on until he came to Hel Gate Bars, where he stepped down from his horse and tightened the girths. He mounted again and plunged his spurs into the animal's flanks. The stallion lept so high there was plenty of twilight between him and the bars. And Hermóðr rode on to the hall of Hel where he got down and went in to see his brother Balder sitting on a throne. Hermóðr stayed with him that night.

Next morning Hermóðr begged Hel to let Balder ride back home with him and went on to tell how greatly the gods were grieving. Hel said it would soon be put to the test that Balder was so beloved by all 'as they make out: if every single creature up in heaven, dead or alive, really mourns him then he shall be restored to the gods. He stays with Hel if but one alone speaks against him or refuses to mourn'.

Hermóðr stood up and Balder saw him outside and he pulled off the ring Draupnir and sent it back to Odin for a memento, while Nanna sent some linen and many other gifts to Frigg, and to Fulla a golden ring.

Then rode Hermóðr back to Asgard and related all his news, everything he had seen and everything he had heard.

At once, the gods sent messengers to every corner of heaven asking all to weep Balder un-dead, and everything did so, both men and beasts, earth, stones, trees, and every metal (you must have noticed how these things weep as soon as they come out of the frost into the heat). When at last the messengers came home, having pursued their errand diligently, they passed a cave where an old witch was crouching. Her name was Þökk and they asked her to mourn for Balder, but she chanted:

Þökk must drop
 only dry tears
  for the beautiful Balder's burial:
 living or dead
I loved not the churl's son;
  let Hel hold what she has!

Everybody guessed that this must have been Loki Laufeyjarson
who had done so much evil among the gods."

3

THE BINDING OF LOKI

"When the gods flew into a blind rage with Loki† (as was to
be expected) he bounded away and lighted on a certain mountain and there built himself a house with four doors to see out
in every direction. Frequently during the daytime he assumed
the shape of a salmon and haunted the waterfall called Frá-
nangr *the Gleaming Water*. He pondered to himself what plan
the gods would likely employ to catch him at the waterfall; and
when he sat in the house he took some linen yarn and knotted
it into the shape we have come to know as a fishing net; and
the fire burned before him as he worked. He saw in the embers
that the gods would make short work of him, for Odin had
already seen from Hliðskjálf where he was. In a second he had
jumped up and into the river, casting his net from him into the
fire as he went. The gods blarged up to the door and the first to
enter was the one who is wisest of all, called Kvasir; when he
saw the fire webbed with white ash where the net had burnt he
realised it had been a trap to catch fish and he told the gods so.
Straightaway, they set about making themselves a net to the
pattern of the ashes of Loki's old one. As soon as it was made,
the gods hurried to the river and cast the net into the waterfall:
Thor held one end and all the gods the other and thus they
dragged it. But Loki flashed in front and hung at the bottom

† *Gylf.* L.

between two stones. They hauled the net towards him and knew from the disturbance that he was in front of them. A second time they went up to the waterfall and cast out the net, having bound it to something so heavy that nothing should be able to pass underneath it. Loki swam in front of the net and when he saw it was only a short stretch to the sea he lept back over the edge of the net and ran up the waterfall. The gods saw where he went and followed to the fall, dividing their party into two groups, one on either bank, while Thor waded behind in mid-stream. They went like this again towards the sea. Now Loki had a choice of two things: his life would be in deadly peril if he fled out to sea, or he could risk diving over the net again; and that's what he did.

Like a flash he dove over the edge cord.

Thor grabbled after him and caught him, but allowed him to slip through his fingers as far as his tail, which he gripped hard (and which incidentally, is the reason why to this day the salmon taper down behind). Loki was now captured unconditionally and lugged off to a cavern.

The gods got hold of three rocks, set them on edge and split a wedge out of each. They then captured Loki's sons Váli and Nari (or Narfi); Váli they charmed into the shape of a wolf and he ripped his own brother Nari to pieces; next the gods extracted his entrails to bind Loki with over the three rocks standing on edge: one stood under his shoulders, the second under his loins and the third under the hollow of his knees. He was then bolted in with iron. Lastly, Skaði got a poisonous snake and prisoned it above him in such a way as to let the venom drop from the snake into his open face. But Sigyn, Loki's wife, always stands beside him holding a basin under the drops. When the basin is full to overflowing she hurries to pour away the poison, and meanwhile the venom drips on to his face, which throws him into a convulsion so terrific that all the earth trembles (that's what we call earthquakes).

And there he lies in bonds until the Twilight of the Gods."

4

THE RAGNARÖK

"The details of the Ragnarök are many and terrible,† and first that the Winter shall come which is called the Monstrous Winter, when blizzards shall drive from every quarter, frosts shall be iron-hard and winds sharp, nor shall the sun afford respite. These winters shall come three in a row with no summer between. But to work up to that there shall be three other winters in which the whole world shall be embroiled in war. For sordid greed, brother shall slay brother; neither father nor son shall show each other mercy in slaughter and fornication. Just as it says in *The Spaewife's Song*:

> Brother fights with brother,
> they butcher each other;
>   daughters and sons
>   incestuously mix;
> man is a plaything
> of mighty whoredoms;
>   an axe-time, sword-time,
>   shields shall be split;
> a wind-age, a wolf-age,
> before the World ends.

Then comes that to pass which is awesome news: the Wolf swallows the Sun. Men shall think that a mighty disaster. The other Wolf shall take the Moon at one bite, an irreparable loss; while the stars shall turn from their steadings in heaven. The next news is that the earth and the mountains shake, woods are torn up by the roots, crags crack from top to bottom and all fetters and bonds are smashed and split. Thereupon, the Wolf Fenrir breaks loose, and a great bore of waters inundates the land as, in a gigantic fury, the World Serpent buckles and boils up out of the sea! Then it comes to pass that the vessel

† *Gylf.* LI.

called Naglfar slips her moorings. That ship is built of the nails of dead men, so here's a warning that if a man dies with his nails unshorn he is adding greatly to the materials for Naglfar (a thing both gods and men would be slow to do). At any rate, poised on this almighty billow shoots forth Naglfar. The Fenris Wolf gallops with his jaws agape, his lower fangs raking the earth, his upper scraping heaven, and wider yet would he yawn were there room enough: flames are sprouting from his eyes and nostrils. The World Serpent blows such clouds of poison that he sprinkles all the earth and sky: he would make your blood run cold as he comes on the other side of the Wolf.

At the height of the clangour the heavens split asunder and through the rift ride Múspell's Sons. Surtr rides first, flinging fire before him and after him both, in his fist the supreme sword more dazzling than the sun. And when they gallop up over Bifröst, the bridge crumbles behind them as was foretold. All the hosts of Múspell plough steadily on to the plain called Vígríðr to meet with Fenrir the Wolf and the World Serpent. There too come Loki and Hrymr who leads all the Frost Giants, while Loki's followers are the Sons of Hel; and the Children of Múspell form an army on their own—a blazing host! The Valley Vígríðr is a hundred leagues wide and a hundred leagues broad.

When this comes to pass, Heimdallr stands forth and blows lustily on Gjallarhorn to turn out all the gods, who fall in together. Then Odin rides to Mímir's Well to seek advice for himself and his people. Yggdrasill the World Ash begins to tremble; no corner of heaven or earth but is seized with terror. The gods and the Einherjar do on their battle harness and march to the field. Odin is riding at their head wearing his golden helmet and a sparkling war coat, and porting his spear called Gungnir. He charges full tilt at Fenrir the Wolf with Thor by his side but unable to help him, for he has enough on his hands to fight with the Serpent of the World. Frey and Surtr attack each other, when a violent conflict ensues before Frey is slain:

FIG. 19 DANISH BRONZE AGE TRUMPET OR LUR

he had sealed his own death warrant when he gave his incomparable sword to his servant Skírnir.

Now the hel hound Garmr, who was chained by the Bottomless Pit, at last breaks free, a fearsome monster. He savages Týr and each of them slays the other. Thor carries death to the Serpent of the World, but staggers away a mere nine steps: then he himself sinks down dead to the earth enveloped in the poison mist the Serpent blew upon him. The Wolf gorges Odin: that is how he dies, but at once Víðarr flies forward and plants one foot inside the Wolf's lower jaw. (On that foot he wears the boot which has been in the making since time first began, cobbled from the snippets of leather which men carve from the toes and heels of their footgear; and for that reason men who wish in their hearts to come to the help of the gods ought to cast away those same pieces). In his fists he grips the Wolf's upper jaw and so rips asunder his maw: and that is how the Wolf dies. But at last Surtr pitches flame over the earth and burns up the whole of heaven. This is the account of it according to *The Spaewife's Song:*†

> Shrilly shrieks the horn
> of Heimdallr up the sky;
>   Odin whispers
>   with the head of Mím;
> Yggdrasill wavers,
> the long-standing World Ash,

† *Völ.* 45 ff.

the old tree judders
and the giant is set free.

What's up with the Æsir?
What with the Elves?
    All Giantland is groaning,
    the gods rush to the Thing;
the dwellers in the crags
the dwarfs are moaning
    by their doors of stone.
    What more will you divine?

From the east sweeps Hrymr
with his shield shoved high;
    the Serpent rolls
    into a giant's rage
beating up the billows;
while the bronze-beaked eagle
    screams slitting corpses;
    and Naglfar sets sail.

From the north a ship sails
with the sons of Hel,†
    drinking the spray
    Loki steers away:
there row the race of monsters
with all their men,
    also in the boat
    is the brother of Býleistr.

From the south drives Surtr
with the scourge of forests;‡
    the sun of the battle-gods
    blazes from his sword;

† MS. has "From the east a ship sails with Múspell's sons" but according to Snorri Múspell's sons ride over the Rainbow Bridge while Loki brings the children of Hel in a boat (as the rest of the stanza bears out).

‡ A kenning for fire.

crag peaks crash as
the kobolds scuttle;
   corpses tramp the hel-way
   and heaven cracks.

Then strikes Hlín
her second great sorrow†
   when Odin fares
   to fight with the Wolf;
and Beli's bright slayer
to battle with Surtr:
   the loved one of Frigg
   is doomed to fall.

Flies Odin's son
to fight with the Wolf,
   Víðarr bores at
   the carrion beast:
with the point of his sword
he pierces the heart
   of the monster's son:
   his sire is avenged.

The glorious heir
of Hlöðyn goes
   valiant to death
   by the venom of the Serpent;
all men everywhere
must abandon their hearths
   when Midgard's defender
   falls in exhaustion.

The sun grows dark,
earth sinks under sea;
   from their steadings in heaven
   the bright stars turn;

† Hlín is Frigg and her first "great sorrow" was caused by the death of her son Balder.

    fire and reek burl
    upwards and break
    with hazy heat
    against heaven itself!

  Such is the myth of the Doom of the Divine Powers called in Icelandic *Ragnarök*. Since in the *Gylfaginning* this is the only occasion when Snorri quotes a *Verse Edda* poem at great length (nine consecutive stanzas and one additional one) it is obvious that he considered his source to be excellent. But there *are* discrepancies (some most important) between Snorri's prose account of the Ragnarök and the account which he quotes from *Völuspá*. If, however, Snorri has to hand additional sources which he considered as good as, or better than *Völuspá* in some details, then it is certain that he would have made use of them. We ought now to try to find answers to two questions: in what do Snorri and *Völuspá* differ regarding their expositions of the Ragnarök, and are there confirmatory sources for any different or additional information which Snorri gives? And perhaps first one ought to make the point that though *Völuspá* is the gem of the eddaic canon, is three hundred years older than Snorri's work and (whether produced in Iceland or not) was composed some fifty years before Iceland was converted, nevertheless the poem is not to be regarded as an infallible pagan mythic source. In fact, there are variations from general mythic belief within *Völuspá* itself, and not insignificant ones: for example, stanza 39 speaks of the wolf who is to steal the moon from the sky, but the wolf who is to swallow the sun is forgotten; instead, the next stanza says "the sunshine grows dark" *svört verða sólskin*, an idea repeated in 59 "the sun grows dark, earth sinks under sea; from their steadings in heaven the bright stars turn . . .". This picture of *Völuspá's* is more nearly paralleled in Christian writ than in any other pagan source, as in Revelations VI 12–14 "(The Lamb) broke the sixth seal; and with that there was a great earthquake, and the sun grew dark as sackcloth, and the whole moon blood-red; the stars of heaven fell to earth, like unripe fruit shaken from a fig-tree, when a high wind rocks it; the sky folded up like a scroll, and disappeared; no mountain, no island, but was removed from its place . . . ".[83] Snorri, of course, sticks to his story of the two wolves Hàti and Skoll who swallow the moon and the sun and he is borne out by *Grímnismál* 40, and 21 where the kenning *Þjóðvitnis fiskr* "Mighty Wolf's fish" is used of the sun, and again by *Vafþrúðnismál* 46 although here the sun swallower is called Fenrir. In the face of this evidence we must believe that Snorri is reporting the true pagan tradition.

Again, Snorri has the story of the Thickmost Shoe which Odin's son Víðarr wears on the foot which he plants in Fenrir's bottom jaw when he avenges his father by tearing the Wolf's gob apart: but *Völuspá* tells nothing of the shoe and says Víðarr stabs the Wolf to the heart. Once more Snorri is supported by *Vafþrúðnismál* 53 "the wolf shall swallow the Father of Men, a deed which Víðarr will avenge in the fight when he rends those terrible jaws apart". As a matter of fact *Völuspá* does not say that the Wolf swallows Odin but that "Hlín's (i.e. Frigg's) second sorrow comes when Odin advances to fight the Wolf". Other important omissions by the author of *Völuspá* are the fact that the hel-hound Garmr despatches the god Týr; and the breaking of the Rainbow Bridge Bifröst or Bilröst under the hooves of the Sons of Múspell (supported by *Fáfnismál* 15). Both Snorri and *Völuspá* forget to mention that Heimdallr and Loki kill each other. *Völuspá* does not remember to muster the Einherjar.

Völuspá presents the only connected account of the Ragnarök to be found among the pieces of the *Verse Edda*, and for that reason, and because Snorri made such use of it for his own account, we might have suspected that this wild tale of the doom of the gods was mainly a creation of the *Völuspá* poet. But since, as I have indicated, Snorri puts forward additional information and different (some radically different) versions of episodes, we may rest assured that this story was widely current among Northmen of Norway and Iceland (if not Denmark and Sweden) at least in Viking times. This assurance is supported by other of the *Verse Edda* poems, by *Vafþrúðnismál* 18 which runs:

> The valley is called Vígríðr
> where converge in battle
>   Surtr and the gracious gods;
> a hundred leagues
> is it every which way—
>   yes, that's the appointed place;

while stanzas 44 and 45 of the same poem allude to the *fimbulvetr* the "Monstrous Winter" which Snorri says will precede the end of the world and which *Völuspá* mentions in stanza 40; again *Vafþrúðnismál* 47 refers to the "death of the gods", stanza 50 to the "fires of Surtr" which have destroyed the world; *Baldrs Draumar* 14 speaks of the time when the destroyers shall come and actually uses the term *Ragnarök*; and not to be tedious with these references, for there are others, I may quote finally *Völuspá hin skamma* 12:

> The stormy sea
> spits in heaven's face,
>   it drives o'er the land
>   and deluges the sky
> from which break blizzards
> and biting winds:
>   for that's the plan
>   when the Powers are doomed.

The conclusions I draw are that *Völuspá* (great poem though it is) is not the only early source for the myth of the Ragnarök; that other sources, just as early, present additional as well as *different* information; that Snorri conscientiously set out all the information available to him (including some no longer extant in any other source) and that he did so even when the pieces of information were mutually contradictory or reduplicating each other.

One such reduplicated myth, I contend, is that of the wolf

swallowing Odin. Some editors have tried to discredit Snorri by suggesting that the *Völuspá* poet has refined the myth by recounting nothing of Odin's being swallowed and by relating that Víðarr stabs the Wolf to avenge his father while Snorri says Víðarr tore the Wolf's jaws apart. But the simple slaying with a sword had no part in the original tale (I am convinced) for there was a valid reason why the Wolf had to be torn open, namely *to let the one swallowed come out again*—just as happens in a folklore version of the story, *Little Red Riding Hood*. I have said this wolf-swallowing myth is reduplicated, and I suggest in four main stories (1) the wolf called Skoll swallows the sun, (2) the wolf called Hati swallows the moon, (3) the Wolf Fenrir swallows Odin, (4) the hel-hound Garmr kills Týr. In the case of Skoll and Hati the central incident is the despoliation of the sky; with Týr, I have noted the myth of his brush with Fenrir resulting in the loss of his hand, and have concluded that the story concerned Týr representing *Djevs the old Indo-European Sky Father: we can hardly be wrong in reading Týr's destruction by Garmr as also concerning Týr as *Djevs; and in the same way Odin who is swallowed by the Wolf Fenrir is not Odin-Vâta the old wind god, but Odin= Týr= *Djevs. In other words, all these manifestations are those of a single original myth dealing with the *temporary* disappearance of the Sky Father caused by his swallowing by a beast and of his reappearance or rehabilitation "explained" by some such story as that concerning Víðarr. Solar myth theories are a bit dusty these days, but I would ask the reader to bear in mind the possibility of such a tale as we are dealing with being an explanation of the daily setting and rising of the sun; of storm clouds covering the sun; or of an eclipse of the sun; or even of a particular northern application such as might "explain" the long darkness of an arctic or sub-arctic winter. Be that as it may, the myth of Odin's being swallowed by the Wolf goes back to Indo-European times, and so does the story of the swallowed-one's return which also lived on to Viking times—how strangely changed we shall see.

At first sight, it is perhaps extraordinary that the Northern mythology should kill off all its important gods in the last cosmic battle: but we may suspect that this nihilistic concept was fostered particularly in the Migration and fatalistic Viking Ages. There are several pointers to a comparatively late origin of the idea of the Ragnarök: first, the parallel pantheons of the Hindus, Greeks and Latins are not killed off; then there is no mention of the Northern *goddesses* being annihilated; but most important, we may conclude from the arguments above that the removal of Odin was at first not a final one and was certainly not part of a permanent cosmic cataclysm. Of the other gods who die at the Ragnarök or just before it, we see that the story of Týr-Garmr is simply reduplicating the Odin-Wolf myth; that Balder was playing out the events of a self-contained myth from Asia-Minor of the god who died into the under-world only to be resurrected again each year; Frey (likewise a "lord") must also owe his death (for the purpose of the Ragnarök at the hands of Surtr) originally to the requirements of the Adonis-type myth.

The Ragnarök is closely linked with what comes after—the return of certain gods to a new heaven, the appearance of a new earth and so on. It will be helpful before further discussion to see what the sources have to say.

5

NEW HEAVEN, NEW EARTH, NEW GODS

According to Snorri, when Gylfi has heard the recital of the events of the Ragnarök he enquires,† " 'But what comes after? What happens when all Creation is burned up, when the gods are all dead as well as all the Chosen Warriors and the Races of Men? Didn't you say before that somebody should live to all eternity in a new heaven?'

The Third answered, 'Many are the abodes which are good

† *Gylf.* LII.

and many which are ill: the best is the one which shall be
Gimlé; and excellent for those gods who find their amusement
in clinking the can is that hall called Brimir which stands in
Ókólnir *the Never Cold*. That too is a good hall which stands
in Niðafjöll (it's made of red gold), called Sindri. There shall
live good men who are pure in heart. At Náströnd *the Corpse
Strand* is a vast hall and an evil one: its entrance faces the cold
north. Moreover, it is rough with coiling snakes as though it
were a wicker work house, while all the snakes' heads look into
the hall and spurt poison in such quantities that it rolls a river
of venom from the hall: and oath breakers and murderers are
forced to wade through it. As it says here:

> I saw a hall
> standing far from the sun
> at Náströnd;
> the door faces north
> drops of poison
> drip through the skylights;
> the hall is bordered
> with the backs of snakes.
>
> Murderers and perjurers
> among dead men
> ever shall wade through
> these baneful waves;

though in Hvergelmir is the worst:

> There Níðhöggr flenses
> the dead men's flesh.

Then Gylfi asked,† 'But will there be any gods alive, or will
there be any earth or heaven?'

High replied, 'Surely the earth shall rise up green and fair
out of the sea, and plants shall grow there where none were ever
sown. Víðarr and Váli shall live on as though neither sea nor
the fires of Surtr had impaired them, and they shall settle in

† *Gylf.* LIII.

Iðavöllr where Asgard formerly was. There too shall come the sons of Thor, Móði, and Magni bringing with them Thor's hammer. After them shall come Balder and Höðr from hel. They shall live in love and talk long together and revive all their old wisdom and shall put behind them all the ancient evils of the Serpent of the World and Fenriswulf. Then in the grass they shall stumble upon the golden chessmen owned by the gods before. Just as this says:

> Víðarr and Váli
> shall view the gods' abodes
>   after Surtr's fires have sunk;
> Móði and Magni
> shall have Mullicrusher
>   when Vingnir's strife shall cease.

Moreover, in Hoddmímir's wood two humans called Líf and Lífþrasir hid themselves against the fires of Surtr. From these two descended so multitudinous a people that they colonised the whole world. It says so here:

> Líf and Lífþrasir
> themselves will lie
>   hid in Hoddmímir's wood;
> they shall drink meanwhile
> of the morning dews
>   and people the plains of Earth.

And you must think it rather surprising when the Sun gets a daughter no less fair than herself who will pace the same path as her mother: as it says here:

> One beaming daughter
> the bright Sun bears
>   before she is swallowed by Fenrir;
> so shall the maid
> pace her mother's way
>   when the gods have gone to their doom.

And now, if you have any more questions, I for one don't know where you'll dig them up; for I never heard anybody tell forth the course of the world at greater length. So avail yourself of what you have heard.' "

Snorri's description of what comes after Ragnarök is pretty sketchy. His first information is of the heavenly places and the hellish ones. From his quotations it is quite obvious that he is merely paraphrasing certain stanzas of *Völuspá*. But there is this important difference: *Völuspá* names these various places and from the context it is clear that they are supposed to exist before and not after the Ragnarök—except in the case of Gimlé.

Because Snorri has so obviously paraphrased *Völuspá* in parts of his description of After the Ragnarök, we must prefer the verse source to him in those particular parts: for in some cases his interpretation of *Völuspá* is not what the poem's creator intended.

Völuspá† says that the earth rises once more evergreen out of the sea, the cataracts fall again from the cliffs above which the eagle flies and below which the fish swims. The "Æsir" meet on Iðavöllr and talk of what has come to pass; they find in the grass the golden tables which belonged to them before. Unsown fields bear ripe fruit; all evils are righted; Balder comes back and he and his slayer Höðr live in "Odin's hall" with other gods. Hœnir comes back to power. The nephews of Odin dwell in heaven. In Gimlé (a hall thatched with gold and brighter than the sun) shall the righteous dwell for ever. There follows in the *Hauksbók* manuscript a half stanza which is not found in *Regius*:

> Then comes a ruler
> to keep dominion,
> a mighty lord
> majestic over all. . . .

Some editors regard this as spurious, some as showing the influence of Christian thought on the author of *Völuspá*. The last

† *Völ.* 58–65.

stanza speaks of Níðhöggr "the dark dragon" flying upwards from Niðafjöll bearing corpses on his wings.

From a comparison of Snorri and *Völuspá* we notice that there is a general correspondence: both agree that the *status quo ante bellum* is in a large measure restored, for the earth comes back fresh, so does heaven and certain of the gods again take up their abodes on high. But Snorri ignores Hœnir and, even more important, the suggestion of the "mighty lord".

Snorri adds material from *Vafþrúðnismál* to the effect that Odin's sons Víðarr and Váli shall live in the new heaven after the Ragnarök; so shall Thor's sons Móði and Magni, who inherit his hammer Mjölnir. Also there shall be a new sun in the sky—a daughter of the old one. But perhaps most important, human life shall be perpetuated through a man and a woman, Líf (*Life*) and Lífþrasir (*Desiring Life*) who shelter from the Monstrous Winter in "Hoddmímir's Wood".

The last stanza of the late (twelfth century) *Völuspá hin Skamma* is reminiscent of the *Hauksbók's* "There comes a ruler etc". It is given significance too by its context, for it follows a description of the sea flooding earth and heaven "when the Powers are doomed" (see page 284). It runs:†

> Then comes one
> who is greater than all,
>   though never his name
>   do I dare to name;
> few now see
> in the future further
>   than the moment Odin
>   is to meet the Wolf.

What are we to make of these shreds and patches? It is easy enough to pick on the references to the "one who is greater than all", the "mighty Lord" and say "Jesus Christ"; to remember Gimlé, the city or hall of gold, and murmur "the New Jerusalem". Snorri himself was nominally a Christian, but strik-

† *Völuspá hin Skamma* 14.

ingly, he makes no reference to the "one who is greater than all"; and although it may be argued that his text of *Völuspá* was without the so-called spurious verse, he certainly knew *Völuspá hin Skamma* and he did accept Gimlé. Presumably the authors of the *Verse Edda* pieces were pagan, but there is every chance that they could have been affected by the Christians all round them in Ireland, England and the continent of Europe. We may argue this way and that, but there are, I contend, definite pointers.

As I have said, the Ragnarök is a comparatively late conception, probably a purely Scandinavian, possibly even only a Norwegian and Icelandic conception. In *Ynglinga saga*, for instance, both the Danish Odin and the Swedish Frey die in their beds and not in conflict with Surtr and the sons of Múspell. The Ragnarök has two fundamental ideas (1) the destruction of the Divine Powers by the Sons of the Destroyers of the World, and (2) the assisting of the Divine Powers by men brave enough to die honourably on the battlefield. But I have already shown that the "everlasting battle", out of which the Einherjar concept grew, already existed unattached not only in Gothonic but also in Celtic myth; and secondly that the destruction of Odin by his being swallowed by a Wolf, and the destruction of Týr by a similar agency are one and the same myth going back to Indo-European times and telling of a *temporary* disappearance. And so the ideas of coming-back, of resurrection, of a new heaven (actually the continuation of the old one) have existed in the body of pagan myth from the earliest times, and there is no need to "explain" these concepts by saying they are borrowed Christian doctrines.

We can see now that the Ragnarök myth (both as reported in Snorri's *Edda* and in the *Verse Edda*) has grown by a process of agglutination: it is a number of different myths stuck together. Already we have recognized (1) the temporary disappearance of the Sky Father (Odin, Týr), (2) the temporary disappearance of the "lord" into the Underworld (Balder, Frey), (3) the Everlasting Battle, (4) the Wild Hunt (of Odin–

Vâta). To pile Pelion upon Ossa, the Northern mythmakers have added at least one, possibly two other tales to the Ragnarök, namely a deluge myth and a myth of a great fire. This is where Líf and Lífþrasir come in. Snorri pictures these two as surviving "the fires of Surtr (*Gylf.* LIII), but in actual fact his source (*Vafþrúðnismál* 44, 45) depicts them as surviving the Fimbul-*Winter*, the monstrous upheaval of the weather of the world. They are said to shelter in "Hoddmímir's wood" a kenning for the World Ash, Yggdrasill. Throughout the world there are supposed to be some four or five hundred deluge myths: many tell of terrible hailstorms and blizzards (*Völ.* 44, *Gylf.* LI), of the sea inundating the land (*Gylf.* LI), of the earth sinking below the waters (*Völ.* 56, *Gylf.* LI). It becomes obvious in such descriptions as this in their account of the Ragnarök that both *Völuspá* and Snorri are dealing with a deluge myth—a myth which concerns the flooding of the whole earth. In such circumstances what happened to the inhabitants? Some tales tell of deliverance through a boat (Noah and his pairs of animals), some of escape by climbing a high mountain (Peru), some by climbing a tree: one version quoted by Bellamy[84] combines all three methods—mountain, tree and boat. We have already come across one Gothonic version of a deluge myth in the story of the giant Bergelmir and his wife who escaped (according to Snorri) by "climbing on to a mill"; when we consider this in conjunction with the evidence just set out to prove that *Völuspá* and Snorri are dealing with a deluge myth, we can hardly suppose otherwise than that Líf and Lífþrasir were originally believed to have saved themselves from a world flood by climbing up the world tree Yggdrasill. A *world* flood, we notice, not a heaven flood: in other words, the story of Líf and Lífþrasir and their deluge had at first nothing to do with a general destruction of the gods.

For good measure we are presented in the descriptions of Ragnarök with a Cosmic Fire myth too. Surtr is at the bottom of this. For a being who appears to play so important a part in Northern mythology we are told very little about him. He is there at the beginning (he plays warder of the realm of Múspell-heim with a flaming sword—according to Snorri) and he is there—almost—at the end: for there is a striking thing which should make us suspicious at once—neither Snorri nor *Völuspá* mentions Surtr again after the Ragnarök; he just disappears from the myth, he has no part to play in the (supposedly) new order. Yet if Surtr had been able to bring down most of the Æsir in ruin and conflagration his power must have been greater than theirs and he should have taken Odin's place.

The name Surtr means "black", an incongruous name for a fire-being until we discover that Agni, the Hindu fire-god is called "black-backed" when he passes through the forest, and at once we see his carbonized track. The ancient Indo-European fire god's most devastating manifestation was long remembered: for the *Völuspá* poet says Surtr had in his hand fire "the scourge of forests". The *Rig-Veda's* description of Agni (vii, 3) is almost word for word what Snorri says of Surtr when he leads the Children of Múspell at Ragnarök: "O Agni, thou from whom, as a new-born male, undying flames proceed, the brilliant smoke-god goes towards the sky, for as a messenger thou art sent to the gods. Thou, whose power spreads over the earth in a moment when thou hast grasped food with thy jaws—like a dashing army thy blast goes forth; with thy lambent flame thou seemest to tear up the grass ... thy brightness comes like the lightning of heaven; thou showest splendour like the bright sun."[85]

Cosmic fire myths are not as numerous as deluge myths, but we can quote examples from the east (Palestine) to the west (American aborigines). An eastern example is to be found in *Revelations*, Ch. VIII; a western example is that of the Yana Indians (California) who tell of five men who set out to steal fire from a mountain top for their race who up to then had been without fire. On the way back, the fire was dropped and set the world ablaze: there were flames everywhere, rocks cracked apart with the heat, the lakes and rivers boiled and dense smoke covered all.

Sometimes it is a god, sometimes a demon, who burns up the world: whichever it is, we can be sure that it *is* the world and not heaven which burns. Surtr is, of course, presented as an inimical being, both to gods and to men: but whether he was originally a god or a demon, whether he was at first identified with Heimdallr or with Loki, we can be certain that he was a world-destroyer and not a heaven-destroyer. It was the later northern pagans who turned Surtr into a fire demon with power over the "joyous gods", and the important thing is not that the gods should have been destroyed, but *why* the Northmen destroyed them.

CHAPTER XI

Conclusion

SOME THEORIES OF THE ORIGIN OF MYTHS

IT is comparatively recently that myths have been taken from the nursery to the study and been invested with an adult importance. For most commentators are agreed on the importance of myths and the more recent the commentary the more important the regard. But in what the importance of myths consists there is still a fair measure of disagreement. It may be helpful to glance at some of the better known mythological theories.

The ancient Greek writer Euhemeros came to the conclusion that myths are based on historic happenings and that the gods are mostly deified men, and their feats only exaggerated traditions of exploits of outstanding primeval, generally national heroes. This is the attitude taken up by Snorri in the Prologue to his *Edda* where, for instance, Thor is made a grandson of Priam of Troy, and his home Þrúðheimr is equated with Thrace and his wife Sif with "the prophetess who is called Sibil"; similarly, in the *Ynglinga saga* Snorri makes the Æsir come from Asia and the Vanir from a land on the river "formerly called Vanaquisl" (*the Don*) and their country "on the Vanaquisl was called Vanaland or Vanaheim".

A variation of the Euhemeristic theory has been fashionable recently both here and in America. An exponent on this side of the Atlantic is H. S. Bellamy, who says on page 70 of his *Moons, Myths and Man* (first published in 1936) "This book endeavours to show that the dragon myths, and their inseparably close companions, the deluge and creation myths, are reports of the cataclysmic end of the Tertiary Age, of the cata-

strophic breakdown of the predecessor of our present Moon."
Bellamy's explanation of the world-wide flood and creation
myths is based on an astronomical theory put forward by an
Austrian, Hans Hoerbiger and published in 1913. According
to this theory, some thirteen thousand years ago Earth had no
satellite, but round about that time "captured" a planet "Luna"
the predecessor of our present moon. Gradually, "Luna" was
attracted nearer and nearer to Earth's surface until by her pull
the seven seas were gathered round the world in a great "girdle
tide". But "Luna" got so close to Earth that she began to
break up and fall upon the Earth, eventually disintegrating
altogether and setting free the "girdle tide" in a monstrous
flood. This cataclysm took place at the end of what geologists
call the Tertiary Age, and it is eye-witness accounts of it from
all parts of the world which (says Bellamy) have left us today
with the deluge and creation myths.

A theory put forward in the middle of the nineteenth century (by Gladstone in *Homer and the Homeric Age*) saw Greek
myth not as something invented by the story tellers but as a
degradation or perversion of an original revelation of the
Christian religion.

The Rev. G. W. Cox in his *Mythology of the Aryan Nations*
(published 1870), scouted Gladstone's theory and plumped
for myths as having their origin in natural phenomena. He
says (Preface to Vol. I, p. vi) "Of one fact, the importance of
which if it be well ascertained can scarcely be exaggerated, I
venture to claim the discovery. I am not aware that the great
writers who have traced the wonderful parallelisms in the
myths of the Aryan world have asserted that the epic poems of
the Aryan nations are simply different versions of one and the
same story, and that this story has its origin in the phenomena
of the natural world, and the course of the day and the year."
An example of a myth interpreted on the assumption that it
originated as an allegory of natural phenomena may be quoted
from *Myths of the Norsemen* by H. A. Guerber and published
in 1909; this example deals with the myth of Balder's death:

"The physical explanation of this myth is to be found either in the daily setting of the sun (Balder), which sinks beneath the western waves, driven away by darkness (Hodur), or in the ending of the short Northern summer and the long reign of the winter season.... From the depths of their underground prison, the sun (Balder) and vegetation (Nanna) try to cheer heaven (Odin) and earth (Frigga) by sending them Draupnir, the emblem of fertility, and the flowery tapestry, symbolical of the carpet of verdure which will again deck the earth and enhance her charms with its beauty."

One of the most recent theories of myth to receive acceptance is that advanced by C. G. Jung. Put crudely, Jung sees the human mind rather like a three-storey building, only one storey of which is (so to speak) above ground. The storey above ground represents the conscious mind, the two cellars the unconscious mind: the upper cellar is the *personal* unconscious and the lower cellar—a sort of communal cellar shared by everybody—what Jung calls the *collective* unconscious. The unconscious in Jung's view "is not merely a cellar where man dumps his rubbish, but the source of consciousness and of the creative and destructive spirit of mankind."[87] Whereas the personal unconscious is mine alone, the collective unconscious I share with all mankind. The manifestations of the collective unconscious are, according to Jung, what he calls the *archetypes* which "bring into our ephemeral consciousness an unknown psychic life belonging to a remote past. This psychic life is the mind of our ancient ancestors, the way in which they thought and felt, the way in which they conceived of life and the world, of gods and human beings."[88] According to one of the accredited exponents of Jung's psychology in English "the archetypes are the result of the many recurring experiences of life: like the rising and setting of the sun, the coming of spring and autumn in temperate climates and of the rains in more torrid zones, birth and death, the finding of a mate, or of food, or escape from danger; it is, however, fantasies rather than actual images of the experience that remain. They typify the triumphs and disasters, hopes and fears, joys and sorrows of our remote ancestors; the men who lived even before the Palaeolithic hunters (who had at least potentially our own qualities of mind) appeared upon the earth."[89] Jung himself says that a "well-known expression of the archetype is myth and fable. But here also we are dealing with conscious and specifically moulded forms that have been handed on, relatively un-changed, through long periods of time."[90] It is from the postu-lation of the "collective unconscious" that Jung explains the belief in metempsychosis or reincarnation and in memories of past lives as well as the finding of myths in similar forms among all people in all ages.

Finally, I may quote Professor Krappe who in *The Science of Folklore* published in 1930, is of the opinion that "myths are merely certain tales, largely of popular origin but utilized and reworked by poets so as often to be considerably modified, loosely connected with certain religions of native growth but never incorporated by them into their creeds and dogmas, only half believed in by the poets and often not taken seriously at all, in short, pieces of popular or poetic fancy as the case may be" (p. 317 f.). Professor Krappe concludes that "myths are, so far as the white man's civilization is concerned, a thing of the past. The last of them died under the hammer blows of the great rationalists of the eighteenth century, and no trick of the demagogue or the obscurantist can bring them back to life. It was left to the nineteenth century to demonstrate by an accumulation of facts, how they had arisen in the first place. Now that they are no more, one may well regret this loss of the blooming fancies of man's childhood. Such regrets are vain, for those lofty creations of the human brain share, alas, the fate of everything else terrestrial and hence but transitory" (p. 334).

Each or any of these theories of the origin of myth may com-mend itself to the reader: or none may. But any theory I myself might put forward could only be one among the rest and, in the present state of our knowledge, just as hypothetical. As far as Northern mythology—our *own* mythology—is concerned, there are I believe, other more fruitful lines of enquiry. Nevertheless, I feel that having come so far with me, the reader is entitled to an exposition of what to my mind may be reasonably held with regard to myths.

2

MYTHS AND TRUTH

The myths of the Indo-European peoples were given their earliest form in verse whether the *carmina* of the Gothonic branch referred to by Tacitus; or the Greek and Latin odes and epics; or the Iranian *Gathas*; or the Hindu hymns of the *Rig-Veda*. In other words, these myths were first shaped by poets, men set apart from the rest by their ability to see farther through a wall than most, men with the gift of being able to glance from heaven to earth and earth to heaven and body forth the forms of things unknown and give to airy nothing a local habitation and a name. But the poets were out of themselves, they were in a "fine frenzy" when they sang their songs: they spoke truer than they *knew*. Knowing is normally taken to be a conscious activity and we may believe that the poets were fishing up truth from the bottom of their own minds, from the well of the unconscious. A myth then, is a combination of conscious and unconscious knowing, and that part of it which proceeds from the unconscious is likely to embody the nearest we mortals will ever get to absolute truth: that is why our ancestors have rated the value of myths so highly, they have kept the songs alive for hundreds, often thousands of years, and for much of that time by word of mouth alone.

A myth is a song: it is also a story. There appear to be three basic requisites for a story, namely characters, plot and what is best expressed by the French word *milieu*—the setting. If we examine the Northern Mythology from the point of view of characters, plot and *milieu* we shall find that much has been consciously shaped. Take the ancient characters for instance, the gods and cosmogonic beings: Allfather, lately Odin formerly Týr and originally *Djevs was the *sky*; but he was sky regarded anthropomorphically as a father, and not only as a sky-father but as an Indo-European house-father with his sons (the gods) living in his house together with their wives (his daughters-in-law) in a communal family even as is still the case today with the Hindu joint family. Whichever way we look at it, we are bound to admit that the pantheon of gods mirrors the ancient family organisation. The individual gods eat and drink and sleep like humans, they beget children, and they observe tribal customs such as those of child adoption, blood-brotherhood and the tribal council of free equals—the *Thing*. All this related as myth is a product of the conscious mind; so is the personification of the elements and man's environment which resulted in the individual gods and cosmogonic beings: the true Odin was originally the wind, Thor was *thunder,* Lóðurr-Rígr-Heimdallr was *beneficent fire*, Loki was *destructive fire* and so was Surtr. In their cases the personification may not at first be apparent, but when the gods' and goddesses' names have remained the same as the phenomenon they personify it would be perverse not to accept their origin in such personification: Jörð = *Earth*, Gefjun = *Ocean*, Nótt = *Night*, Dagr = *Day*, Sól = *Sun*, Máni = *Moon*, Nörvi = *Dark Moon*, Bil and Hjúki = *the Waning and Crescent Moon*, Urðr and Verðandi and Skuld = *the three phases of the Moon*, and so on. The giants too are personifications of the mountains (*bergrisar*) or of the powers of frost (*hrímþursar*) together with qualities inimical to our ancestors such as cannibalism, a trait most likely labelled in the name *jötunn* = ettin or giant as an eater of human flesh.

"The oldest archeological finds in the north reveal a people under the absolute necessity of seeking their subsistance in hunting and fishing."[91] Such hunting peoples were parasites on Nature through the animals and fish they preyed on, living in a state of utter dependence on Nature and for that reason more religious than people of higher cultures since the sense of dependence on mysterious external powers was stronger with them. While the primitive hunter sees a vague undifferentiated supernatural power manifest in sun and cloud, storm and thunder, fire and water, beast and plant in a sort of primitive pantheism, it is undoubtedly from such an attitude that the personification of these forces in myth at last occurs.

But there are other Northern gods (and goddesses) who appear to be something more than personifications of natural phenomena. I mean, of course, Balder, Njörðr, Frey and Freya, here too we may group Frigg as Jörð's latest apotheosis. None of these five is native to the Gothonic cosmogony: they are immigrants from Asia Minor, from lands where farming first began. The basic qualities of these five are those of the mother (the one fertilised) and the lover (the fertiliser). These gods and goddesses are those of the Peasant religion as opposed to the others I have spoken of who come from the pantheon of the Hunter. Even as farming was at first the preserve of the woman and the provision of food depended on her ability with the digging-stick and the hoe and not on the agility of her husband as a hunter; and possibly because our primitive ancestors did not know of the connection between copulation and conception; so we find the Earth Mother first and pre-eminent in the Peasant Religion. Njörðr (Tacitus' *Nerthus* "Mother Earth" having suffered a change of sex), Frigg and Freya are manifestations of the Earth Mother. To her the domestic animals are sacred, the goat, sheep and pig, and especially the cow. We suspect now why Freya was called Sýr (*sow*), why she and her brother Frey were associated with boars, why Heimdallr even is represented with goat's horns, and why the cow Auðumla was the first nourisher of Ymir and the means of licking Búri from the primeval ice. But the earliest agriculture (horticulture rather) was not characterized by the use of domestic animals and so for a time the Earth Mother stands alone: when animals came to be domesticated and used in cultivation, then for the man the old idle life of the savage, in which the women do most of the work while the men hunt and fight, passes away. All the productive forces of the community are employed, the men in the fields and the women at home. It is now that a second figure is seen alongside the Earth Mother, her divine son and lover who personates fertility and the vegetative life of Nature and who embodies in his person the great cosmic mystery of the annual death and resurrection of Nature. Now we begin to see why Balder must die (and Frey) and we can understand why our near ancestors the Angles and Saxons saw an identity between Balder and Christ, and why they called Jesus the Frey of Mankind.

But when we have outlined this mythic "plot" of the dying god we have not said all: an anthropomorphic figure may be loved and he may die through a wound; he may die and then be restored to his lover: and such characters and events may be explained as conscious creations in the mind of a poet, but there is still an unconscious acceptance of a relationship between man and his environment which can be felt rather than understood. This is the truth of myth, and it is no part of my intention to try and show what is the truth of the "plot" of each Northern myth.

Again, if we consider the *milieu* of these myths, we may trace anthropomorphism in the buildings and topography of Asgard, hel and Jötunheim: in Asgard the climate is always equable, the cloud-capped palaces are built of gold—but there *is* weather and the palaces reduced to essentials are four walls and a roof; hel is the "place of concealment" and may be traceable to the cold dark grave even as may be Valhalla; Jötunheim is a country of vast mountains and strong rivers, an exaggeration of Scandinavian scenery: but behind all this, there is still the unconscious shaping. As I remarked at the end of Chapter II, the conception of Midgard, Asgard, hel and Jötunheim partakes of the mysticism of the mandala, with truth lying at its centre: truth, which can never be handed to one on a plate, but which each person needs must find for himself. The way to truth may lie up a steep hill, but at least our ancestors believed that Myth would help to find it.

3

THE REJECTION OF ODIN

Of course, the obvious objection to these last remarks is that one by one the Gothonic tribes forsook or rejected their ancient myths: we know, for instance, that our English ancestors accepted Christianity some two hundred years after they came to these islands, and Norwegians, Danes, Swedes and Icelanders were proselytised round about the year A.D. 1000. But let us look a little closer at what actually happened. As I have argued before, the men of the north who conceived the Ragnarök, the general destruction of the gods, were influenced by two things: first the myth of the dying god Balder and second the myth of the Sky Father (whether depicted as Odin or Týr) being *temporarily* swallowed by a wolf. In both cases, the reappearance of the god—his resurrection—was originally essential to the myth: it is the later transcribers who emphasised the Doom of the Gods and minimised or forgot the return of Balder and the others. It was the aristocratic warlike and fatalistic kings and jarls together with their skalds who developed the nihilistic side of the myth: and it is just this side of it which was finally rejected when the various Northern peoples accepted Christianity. But the fundamental truth of the myth they clove to: for if we look now at the new religion adopted by the people, the ordinary people, what is it to them? Certainly not the thirty-nine articles nor the Pauline doctrine nor even the tenets of the Sermon on the Mount. It is a story of a child born miraculously of a virgin mother, born in the dead of winter, surrounded significantly by the beasts of the field, the ox and the ass with the sheep and the shepherd hard by. It is the story of a baby whose birth was mystically connected with a time of peace over the whole earth, who grew to manhood, suffered a bloody wound and died to be resurrected again from the dead. And perhaps most important, the death of Jesus was a necessity that the world might live. This is what the new story, the new myth, the new religion meant to the ordinary people, and it was compatible with many fertility rites and observances such as the blessing of the plough, of rivers and the sea, with conjuration of fruit trees, with prayers for good seasons, rain and the general fertility of the earth, with thanksgiving at harvest, with mourning at Easter for the death of the god and with rejoicing for his resurrection.

If we look at the change from paganism to Christianity in the common people of this land in this light we must surely accept that the one flowed imperceptibly into the other. Today Christianity is suffering a decline, its churches are emptying. Where then are we to look for our life-giving myths? Back to our peasant heathen ancestors lodging close to mother earth or to the great wens of cities in which we now live? These cities with their bricks and mortar, their great slabs of concrete paving stones and tar-macadam, their smog-laden air, have effectively cut us off from the soil our mother and the sky our father. Must we look for our myths to the cities, to the internal combustion engine and the atomic pile? I wonder.

NOTES

1 According to Ethelweard, aldorman of West Wessex telling the story some 200 years later. *v. Monumenta Historica Britannica*, ed. H. Petrie and T. Sharpe (1848).

2 The *Chronicle* says that the heathens came in "January". A scribal error: the Northmen's boats were unsuitable for winter expeditions. Probably "June" is correct.

3 *N.E.D.* gives 1807 as first appearance of "vikingr" (noun) and 1847 "viking" (adjective).

4 *The Aryans*, V. Gordon Childe (London 1926).

5 Tacitus, *Germania*, II.

6 Mawer, *Problems of Place-Name Study*, pp. 59–61 (1929).

7 R. H. Hodgkin, *A History of the Anglo-Saxons*, Oxf. 1935, I, p. 244.

8 Ari Thorgilsson writing in the twelfth century fixed the date of the battle of Hafrsfiord at *c.* 872. Vigfusson and Powell argued that Harald Fairhair's reign was much later, i.e. 900–945.

9 O.N. *papar*, Irish *pab(b)a*, Lat. *papa*. This word meant in Irish a monk or anchorite.

10 William Jackson Hooker, F.L.S., *Journal of a Tour in Iceland in the summer of 1809*, printed by J. Keymer (King St., Yarmouth) 1811, ("Not published").

11 Alastair M. Dunnett, *Land of Promise* in the *Sunday Times*, 27 Sept., 1953.

12 In a paper read before the Viking Club, 15 Nov., 1895.

13 *Adam of Bremen*, IV, 26.

14 *Hauksbók c.* 1310.

15 Vigfusson and Powell, *Corpus Poeticum Boreale*, II, pp. 642 and 644 (publ. 1883).

16 *Heimskringla*, translated by S. Laing, Everyman ed., p. 4.

17 *The Prose Edda*, translated by A. G. Brodeur, O.U.P. 1916, p. 97.

18 *The Gods of the Greeks* (pp. 20–21), C. Kerényi, Thames & Hudson, 1951.

19 *The Prose Edda*, translated by A. G. Brodeur, O.U.P. 1916, pp. 4–5.

20 *Op. cit.*, Vol. I, p. 218.

21 *Iliad*, 14, 201.

22 *Iliad*, 14, 246.

23 *E.g.* Vigfusson and Powell, *Corpus Poeticum Boreale* (1883), and A. G. Brodeur, *The Prose Edda* (1916).

24 *V. Oxford Book of Nursery Rhymes*: Jack and Jill.

25 *V.* H. S. Bellamy, *Moons, Myths and Man*, p. 138 ff.

26 *C.P.B.*, I, p. 199.
27 *The Road to Hel*, p. 86, H. R. Ellis, C.U.P. 1943.
28 The dark moon—according to Vigfusson and Powell, *C.P.B.*, II, 468.
29 *Cf.* Yorkshire dialect *swither*.
30 *Midsummer Night's Dream*, Act II Sc. i.
31 *Riders in the Sky (A Cowboy Legend)*, by Stan Jones, Copyright 1949, by Mayfair Music Corp., New York, Edwin H. Morris & Co. Ltd., 52 Maddox Street, W.1.
32 G. Schütte, *Our Forefathers*, Vol. I, p. 228.
33 *Cf.* Cuchullain in *Táin Bó Quailgné*.
34 *V. Edda and Saga*, B. S. Phillpotts. Cf. the Cross as "Christ's Palfrey", *C.P.B.*, II, 460.
35 *Cf.* Cuchullain's weapon "gae bolg".
36 *C.P.B.*, II, 433.
37 Schütte, *Our Forefathers*, Vol. I, p. 219.
38 Cleasby-Vigfusson, *Dictionary*.
39 Schütte, *Our Forefathers*, I, 220.
40 From a fourteenth-century charm printed by George Stephens, *Archaeologia*, Vol. 30, p. 503.
41 *V.* George Stephens, *Runic Monuments*, Vol. 1.
42 *Tacitus on Britain and Germany*, translated by H. Mattingly, Penguin Classics.
43 *Flateyjarbók*, II, 337.
44 *Adam of Bremen*, IV, 26.
45 *Herodotus*, IV, 94, 95.
46 *Adam of Bremen*, IV, 26.
47 Saxo, IX, 301.
48 *C.P.B.*, I, 178.
49 H. A. Bellows, *The Poetic Edda*, p. 203, O.U.P.
50 *Ibid*. p. 3.
51 *C.P.B.*, II, 434.
52 *C.P.B.*, I, cii.
53 *Ibid*.
54 *E.g.* H. A. Bellows in *The Poetic Edda*, p. 9.
55 Þjóðólfr of Hvin in *Haustlöng*.
56 *V.* A. C. Haddon, *Head Hunters: Black, White and Brown* (1901).
57 Tacitus, *Germania*, 45.
58 *Ibid*. 40.
59 *V.* p. 155–156.
60 *Adam of Bremen*, IV, 26.
61 Eyvindr Skáldaspillir tells in *Haleygjatál* of the time when Skaði lived *i Manheimum* with Odin and had many sons by him. *Manheimar* means that part of the world lived in by man; it was also an old name for part of Scandinavia.
62 *Þórsdrápa*, by Eilífr Guðrúnarson (*C.P.B.*, II, p. 21, lines 62–63).

63 The Northman's hundred is the "long hundred", i.e. 120. These numbers are used to express infinity.

64 Viktor Rydberg in *Teutonic Mythology*, pp. 470–471, claims that "Þjóðvitnir's fish" means the Rainbow—Bifröst Bridge: his evidence is unconvincing, but even if Rydberg is right, Þund must still be the River of Air. Cf. also *Fáfnismál*, 15:

> It's called Óskópnir
> where all the gods
> are bound to battle at last;
> Bifröst breaks
> when they crowd the bridge
> and steeds shall swim in the flood.

65 *C.P.B.*, I, 480.

66 *C.P.B.*, II, 422 ff.

67 According to *Fagrskinna*.

68 Haraldr Hárðráði's saga LXXX, translated by S. Laing (Everyman Lib.).

69 *Ibid*. LXXXI.

70 Sweet, *Anglo-Saxon Reader*, p. 95.

71 Early English Alliterative Poems, E.E.T.S. 1864. *Cleanness*, line 1577.

72 "Tisifone", "Eurynes", "Herines", in eighth-century Corpus Christi MS. CXLIV (ed. T. Wright, *Vocabularies*, 1873): II, 122.34; 107.43; 110.34. "Herines", "Allecto", "Bellona", in eleventh-century MS. Cotton. Cleopatra, A. III, II 43.2; 5.70; 12.12; 94.15.

73 *The Gods of the Greeks* (C. Kerényi, Thames & Hudson, 1951), pp. 46–48.

74 *Narratiumculae Anglice conscriptae* (ed. Cockayne, London 1861), 34.6.

75 Aldhelm, *De Laudibus Virginitatis* 4449 (*Old English Glosses*, ed. Napier, Oxf. 1900, p. 115).

76 *Codex Regius*, and from stanza 20 onwards *Arnamagnaean Codex*.

77 *Hilde-Gudrun* (Halle 1901), p. 330.

78 Translated by T. P. Cross and C. H. Slover from the *Otia Merseiana* (*Ancient Irish Tales*, Chicago 1935), p. 523.

79 *Gods of the Greeks*, p. 32.

80 *Ibid*.

81 *The Poetic Edda*, p. 234.

82 *Ibid*. p. 115.

83 *The New Testament*. Newly translated from the Vulgate Latin by Mgr. Ronald Knox, London 1945 (p. 574).

84 H. S. Bellamy, *Moons, Myths and Man*, pp. 95–96.

85 Quoted by Rev. G. W. Cox, *Mythology of the Aryan Nations*, II, pp. 122–123.

86 H. A. Guerber, *Myths of the Norsemen*, Harrap & Co., 1909, pp. 213, 214.

87 Frieda Fordham, *An Introduction to Jung's Psychology*, Penguin Books Ltd., 1953, p. 27, 28.
88 C. G. Jung, *The Integration of the Personality*, Routledge, 1940, pp. 24, 25.
89 Frieda Fordham, *op. cit.*, p. 25.
90 C. G. Jung, *op. cit.*, p. 53.
91 *Scandinavian Archaeology*, Shetelig, Falk and Gordon, p. 305.

BIBLIOGRAPHY

This list is not intended to be exhaustive but is given as a guide for English-speaking readers. In quoting from the Verse Edda I have used Finnur Jónsson's numbering in the edition given below.

SOURCES

Finnur Jónsson (editor), *Sæmundar-Edda* (i.e. the *Verse Edda*), Reykjavik, 1926.
Finnur Jónsson (editor), *Snorra Edda* (i.e. the *Prose Edda*), Reykjavik, 1907.
Vigfusson and Powell (editors and translators), *Corpus Poeticum Boreale* I and II (eddaic and skaldic verse), Oxford, 1883.
A. G. Brodeur (translator), *The Prose Edda*, American Scandinavian Foundation and Oxford University Press, 1916.
H. A. Bellows (translator), *The Poetic Edda*, American Scandinavian Foundation and Oxford University Press.
Saxo Grammaticus, *Danish History* translated by O. Elton.

HISTORY

Fridtjof Nansen, *In Northern Mists*, London, 1911.
W. Hovgaard, *The Voyages of the Norsemen to America*, New York, 1915.
G. M. Gathorne-Hardy, *The Norse Discoverers of America*, Oxford, 1921.
V. Gordon Childe, *The Aryans*, London, 1926.
Knut Gjerset, *History of the Norwegian People*, New York, 1927.
Gudmund Schütte, *Our Forefathers* I and II, Cambridge, 1929, 1933.
T. D. Kendrick, *A History of the Vikings*, Methuen, 1930.
Bertha S. Phillpotts, *Edda and Saga*, Thornton Butterworth, Ltd., 1931.
R. H. Hodgkin, *A History of the Anglo-Saxons* I and II, Oxford, 1935.
Shetelig, Falk and Gordon, *Scandinavian Archaeology*, Oxford, 1937.
A. W. Brøgger, H. Shetelig, *The Viking Ships*, 1951.
G. N. Garmonsway (translator), *The Anglo-Saxon Chronicle*, Dent, 1953.
G. Turville-Petre, *Origins of Icelandic Literature*, Oxford, 1953.
Gwyn Jones, *A History of the Vikings*, 1962.
J. Brøndsted, *The Vikings*, Penguin Books Ltd., 1965.
D. M. Wilson, O. Klindt-Jensen, *Viking Art*, 1966.
Knud J. Krogh, *Viking Greenland*, Copenhagen National Museum, 1967.
Jacqueline Simpson, *Everyday Life in the Viking Age*, B. T. Batsford, 1967.
Olaf Olsen, Ole Crumlin-Pedersen, *The Skuldelev Ships*, Acta Archaeologica Vol. XXXVIII, reprint Copenhagen, 1968.
Eric Graf Oxenstierna, *The World of the Norsemen*, Weidenfeld & Nicolson, 1967.
R. L. S. Bruce-Mitford, *The Sutton Hoo Ship Burial*, British Museum, 1968.

P. Foote, D. M. Wilson, *The Viking Achievement*, Sidgewick & Jackson, 1970.

MYTHOLOGY
Rev. G. W. Cox, *Mythology of the Aryan Nations* I and II, London, 1870.
Viktor Rydberg, *Teutonic Mythology*, London, 1889.
H. S. Bellamy, *Moons, Myths and Man*, Faber, 1936.
C. G. Jung, *The Integration of Personality*, Routledge, 1940.
H. R. Ellis, *The Road to Hel*, Cambridge, 1943.
Frieda Fordham, *An Introduction to Jung's Psychology*, Penguin Books, 1953.
Brian Branston, *The Lost Gods of England*, Thames and Hudson, 1957 and 1974.
G. Turville-Petre, *Myth and Religion of the North*, Oxford, 1964.
H. R. Ellis Davidson, *Gods and Myths of Northern Europe*, Penguin Books, 1964.
Brian Branston, *Gods and Heroes from Viking Mythology*, Eurobook, 1978.

MAPS
Colin McEvedy, *The Penguin Atlas of Medieval History*, Penguin Books, 1961.

Acknowledgments are due to the following for kind permission to quote:

Oxford University Press (*A History of the Anglo-Saxons* by R. H. Hodgkin; *The Prose Edda*, translated by A. G. Brodeur); Penguin Books Ltd (*Tacitus on Britain and Germany*, translated by H. Mattingly; *An Introduction to Jung's Psychology* by Frieda Fordham); Burns, Oates and Washbourne (*The New Testament*. Newly translated from the Vulgate Latin by Mgr. Ronald Knox); the Kemsley Press and A. M. Dunnett; Methuen & Co., Ltd (*Ballad of the White Horse* by G. K. Chesterton); Macmillan Publishers, Ltd (*Danegeld* by Rudyard Kipling); Faber & Faber, Ltd (*Whispers of Immortality* by T. S. Eliot).

INDEX